THE LIB
ST. MARY'S COLLEG
ST. MARY'S CITY,

AH φ

rec. 9/92

Museums 2000

Record of a Museums Association Conference on the future of museums held in London, May 1989, as part of Museums Year 1989, celebrating the Association's Centenary.

Museums and art galleries have never been so much in the news as over the past decade. Yet the public focus at both professional and non-specialist levels has been remarkable for what has been accidentally or deliberately left out of the debate. Moving beyond the narrow issues of professional practice, *Museums 2000* probes instead the political, economic and cultural realities which affect museums today. And because the contributors are drawn from both the museum profession and the wider political, academic and business communities worldwide, the book is truly international, reflecting the issues which affect all museums.

Editor in chief   Andrew Wheatcroft

The Heritage: Care–Preservation–Management programme has been designed to serve the needs of the museum and heritage community worldwide. It publishes books and information services for professional museum and heritage workers, and for all the organisations that service the museum community.

The programme has been revised with the advice and assistance of the leading institutions in the museum and heritage community, both at an international level, with ICOM and ICOMOS, with the national and local museum organizations and with individual specialists drawn from every continent.

Forward Planning: *A handbook of business, corporate and development planning for museums and galleries*
Edited by Timothy Ambrose and Sue Runyard

The Industrial Heritage: *Managing resources and uses*
Judith Alfrey and Tim Putman

Museums and the Shaping of Knowledge
Eilean Hooper-Greenhill

Museums without Barriers: *A new deal for disabled people*
Fondation de France and ICOM

The Past in Contemporary Society: Then/Now
P. J. Fowler

Museums 2000
Politics, people, professionals and profit

Edited by
Patrick J. Boylan

Museums Association
in conjunction with Routledge

London and New York

First published in 1992
by Routledge
11 New Fetter Lane, London EC4P 4EE

Simultaneously published in the USA and Canada
by Routledge
a division of Routledge, Chapman and Hall Inc.
29 West 35th Street, New York, NY 10001

© 1992 Museums Association

Printed in Great Britain by Butler & Tanner Ltd, Frome and London

All rights reserved. No part of this book may be reprinted or
reproduced or utilized in any form or by any electronic,
mechanical, or other means, now known or hereafter invented,
including photocopying and recording, or in any information storage
or retrieval system, without permission in writing from the
publishers.

British Library Cataloguing in Publication Data

Museums 2000: Politics, people, professionals and profit.
 I. Boylan, P. J. (Patrick John)
 069.0941

Library of Congress Cataloging in Publication Data

Museums 2000: politics, people, professionals & profit/[edited by]
 Patrick Boylan
     p.   cm.—(Heritage)
  Proceedings of a Museums Association conference held in London,
 May 1989, celebrating the Association's centenary.
  Includes bibliographical references and index.
   1. Museums—Management—Planning—Congresses. 2. Public
 relations—Museums—Congresses. 3. Cultural property, Protection
 of—Congresses. I. Boylan, Patrick. II. Museums Association.
 III. Series.
 AM121.M89   1992
 069'.5—dc20   91–30976

ISBN 0-415-05455-9
ISBN 0-415-07129-1 pbk

Printed on permanent paper in accordance with American NISO Standards

Contents

Contents

Museums 2000 and the future of museums

Patrick J. Boylan

Introduction

Although museums and art galleries have never been so much in the news as they have been over the past decade, the public focus at both professional and non-specialist levels has been remarkable for what has been accidentally or deliberately left out of this debate.

Any priority list of factors of central importance to museums and art galleries in recent years and at the present time should have included the impact of politics on museums at both national and local levels, the relationship between museums and ordinary people, the nature and future of the museums profession, and the changing financial climate for museums, especially the drive for profit (or at least the political agenda of seeking to switch responsibility for museums from public to private funding), and these seem certain to remain central issues for the foreseeable future.

Museums Year 1989

The City of York has played an important part in English national history for almost two millenniums. However, its oldest museum, The Yorkshire Museum, though immensely rich in its collections and a model of its kind in terms of its exhibition, communication and other public services, is still quite a small institution. It was founded in a wave of local scientific zeal and Yorkshire patriotism in 1824 in order to keep in the county some of the remarkable and highly controversial fossil mammal finds from Kirkdale Cave discovered at the end of 1821 (described by Professor Adam Sedgwick, one of its first honorary members, as 'our Yorkshire Hyaenopolis'!). Yet during the past century and a half the Yorkshire Museum has had the unique distinction of launching not just one, but two, world movements, each aimed at promoting the public understanding of, co-operation in, and the professionalizing of both science and the arts.

In 1830 a small group of scientists (although they did not call themselves that since the very word was not to be invented for another seven years) gathered together in the Yorkshire Museum to create the world's first national 'Parliament of Science' – as one of the founders called the British Association for the Advancement of Science. From these small beginnings has grown the still healthy and expanding British Association which meets in both plenary sessions and over twenty specialist Sections, every autumn in a different city of the United Kingdom (and sometimes overseas too), and which also plays a major role in science education and the public understanding of science throughout the year. Further, demonstrating the old saying that 'Imitation is the most sincere form of flattery' the aims of those 1830 Yorkshire Museum pioneers have been followed in similar national organizations in many other parts of the world, most notably in the USA, where the 'Triple A–S', the American Association for the Advancement of Science, has long since outgrown its UK model in terms of both size and influence.

Precisely the same spirit of co-operation, fellowship and the hope of 'advancement' within their chosen field filled a still smaller group of less than a dozen museum curators and governing body representatives from across Britain who met in the office of the Keeper of The Yorkshire Museum on 20 June 1889. These pioneers, perhaps prompted in part by concern about the organization and health of museums expressed by the British Association itself in several critical reviews of the state of the museums of Britain over the preceding two decades, quickly resolved to establish the world's first national (and indeed international) organization for museums – The Museums Association.

It should be noted that even today it is 'The' Museums Association, not the UK (or English) Association, because when it was set up it was the only organization of its kind in the world. Indeed from an early date the Association had international members, both museums and individuals, and although the proportion of overseas members has fallen as national museums associations modelled on it developed elsewhere, the Association still has, and very much welcomes, foreign members. However, the British model has been taken up in most other parts of the world – most spectacularly in the United States, where the American Association of Museums now has more than 9,000 members (three times the membership of our Association) and regularly attracts 3,000 or more delegates to its Annual Meeting.

The Museums Association represents both museums as institutions and the museums profession, with the central aim of enhancing the quality of service, professionalism and standing of the museum community, throughout both the public and private sectors. Its four primary activities are professional support, publication, research and information, and parliamentary and public affairs.

These are all directed towards four primary objectives: enhancing the quality of public service and collections care through career-long professional development for museum staff; enabling the museum community to seize opportunities to meet people's needs, traditional and changing, from museums, arising from the rapid social, educational, economic and demographic changes in society; representing the views, needs and values of the museum community and its users to national and local government; and the facilitating of the exchange of information about new initiatives, best current practice and likely future trends in the museum community.

Almost six years before the Association's centenary year its Council, under the leadership of Lord Montagu of Beaulieu as President, recognized that the 1989 centenary offered a special opportunity for the Association and its membership, both institutional and professional, to review the current museum scene, to promote museums and galleries individually and collectively, and to look into the future of the museums within the UK and further afield. After long periods of discussion, the Association developed the concept of seeking support from both the museum movement and the various UK official bodies, including Government, the Museums and Galleries Commission, the Arts Council and the British Tourist Authority, for a year-long nationwide festival and celebration of museums, the arts and sciences – on a scale that had never been attempted anywhere else in the world.

Over 900 individual museums, galleries, and other heritage buildings and sites in over 400 cities, towns, villages and other localities registered one or more different types of special events and activities officially linked to and promoted as part of Museums Year, covering an extraordinary and often ingenious range of special promotions. Indeed, some linked several dozen special exhibitions, lectures, visitor activities and other special events to Museums Year. The original ambition of mounting much the largest national festival of the arts and sciences the world has ever seen was therefore fully realized.

We were very fortunate in having the very active support of the Royal Family, especially the Queen Mother as Patron of the Association itself, and HRH The Duchess of York as an extraordinarily active Royal Patron of Museums Year itself (undertaking thirty-one days of Museums Year events, frequently in the smaller museums which rarely get national publicity), and indeed every one of the adult members of the Royal Family undertook at least one Museums Year engagement, giving us support that was of enormous benefit in publicity terms.

Some of the special events linked to the Museums Year promotion were on a major scale – for instance the opening of the new national Design Museum, or the reopening of the totally remodelled Imperial War Museum by the Queen and the Duke of Edinburgh, while others were very modest indeed – a series of small-scale community events for disabled or otherwise disadvantaged people in a small local museum, for example, but equally effective in their own way and in relation to their own locality and community.

However, Museums Year was not without its problems in the planning stages not least because few potential major corporate sponsors could understand how they could relate effectively to such a diverse and dispersed programme of activities. Many potential corporate sponsors could see the mutual benefits of sponsoring individual events, whether national or local, and probably in total several hundred different businesses and other organizations were involved in this way, and both the individual museums and the Association were extremely grateful to these.

For example, Rank Xerox sponsored this 'Museums 2000' Conference on the future of museums. Similarly, the international accountants and management consultants, Touche Ross, gave generous support to our Centenary Conference in York (the Association's birthplace), which enabled the Association to offer no less than one hundred free places to the younger members of the profession who are usually at the bottom of the list, way below Trustees, Councillors, Directors and Senior Curators, when museums are sharing out the budget for our annual Museums Conference.

Fortunately, Times Newspapers Ltd (part of News International) saw the wider benefits of being associated with such a broadly based national festival and gave enormous support as the principal sponsor of Museums Year 1989. This included covering the costs of the Association's own central co-ordinating role for Museums Year, organizing (in partnership with Spero Communications) an innovative *Museums Year Guide and Passport*, which together offered up-to-date information in a pocket-sized guidebook format to participating museums together with – through the 'passport' facility – a wide range of material benefits to the passport purchaser, such as admission and shop concessions, or invitations to special Museums Year events.

The Times also ran a weekly feature half page on Museums Year every Saturday in addition to excellent general news and review coverage. Special tribute is due to Simon Tait of *The Times* for both his news and reviews writing on Museums Year, and for his participation in the *Museums Year Guide and Passport* scheme.

The benefits of Museums Year proved very substantial for many of the participating museums of all sizes. Despite some initial hostility from other sectors of the national media because of our sponsorship by *The Times*, a rival newspaper, Museums Year had the desired effects of benefiting individual museums while at the same time getting over to decision-makers in both the governmental and corporate sectors that museums are of central importance to our national educational, cultural and scientific life. Certainly the museums and heritage sector had never before been so much at the forefront in the media and public understanding.

In particular, from the central organization by the Association itself, we tried to get over the (entirely truthful) messages that in the UK museums and related facilities succeed in achieving their mission on generally very limited resources, and that they would be even more effective and successful given quite modest additional investment from both public and private (especially corporate) sources. In other words, both as a nation and at the more local and individual institutional level, we need to build on the success and proven track records of our nation's museums, large and small, both individually and collectively.

As a final indication of the success of the promotion, it is good to be able to record that Museums Year 1989 also saw record attendances throughout the sector (especially in those areas and institutions who made best use of the opportunity, for example the museums and galleries of the Yorkshire and Humberside region). The English Tourist Board recorded 72 million visits within Museums Year 1989 to museums and art galleries in the narrow sense, plus a further 66 million visits to historic buildings, monuments and other 'heritage' sites, giving a remarkable overall total of 138 million visits.

'Museums 2000' Conference, May 1989

As part of the programme of Museums Year 1989, the Association brought together in London for two days in May 1989 a panel of twenty-one members and guests from across the world. They came from a wide variety of backgrounds both within and outside the museum movement with the objective of debating with no holds barred the future of museums looking towards the new millennium, in front of, and then with, a capacity audience.

Eight different debates were held on the four central themes of the future of museums in relation to politics, people, professionals and profit, presented in the sequence followed in this book. In each case there was a prepared keynote address, followed by a discussion amongst a number of the invited keynote speakers and panel members, which was then broadened into a wider debate bringing in contributions from the floor of the 'Museums 2000' Conference.

Both the prepared keynote addresses and the subsequent discussions were recorded and transcribed verbatim. Consequently, by close adherence to the substance of the transcripts, this book attempts to give not just the argument but also the flavour of this challenging and stimulating conference: it is as complete a record as is practicable, with only minimal text editing.

The success or otherwise of a public debate such as 'Museums 2000: Politics, People, Professionals and Profit' depended very much on all those participating – not just the invited speakers. Both the Museums Association's Museums Year 1989 celebrations and our principal Conference sponsor, Rank Xerox Ltd, were very well served in this respect. The very brief biographies as at May 1989 provided for the conference programme by the keynote speakers and panel members are reproduced at the end of this book (Chapter 11), but where appropriate in this introduction I have briefly amplified these (using the transcript of my welcome and introduction to the conference which has not been reproduced).

We were particularly delighted to have HRH The Duke of Gloucester to open the Conference, because of his long interest in museums and the heritage both professionally as a practising architect and through his distinguished and very active public service in the sector. The latter has included a long period as a Commissioner of English Heritage – the Historic Buildings and Monuments Commission (and a full term as Vice-Chairman), and a long and continuing period of service as a Trustee of the British Museum.

The Association's choice as my co-chairman for the Conference, Lord Montagu of Beaulieu, was an especially appropriate one, since it was during his period as Museums Association President in 1984–5 that he initiated the concept and planning of the Association's 1989 Centenary Year.

Having founded the original Montagu Motor Museum at Beaulieu almost forty years ago as a small additional attraction for visitors within Palace House, he led its growth and development into the present internationally known and respected National Motor Museum. He has also served many different organizations within the museum and heritage movement, including the Historic Houses Association (founder President), the Association of Independent Museums, and above all as the founder chairman of English Heritage from its creation in 1983.

Museums and politics

Bearing in mind the scale of the recent expansion in museum provision (with more than half of the museums and galleries in Britain being less than forty years old), and the great majority being at least partly publicly funded, the relationship between museums and the political system and the future of public funding ought to have been central issues throughout the 1980s. Similarly, the relationship between the museum and the general public, and the internal relationships of the museum employees themselves – is there at last a museum profession emerging? – should have been major issues as well.

Yet none of the vitally important issues of the relationships between museums and politics and between museums and the non-specialist public, the nature and future of the museum profession, and the relentless drive of the profit motive have been at the forefront of the recent United Kingdom museum agenda, at least in terms of either public or professional debate. The first of the four major themes of the 'Museums 2000' Conference was therefore the exploration of the relationship between museums and politics.

The UK museums profession seemed through much of the 1980s to have been very much on the defensive. There have been growing challenges to the traditional, and still central, museum values of public service, education and scholarship, and a marked downgrading of the status of the local museum director or curator in his or (increasingly) her local community. A small minority of public and quasi-public (grant-aided 'independent') museums (or perhaps more accurately some key senior staff and governing bodies of these) have responded by attempting to adopt the political, economic and social agenda of the 1979 political revolution that quickly became known as Thatcherism. However, many more UK museum professionals reacted to what they rightly or wrongly viewed as a frontal onslaught on them and their institutions by a retreat into a wholly distorted view of what were (not wholly correctly) regarded as traditional curatorial values, with a major emphasis on issues such as collections management.

The opening keynote speaker, Lorena San Roman, was at the time of 'Museums 2000' the General Director of the National Museum of Costa Rica, Central America. Originally a researcher in tropical forest ecology, a field in which she retains a very active interest, Lorena San Roman developed a very clear view of the role of museums in a political environment, and as a servant of and fighter for national education and identity.

As her keynote address 'Politics and the role of museums' made clear, she was willing to risk all in placing her museums at the service of the nation, its people, its democratic traditions and its unique 1948 Constitution, which amongst other things totally abolished all armed forces and relies entirely on the force of moral argument and international law for its national defence, a policy that has been successful through more than forty years of regional instability throughout the rest of Central America.

Indeed, as I mentioned in introducing her to the Conference, Lorena San Roman faced great personal risks in her 1988 unarmed and undefended investigation for the Costa Rica government of the ecological effects of illegal military activities of Nicaraguan Contras and their US military advisers in the virgin rainforest of northern Costa Rica near to the Nicaragua frontier, as a result of which much of these border zones of both countries are now protected as an international heritage natural park because of their world importance.

She was forthright and challenging from the opening remarks of her keynote address, insisting that museums must have a central role in relation to not just the allegedly dead past, but also to their society and community and the current concerns of that society, and also stressing the political context within which museums operate, quoting the view of the President of her country's National Congress that national culture both influences politics and politicians, and is in many ways in turn determined by past and current political action.

Amongst her case studies was her own handling of the National Museum's 1988 exhibition on the history of the Nobel Peace Prize in the context of its award in 1987 to Costa Rica's retiring social democrat President, Oscar Arias. The Nobel judges made the award in recognition of his role in achieving an international peace agreement in Central America after two decades of regional conflict. Lorena San Roman also referred to her plans to mark later in 1989 the centenary of democracy in Costa Rica (arguably the most truly democratic nation in the world in terms of both constitution and practice, and certainly one of the most civilized in every sense of the word).

Her unambiguous declaration that 'Today, museums cannot be useless, because if they are they will disappear. They must play a role in the polemics of the country and in its socio-economical development' was a frontal assault on the declared aim of the UK museum movement throughout recent times (and indeed enshrined in the guidelines under the Museums Association's Code of Conduct for Museum Curators) of retaining what we regard as strictly non-political and non-controversial 'balance' (though this is often perceived by the disaffected in our society as in fact showing massive bias – but in favour of the political middle ground and middle-class social values).

In fact, following the change of government in the 1990 national elections Lorena San Roman paid the price of her convictions and resigned from her post in the interests of the National Museum a few days before the incoming liberal democratic (conservative) government could act. Although the post of National Museum Director was nominally the responsibility of an independent (though government-appointed – as in the UK) body of trustees, she believed that if she insisted on her rights under her terms of employment and stayed in post the museum would suffer indirectly because of her close association with the outgoing government, or perhaps through direct pressure such as reductions in funding and other support, because of the expectation that the new government would want the policies and priorities of the National Museum to reflect more closely the changed national agenda. Instead, she now grows mangoes, directs a ecological conservation project in the north of the country and teaches forest ecology and conservation part-time in the National University.

These subsequent events show that much of the formal and informal discussion about her contribution to 'Museums 2000' was highly prophetic and gives added weight to both her own contribution and to the discussion of the theme.

The second keynote speaker on the 'Museums and Politics' theme was Eric Moody of the Department of Arts Policy and Management of The City University, London, and hence now a colleague of mine following my move to the University in 1990. He is a practising artist, and has worked as both a teacher and gallery administrator. At City University, after a long period of participation in its full-time and part-time postgraduate arts administration courses, he established in addition a successful 'mid-career' MA in Museum and Gallery Management, and also contributes to the Department's innovative MA in Arts Criticism. His

Ph.D. research was on the relationship between the art market and the state, including the relationship between private commerce and public support of the arts.

In planning 'Museums 2000' we had asked him amongst other things to review the current relationship between national and local politics and the arts. With this keynote theme too the whispers were at last out into the open, with Eric Moody's frank recognition of the hostility of some museum professionals, especially in Britain, to the linking of museums and the arts as virtual synonyms within the political (and indeed media) context.

He also shook the gathering by his forthright comments on the currently fashionable conception of Art (always with the capital 'A') as something essentially exclusive, egocentric, and solely concerned with individual self-expression, describing this view as hanging 'like the albatross of the Ancient Mariner around the neck of artists, arts managers and those condemned by association'. One of the panel members, Kenneth Hudson, a gadfly commentator on and critic of the museum scene for nearly two decades, took up this cue and expressed again in typically abusive terms (both literally and metaphorically) his long-held antipathy to non-representational modern art and those who purvey and support it.

Eric Moody also challenged the view, so commonly expressed in Britain today, that 'art, the new religion, is required to achieve all sorts of impossible goals, like helping to revitalize economies and regions', and argued that the more secular societies such as the United States and France are better at understanding and supporting 'the new religion' of art. Another near taboo was broken in his questioning of the distinctively British (and comparatively recent – post Second World War) notion of the 'arm's length principle' of arts funding, pointing out that in Britain this is seen as very much a one-way process, preserving the arts from any control from, or responsibility to, their funders, whether public or private sponsors.

The discussion of Lorena San Roman's opening address had been somewhat muted at first and then virtually unanimously supportive of her argument, perhaps because most of the panel and the audience were stunned by what was to many so novel a view of the proper role and future of museums. In contrast with this, Eric Moody's paper, presenting as it did a non-traditional perspective on one of the most frequent areas of both political and professional debate, provoked a much greater divergence of views and not just between the politicians on the panel.

The two Members of Parliament, Sir Philip Goodhart of the Conservative Heritage Group, and Mark Fisher, Labour Shadow Minister for the Arts, demonstrated the consensus between the major political parties on the continuing governmental responsibility to support the arts and museums, though they divided predictably between government and opposition over the prospects for future changes in policy and for significant expansion in government funding. In the absence of anyone supporting the views of the small minorities on the ultra-libertarian or ultra-populist right, it was left to Kenneth Hudson to argue for an actual reduction in investment in the arts, and specifically in art museums.

Museums and the general public

Turning to the second major theme of 'Museums 2000', 'Museums and People', most in UK museums would hotly deny any accusation that they and their museums have been ignoring ordinary people in the planning and provision of their services. What about the extensive attempts to apply market research techniques such as visitor surveys through the 1970s and early 1980s, or the current and burgeoning concern with the visitors as 'consumers' of museum and gallery provision, whether paying or non-paying customers, and hence the rapidly expanding demand for 'customer care' training?

But these approaches have in my view been over-concerned with people as actual or potential purchasers of a distinctive product (the museum visit) as a market commodity within a 'leisure' (or – less frequently – educational) market-place, rather than with the people of the museum's actual or identified potential community themselves. Further, as I have previously commented, a substantial proportion of the museum pro-fession felt themselves beleaguered in the face of the pace of change, the devaluing of the professional status and responsibilities following the local government changes of the early 1970s and the economic problems and political changes of the late 1970s and early 1980s.

Nowhere was the impact of the new national mood and the museum profession's reaction to it more clearly seen than in the Museums Asso-ciation's own revised definition of museums and the museum profession adopted in 1984. Seven years earlier, the Association had unanimously adopted as its formal policy the world-wide definition adopted by the International Council of Museums (ICOM) at its Copenhagen, 1974, General Conference, with its unambiguous and confident assertion of the primacy of the museum movement's commitment to the service of society and to development:

> A museum is a non-profitmaking, permanent institution in the service of society and its development, and open to the public, which acquires, conserves, researches, communicates, and exhibits, for the purpose of study, education and enjoyment, material evidence of humankind and its development.

In contrast with this, the Association's 1984 definition was pared down to the narrowest of collections-orientated perspectives:

> A museum is an institution which collects, documents, preserves, exhibits and interprets material evidence and associated information for the public benefit.

Not least because of the growing concern within the Association about the apparent narrowness of the Association's official position on the nature of museums, the aim of the second major 'Museums 2000' theme: 'Museums and People' was to look at the present state and future prospects of museums in relation to everyone within the museum's actual or potential constituency. In particular, there was a clear implicit assumption that 'people' in the subtitle of the Conference meant the whole of the available population of the museum's territory, not just those who chose and are able to use the museum and its facilities without any actual or self-perceived limitations of access (whether because of geographical, physical, educational or financial restrictions).

The opening keynote speaker on the theme was the distinguished Australian, Donald Horne, the Chair of the Australia Council. He is an internationally known academic, and before his retirement was Professor and Chair of the Arts Faculty at the University of New South Wales. Outside Australia, he is perhaps best known for his writing on the arts and culture, and especially for his *The Great Museum* (1984) in which amongst many other things he drew a provocative but telling parallel between perceptions of museum objects and the veneration of holy relics, and argued that cultural tourism is the modern equivalent of the religious pilgrimage.

He opened his contribution with a challenging view of the relationship between the general public and museums, and the way in which non-specialists – in his word – 'read' museums. Using Zola's witty description of the couple sheltering from the rain in the nineteenth-century Louvre on the afternoon of their wedding day, he began by analysing the classic and still all too frequent public perception of the purpose of the museum visit, and the traditional alienation of much of the public from the cultures and scholarship that are regarded as central features and responsibilities of at least the major art and 'international' museums, but which have much wider echoes throughout the world museum movement.

Nor did Donald Horne ignore or gloss over the class bias that museums in general, and the great museums of the world in particular, inevitably represent as children of their own history. Especially valuable was his insistence that 'we are all of us, however ill-educated or highly educated, critics of existence and as such, we approach a museum not on the terms of the museum, but on our own terms': hence the need for everyone to learn to 'read' museums.

Nevertheless, his main message was a more optimistic and hopeful one, stressing the potentially liberating role of museums in the future, as what he termed 'a configuration of knowledge'. Could not the present artificial boundaries between different types of museums and of subject treatment within them be broken down, for example current distinctions within museums between rural and industrial ethnography, or between 'Art' and the rest of the historical and/or geographical context in which it was created? He quoted with particular approval the successful integration of all three in Amsterdam's excellent Tropical Museum, and the 'reconfiguration' of Australian aborigine culture in progress at the present time.

Finally, but by no means least, Donald Horne's keynote address challenged the issues of nationalistic identity, bias and the pressure for conformity rather than eccentricity and individualism, both from society and from the profession: 'the Duke of Wellington was allowed to die but not his chair'.

In the discussion, which was generally highly appreciative and supportive of Donald Horne's thesis, Barry Lord introduced the nineteenth-century English term 'edification', 'the broadening of one's perspectives, the sharpening of one's interests, the loosening of one's prejudices and beginning to see the relationship between things that one didn't see before', as a valuable synthesis and resolution of the traditional argument about the role of museums – whether these exist for education or entertainment?

A distinguished conference participant from the Netherlands, Frans Schouten, quoted research in the USA on the popularity of video games, which had identified the need for a challenge, the raising of curiosity and element of discovery amongst those playing them for the games to be successful. He suggested that this consumer research was relevant to museums as well, and believed that measured against these tests traditional nineteenth-century museums sometimes offered more of each than do modern museums and their displays. In my own contribution to the discussion I drew attention to the insularity of the UK museum profession and the lack of resources and opportunities for training and career development, and to enable our museum staff to gain experience of non-British museum issues and perspectives, a view that was strongly supported by Lord Montagu of Beaulieu among others.

However, perhaps it was Tomislav Sola who summed up best the mood of the Conference on the issues, with his quotation from Goethe: 'You only learn from those whom you love', and his argument that museums must achieve this place within the public perception, otherwise, in Tomislav Sola's view, 'there won't be communication or any sort of understanding between the public and museums'.

For the second keynote address on the 'People' theme, we turned to a distinguished museum professional, Saroj Ghose of India. He is Director-General of the National Council of Science Museums, which is one of the spearheads of the Indian Government's highly imaginative and ambitious programme to bring science to the whole of the population, and especially to young people. Unfortunately, no written report can convey the vivid video images he showed to the Conference of children learning and, equally important, enjoying science in both established Indian science museums and their supporting mobile 'Museum Bus' programmes, and in a few of the 1,000 new science museums and science centres across that vast nation that the National Council of Science Museums is developing during the current national five-year plan.

His keynote address on 'People's participation in science museums' outlined the role of the science museum as what he termed an 'information tool', stressing his view and experience that it is essential for the visitor to participate interactively if they are to discover and understand science. This in turn makes it essential for museums to become 'more people-minded'.

He also described, partly in his text, but even more vividly in his selection of video images of real science museums doing real work with real people of all ages, the role of science museums in public education and communication at all levels in India. Indian science museums draw very much even today on the original and still entirely relevant inspiration and national agenda of the founder of modern India, Jawarharal Nehru, who was a strong supporter of both science education and science museums.

Particularly telling was Nehru's concept of 'scientific temper', which he quite frequently used 'as a goal to achieve through the science and technology planning of the country. This is something like generating a new line of thinking, a new culture, a new ethos.' Saroj Ghose ended his prepared address with a reference to what he believed to be the 'burning question for 2000 AD', and one that was to be the central theme of the General Conference of the International Council of Museums (ICOM) later that year (The Hague, Netherlands, September 1989): 'Will museums succeed in becoming a generator of new cultures rather than projectors of old heritage?' – leaving the Conference in no doubt as to his own view as to the way in which museums now and in the future need to relate to and serve the people.

In the discussion, I was able to amplify and commend the Indian approach, and argued for the integration of the interactive approach to presentation and learning into the displays of the real collections, and not just use these in separate science centres, and I was supported in this by the rest of the panel. Paul Perrot stressed the need for the formal educational system to cover learning from objects, as a key step in making museum visiting meaningful, while Hazel Moffat, Her Majesty's Inspector of Schools, referred to the potential for learning from museums in relation to the new National Curriculum for Schools in England and Wales.

The discussion then broadened into considering the wider issues of the non-specialist public and the museum: who should determine what the museum presents, and how should the interests and needs of the general public (including the non-visitor as well as the paying or non-paying 'customer') be ascertained and then responded to? The need for museums to respond to the needs of the increasingly multi-ethnic and multi-cultural societies of our large cities was also an important concern of panel members and conference participants. However, if the museum does identify what the public appears to want, and responds by providing this, are we de-professionalizing museums and museum work or is this the very essence of true professionalism? Whatever the answer to that, the Conference recognized that people, including children and non-specialist adults, must be a central and growing concern of our museums and galleries, both now and into the future.

The museum profession

The second day opened with two viewpoints on 'Professionals and Museums'. The first of these was given by Tomislav Sola of the Museum Studies Centre of Zagreb University, Yugoslavia, who has both taught and researched extensively both the theory and practice of museology, and who has been actively involved in the programme of research and discussion about the subject within the International Committee for Museology of the International Council of Museums. His provocative title: 'Museum professionals – the endangered species' led him straight into a lively and equally provocative, iconoclastic opening, slaying real and imaginary museum and museum profession dragons left, right and centre!

In particular he demonstrated the wide dichotomy of views within the profession as to whether either museology or the concept of a museum profession are valid: 'Most museum professionals . . . think museology is some kind of fiddling'. They also argued that museums '. . . are used and manipulated, they obey their bosses and because they are, for the most part, like them: being concerned with power, profit and conquest'.

In a more serious vein, he argued that despite being 'disguised with its modern buildings and heaps of modern technology' the predominant contemporary museum model is still essentially a nineteenth-century one; hence, despite the near exponential growth in the numbers of museums, there is at the philosophical level 'a serious crisis of institutional identity and a crisis of concept'. He challenged many of the most precious and central assumptions of the contemporary museum profession, comparing the current central place of museums in the care of the heritage as equivalent to the Earth-centred universe of Ptolomy's astronomy, while he too questioned the prevailing curatorial and conservation ethic that refuses to let any 'dying' object in the museum finally die, saying that many modern museums already look like hospital intensive care departments.

He questioned and by implication rejected most if not all of the current measures of judging the success or otherwise of the museum curator – especially the expansionist 'man of action' model (what I have termed elsewhere the macho museum management heresy), and the continued increase in specialization, arising at least in part from a lack of professional theory. Instead, he suggested that a more contemplative style and broader vision is the way forward: 'the time of synthesis has come. We need clear vision, panoramic view, synoptic insight, and a holistic approach.'

Tomislav Sola developed this argument much further and in considerable detail, through what he termed 'the third wave' community and environment-orientated museums, termed ecomuseums by the New Museology movement in France and elsewhere, and leading on to an integration of all heritage preservation and interpretation, which he has previously termed 'heritology', or the cybernetic philosophy of heritage. The consequence of these changes in the nature, objectives and operations of the museum institution will be profound for the museum profession, but he ended on an optimistic note, predicting that the museum profession will continue to exist, though perhaps in an modified form, but as part of a broader heritage preservation profession.

In the light of his own research on European museums for the Institut La Boëtie, Claude Labouret began the discussion with the argument that if museum professionals are an endangered species, then a conservation programme is needed. He also commented on the difference between museums and business in terms of the speed and management of change: museums need to follow business and put human resources management, especially management for change, at the top of its priorities. Victor Middleton took this argument further, arguing that in the future museums will need to be headed by someone in a general manager role, whose job would include establishing goals and practical targets, resolve conflicts, motivate staff and manage business information, suggesting that such general managers may or may not have a traditional museum background, but could instead come from a general management background.

Donald Horne took up the general problem of over-specialization of intellectual labour in the modern world, while Paul Perrot urged the Conference not to concentrate solely on the museum curator when discussing the museum profession, pointing out that 'in many museums, *de facto*, there is a whole congregation of professions that work together' covering conservation, preservation, communication, education, public affairs, publication, etc. However, he totally rejected the idea that 'bankers, lawyers and former ambassadors' are better able to run museums than those with a lifetime experience in the field, and further suggested that multinational businesses may eventually discover their present fashion of having what he termed 'manipulators' at their head, rather than those with a knowledge of the business, may not be in the best interests of either their shareholders or their customers.

Another Past President of the Museums Association, Neil Cossons, Director of the National Museum of Science and Industry, gave the second keynote address on the 'Professional and Museums' theme, under the title 'Rambling reflections of a museum man'. He too was very provocative about traditional museum values and practice, speaking as someone 'with a deep suspicion of professions but an overwhelming admiration for professionalism'.

He discussed in particular traditional professional views about collecting and collections, and 'a really quite alarming situation in which large museums of long-standing now tend to see their collections almost as liabilities rather than assets, despite the fact that the reason for the museum's existence is to have and hold collections, and indeed to do things with those collections'. He contrasted preventative with remedial approaches to the care of museum collections, arguing for strategic investment in long-term preventative care, which in turn needed to be linked to new approaches to the collecting of contemporary collections, particularly in areas such as contemporary science, where perhaps large numbers of items should be collected initially on an interim basis for an initial period of some decades, during which period the long-term retention or otherwise of each object would be regularly reviewed.

He also considered that the traditional staff structures and specializations within museums needed to be challenged and changed, in order to make these more relevant to the current needs of their museums. Such changes could well involve far fewer staff directly on the payroll, and much greater use of short-term contracts for some categories of staff. However, he too was convinced that whilst high managerial qualities are needed to run museums, these need to be built on a foundation of scholarly object-based understanding: 'I am not at all persuaded that museums can be run by managers who haven't their roots in a passion for the collections.'

In the discussion Saroj Ghose emphasized the scale of the growth of collections in the science field and the need for proper acquisitions and collections management policies, and Barry Lord drew attention to the emergence of museum planning as a key discipline in its own right, and which can assist in establishing development and collections plans. Saroj Ghose raised a new point in stressing the need for the closest possible links between museum training centres and the leading museums in order to ensure the continued relevance of professional training, and the feedback of best practice from museums to the training programme.

Both Paul Perrot and Tomislav Sola referred to the Swedish SAMDOC contemporary history documentation and collecting programme, which involves both close documentation in advance of actual collecting, and carefully planned co-operation and specialization involving a considerable number of different museums, as a further model for contemporary collecting.

The discussion on this part of the Conference was particularly wide-ranging, as can be seen from the full transcript. With so many museum professionals present and taking part, it was not surprising that the present state and the future of the museum profession were of special interest and concern. In general, most contributors accepted that both museums and their employees need to change and will change over the coming years, with increased specialization (despite Tomislav Sola's strictures) and much greater emphasis on planning, and better standards of management and leadership. However, most felt that there is still a very good future for the museums profession and that museum professionals, properly trained in the special skills needed for the leadership of their institutions, rather than imported general managers, will continue to be the proper people to run museums.

Museums and money

The first of the two keynote speakers for the 'Profit and Museums' theme was a distinguished American (though French-born) colleague, Paul Perrot, who has during his career worked in a private museum, the Corning Glass Museum, a national museum at the Smithsonian head-quarters in Washington, and now in the local government sector, as Director of the Virginia Museum of Fine Arts, based in Richmond, Virginia, which also runs an outstanding state-wide outreach and pastoral care programme.

In his 'Funding, sponsorship and corporate support' keynote address he drew on the American experience of private support and sponsorship to review both the practical and professional (including ethical) impact on museums of external funding of museums, especially that from the business sector. However, he stressed the potential and actual value of a large membership organization in support of the museum: this may not produce much money if it is a broadly based non-exclusive society, but results in 'a nucleus of supporters throughout the community and this can have enormous value, not only in appealing to the public sector, but also to the corporate sector'.

In relation to business and similar sponsorship it is particularly important to have in advance a clear definition of the museum's purposes and to be 'unswerving in presenting them and defending them'. He also drew attention to the selectiveness of many sponsors, in terms of the content of the proposed exhibition or special event (with ideas for potentially controversial subjects rarely receiving support), or perhaps in terms of geography (with some major companies only willing to support activities in towns where they have a particular business interest). In contrast with this the national museum – the Smithsonian Institution – has much greater freedom because although it receives government funds its operations and governing body are totally independent of all branches of the govern-ment, all members of the governing body (citizens' Regents) being appointed by joint resolution of both Houses of Congress.

The pressures of sponsorship in relation to the expanding numbers of, and inter-museum competition in, 'blockbuster' exhibitions was also clear, as are both their positive and negative effects. However, as a counterbalance to these Paul Perrot stressed the need even within the US sponsorship system and tradition 'to do much more to sell the idea that the museum is an instrument for the service of the total community, and that as part of this community, both in the large and small cities the company has a role to play to enhance the quality of life for all, at relatively little cost'.

Claude Labouret, from his lifetime's experience within the business community and from his research, questioned whether the bargaining with potential sponsors is on an equal basis: do museums know the real value of what they are offering to business people? He believed that 'what they are buying with their sponsorship money is acceptability in the world of art and culture. They are bargaining for their acceptability and prestige'.

There was a good deal of scepticism at the Conference about the current UK view of sponsorship through rose-tinted spectacles and as the long-term salvation of museums, as Barry Lord pointed out. Paul Perrot confirmed that the US tax regime and in particular the availability of tax deductions had been a major factor in the private giving from business and individuals. He drew attention to the fact that gifts to American museums had recently dropped by 60 per cent when these tax advantages were reduced.

Ian Spero, a professional consultant working in the field of sponsorship (who arranged the Museums Year 1989 sponsorships for The Museums Association, including that for the 'Museums 2000' Conference), pointed out that actual and potential UK-based sponsors needed to be shown both sides of the equation in the sponsorship proposals. Museums were usually very good in drafting what they needed from the sponsor, and what they would do with the money, but far less frequently showed what the sponsor's benefits would be.

The final keynote speaker, Frans Verbaas, moved from the Dutch business community ten years ago to run the joint Dutch Museums Association/Ministry of Cultural Affairs Museum Year Pass Foundation, a highly successful joint marketing and annual admission ticket scheme with over 500 museum members and annual sales of over a quarter of a million Year Passes. His theme was 'Options and unique commercial opportunities for museums now and in the future', and after outlining the Pass scheme he explained how the Dutch museum situation had changed over the past decade. The predominant agenda items today were topics that were never mentioned just a few years ago, such as possible privatization, visitor numbers and fund-raising. He believed that so far as Dutch museums are concerned 'the next century is already here'.

Within this context he also drew attention to the changing museum culture in terms of management needs, style and training, all of which, in his view, need to change in order to cope with the new situation and the future needs of museums, arguing that the corporate culture and the personal objectives of the staff need to grow towards each other. If this is not achieved members of staff will each have their own values and objectives and the institution will pull apart, as Frans Verbaas believes is happening in a large number of museums today. This new museum culture has to begin with leadership from top management, and must have an integrated, interdisciplinary approach, within which marketing is totally integrated.

The final discussion focused very much on marketing in relation to museums – a very appropriate final theme in view not only of the major focus on marketing within museums, especially the nationals, at the present time, but also because Museums Year 1989 was primarily a cooperative marketing exercise. However, it was agreed that in its true sense marketing is not solely a device for increasing visitor numbers and income: it can equally be used to reduce numbers at an over-visited museum for conservation reasons or in order to improve the quality of the visit or other service, or to reposition the museum in terms of its audience.

In contrast with these assumptions, Max Hebditch, Professional Vice-President of the Association, pointed out that in the 1970s the Association produced models for the structure of museum provision in Britain based on a concept of service derived from traditions of the British welfare state, and asked: 'Are we quite certain as a profession that we do actually want to abandon that model in favour of what is essentially a public limited company?'

The final word of the Conference was from a Conference participant, Don Filleul, a trustee of the Jersey Museum Service, who summed up both the Conference and the future prospects for museums into the new century:

If I have learnt anything this week I have been privileged to feel the pulse of how museums seem to operate here and I think that the international contributions have been marvellous. But I do hope that we all want to make museums lively places. And I think if there is anything for museums in 2000 and onwards it is that we want more and more participation by more and more people to make museums not dusty, fusty and musty, but the liveliest centres of social intercourse in our countryside.

2 Opening address: Museums 2000

HRH The Duke of Gloucester

If we can be complacent for a moment, the twentieth century has seen a great advance in museums, not just in this country but all over the world. I remember reading how in the previous century at the British Museum there was a man on the gates who was there to turn away anybody who wasn't respectably dressed. I think we have seen a lot of changes since the time when museums were reserved for the educated elite. We now like to hope that everybody is educated whether they are elite or not.

I think the reason that museums have become more popular is primarily because that is what their directors and their staff have wanted. They have found not only justification for museums but also greater personal satisfaction in extending their own interests and obsessions and trying to share them with a great deal more numbers of people. In fact, in this country this year, 80 million people will be visiting different museums, and the creation of new museums for so many different things increases at a rate of roughly fifty a year.

Included in that figure are historic buildings and houses and I think whereas museums can be created in exactly the right places, historic buildings and monuments can only be where they are, which is very often in the wrong place as far as the population is concerned. One of the new departures of museums is treating buildings (and not only the largest and finest of historic buildings) as portable objects and collecting them together in villages and industrial museums. I think that will probably continue in many places – it has been successful in Scandinavia and many other places where they have moved historic buildings that were in the wrong place and put them all together as if they were more portable objects.

That is a particularly significant method for those who want to create industrial museums. There were so many industrial processes that were created by pioneers of one sort or another who produced an economic success initially and then were replaced by further techniques in other countries and other places and so disappeared. Unless there was somebody who was prepared to collect the historic evidence together and present it, it would disappear totally. I think that this is one of the most significant new fields in British museums – creating industrial archaeology as a potent and interesting display.

I have also noticed that one of the problems with historic monuments is that they can become victims of their own success and if you get some that are hugely popular there is a tendency to create more of them and rebuild more. It is a tendency that has been rejected mostly in this country but I have certainly come across it in other countries where you suddenly find that the site you saw a few years before is twice as big and there are twice as many monuments as when you went there before. One can see why a Tourism Department has insisted that the Archaeology Department increases its output. Again this is something which I think many people are worried about in terms of authenticity.

Of course, in the traditional definition of museums, historic houses and monuments shouldn't really be included, as a museum is a specifically built building to house a particular collection, and the purpose of that museum is therefore the scholarship that is used to understand the collection, to verify its importance and to display them to the public. I think that a lot of people just assume that museums are static but it's very obvious that the best museums are the ones where the scholarship attached to the collection is a lively, vibrant thing, and not something that is dead and stultified, and because the scholarship goes with the study of the collections it is what is transmitted to the public in terms of understanding and enthusiasm.

What we are going to see in the next century is a lot of competition. There is going to be competition for the kind of objects that museums want to display. I am very fortunate to be connected with the British Museum which is a wonderful collection of objects from all over the world, but it is very obvious from visiting the kind of countries that these objects have come from that they are now creating their own national museums and some of them are very fine buildings. They are going to want better collections of their own native cultures than can be found in international museums like the British Museum. So there will be competition to collect the same objects – let's hope there will be enough around for everybody.

There will also be competition for funds, particularly government funds, because there are so many museums. There will be competition for staff – in this country we haven't been breeding fast enough and there is soon going to be a shortage of students and of graduates. Although that may be quite good news for the graduates themselves it does mean that there is a great shortage of the kind of trained intelligence that is necessary for museums.

It is difficult to know whether we are all going to be competing for the same visitors. I am inclined to believe that the more museums there are that are really interesting, the greater the demand for museums is thus created. I think if the whole process of going to museums can be made more attractive, whether it is better transport or easier parking or whatever, the whole process becomes easier rather than more difficult. I think more people are going to want to go out and see things for themselves rather than expect to sit in front of the television and be told exactly what to look at and what to think.

There will also be competition for sponsors because, whether public or privately funded, museums are always a good and noble cause. For many years we have expected the government to pay for the national museums but it's not something as far as this government is concerned that is a bottomless pit. They expect museums to pay for themselves (not entirely for themselves) but if they are free to the public then they expect them to get sponsorship from other people. Although this is a difficult route to undertake I certainly know that at the British Museum the fact that we have had to look at this to consider how we are going to make the shortfall has made us much more aware of our relationship with the public and how we should go out and seek the interest of particular people who may be able to help us: that in many ways has made us much more open to outside ideas. It has also made us much more aware of our public image and how we can make the best use of our connections to increase that public image.

Politics and museums 1

3

Politics and the role of museums in the rescue of identity

Lorena San Roman

Museums, as mirrors of past and present societies, show their progress and development, as well as their link with other societies influencing the world's development.

Museums, in one way or the other, are reservoirs of the natural and cultural heritage, and always rescue part of the identities of the communities, not only showing their history but also the current events of a given area of the world, and they must present events of a given area of the world. They must communicate through objects, designs, lectures and other activities, non-tangible values of each society.

Through museums, each country or city can present both events that occurred recently in history, or point out past events. Many of these are the product of the political decisions of the governors and the governed of the time in question.

In this sense, in our small country, we are elaborating, in the National Museum of Costa Rica, an exhibition to present our national reality, showing our natural history, our archaeological history, and past and recent developments of culture. It is intended for both Costa Ricans and also for foreigners who want to know us better. Since we are seeking, with this exhibition, the reinforcing of our identity, we are presenting the decisions the rulers take for the development of our country, as well as the opinions of the community, either in favour or against any historical event.

Politics and role of museums

If museums make exhibitions of this kind and present the message the current rulers want to give in relation to the development of the country, they must also present other opinions of the community. The museums must, in my opinion, be pluralistic. So, in any subject chosen for an exhibition, or within lectures or any other activity, we must present the opinions of the majority, as well as the ones of the minorities, not forgetting the cultural and non-cultural expressions in the country or abroad.

We must remember that museums must present all the community's feelings or at least their principal ideas. That is why they must present the range of different opinions on a theme, as I said before, and for that reason proper, wide-ranging, research by curators is so important for an exhibition.

The part of our museum that will be presenting Costa Rican history from the fifteenth century to the present day, will show the history of those centuries, as well as the history of the present times. It will include different political ideas during all these years, and the different situations of the world during the various periods, for example, showing how the world dealt with us and how we fit in this big world. In order to have a complete presentation, we have turned to historical situations and the problems that they face at each moment. The result of our dynamic effort will not produce solutions, for that is not our purpose. Instead, it will create a didactic attitude towards the complex historical facts. Then, we will present a complete frame of manifestations of the problems.

In Third World countries museums often present exhibitions without enough research. Exhibitions may lack an objective point of view, and also fail to present the plurality of ideas. In some cases this happens because we don't have enough training. In other cases it is because the ministers, directors or curators themselves want to present their own subjective point of view on the theme of the exhibition. This last situation is a most dangerous one. To train people without experience is not so difficult, but to change the way of thinking of a person, who is used to doing things or thinking in one way, is quite difficult, and they often refuse to accept the different ways of thinking of other sectors of the community. That is why directors and curators of the museums must be very well chosen, and must know the importance of the interdisciplinary work in museums. They must also find a way of advising and guiding politicians on different programmes they want to develop in, or with the aid of, the museum.

In my opinion, museums, especially ones depending on the central government must, to a certain point, collaborate in presenting some exhibitions which accord with the policy of the government. We must accept this fact because museums must collaborate closely with the formal education system, and formal education is generally directed as part of government policy. However, museums must never lose the scientific and objective base of the actual historical events, or other subjects covered.

Also, the museums must be critical institutions in which the people can see the consequences of the decisions of the government or other governors. The public will then be able to analyse better what they want for their present and future in relation to current policies of the government.

The museums must offer all the information needed to know the reality and points of view of any situation, so that with these tools people will be able to discuss the theme knowledgeably. All of this, with a good direction, is necessary for the development of democracies all around the world.

The President of the Congress of Costa Rica, Mr José Luis Valenciano, in an interview stated: 'The cultural facts had a big influence on the thinking or ways of going on of the politicians, but also the cultural facts are in many ways determined by political actions now and before in history.'

He considers also that a certain time must pass before exhibiting recent historic events. For instance, under a political decision in the 1950s, a museum in Hawaii exhibited how American men died in action during the Second World War, and the treason of the Japanese. If this museum was being created instead, I think perhaps the Marines of the United States would have made a museum exalting the heroes of both groups.

In recent years, museums world-wide have been discussing and executing activities, so that our museums can improve their public relations and their status in the community, as well as to raise more funds to run our institutions. I remember the British Council Seminar in 1985 when Neil Cossons discussed this with us and the importance of improving these aspects of museums. Many have succeeded in these activities. But we also already know that, because of our better status and through getting involved in the different activities of our communities, we are under more political pressure from the different parts of the government as well as from the community and private enterprise. All of them ask for more and better information on the different aspects of the identity or development of the country.

Politics and role of museums

The museums are beginning to be more and more important for politics each day, especially in underdeveloped countries, since the politicians know they are important tools for presenting their points of view in a serious and nice way, as well as showing the opinions of the opposition.

As far as I know, European museums have been outside the political conflicts of the country, while in Latin America that condition on many many occasions has been difficult to obtain. I think we deal in our conscience with politics daily and perhaps it could be that sometimes 80 per cent of our time is dedicated to dealing with this.

Museums can be an active voice in national debates on different events: let's say from a debate on conserving a building, to the political decisions of the government. For example, you can see a structured and planned museum such as the Museum of the Centre of the World in Ecuador, the Museum of London, or the Milwaukee Public Museum in the United States. All of these museums and many others around the world present exhibitions that include the results of research on the themes of history in a serious and pluralistic way. After going through the Museum of the Centre of the World in Ecuador, do you seriously think of the Ecuadorian reality in recording and presenting the identity of that country? This is a good example, which must lead us on to a reflection on our role in managing museums.

In our particular case, the National Museum that I run opened in October 1988 an exhibition on the Nobel Peace Prize to celebrate the first anniversary of the award of this prize to our President. Analysing it, we must say that this prize has an international recognition and that the award is very important in the political situation of Central America today. Also, this exhibition for the National Museum was an opportunity to show an event that reinforced the civic values of Costa Rica, and that prepared the Costa Rican community for the celebration of one hundred years of democracy on 7 November 1989, and for attracting the attention of the media with the polemics they develop. I think for the first time in the history of our museum we have had about six months of polemics on both sides. All the media were bringing the National Museum to the attention of the politicians and the community, which for many years had thought that the museum was just there, like Cinderella with money, standing in the centre of the city and nothing more. Now we began to discuss what we were doing, not only the Nobel Peace Prize.

Also, I must mention that we complemented this exhibition with a symposium called 'Democracy and Political Culture in Costa Rica', in which the main philosophers, historians and anthropologists of the country, of every tendency, discussed this important national event. For the first time we sat at a table – people from private enterprise, people from the trade unions, and people from the Congress, to discuss this matter, and it really was quite interesting to hear them.

From another point of view, perhaps for the politicians this was seen as a way of reinforcing the work done by the President and the political party in power. But for the museum it was a way, as I said before, to show a continuity of our civilian tradition, to improve the museum's status, to attract the attention of both the media and of the government, and to obtain political decisions needed for the approval of our big project for the expansion of the building and other future developments, agreed in principle as projects sponsored by the United Nations and UNESCO many years ago.

We must remember that using a museum as a political instrument must be avoided. That is why Museum Boards and Directors must analyse and be very careful in their relations with the government and the community, including private enterprise. Many times museums want to do a project without knowing the whole situation of the matter or ask more than is possible, in exchange for the aid they give. So, with a lot of care, we must explain to them the way we can do the project in a technical and scientific way if we decide to do so, or if we don't accept the project, explain in a logical and polite way the impossibility of what they are asking for.

Ms Ulla Keding Olofsson in her article 'The Swedish Center for Itinerant Exhibition: from the Itinerant Exposition to the Creation of a Center of Information' (*Museum*, no. 152 (1986)) discussed the goals of this centre, indicating among others that they seek the protection of the liberty of expression, as well as giving the opportunity to individuals to realize their creativity in favour of the social relations.

She discussed also the questioning by the Swedish Parliament of Mr Olaf Palme, at that time Minister of Education and Culture, whether museums were good places for exhibitions with a political character, and if it was legitimate for an exhibition funded by the state to be converted to political proselytism. He answered, after giving a brief explanation of the cultural policy of the government: 'Nothing accords more with the spirit of democracy than to give support to different initiatives, whether you like them or not.'

So the museums are entities of expression for the life and development of the communities, and because of the dynamism they are acquiring through us, they are becoming more and more important in the life of our communities. This means accepting more challenges and more responsibilities towards the community instead of being inactive and contemplative.

Today, museums cannot be useless, because if they are they will disappear. They must play a role in the polemics of the country and in its socio-economical development. For example the role of the Cité des Sciences et de l'Industrie at La Villette in Paris, France, and the Rural Museum of Chordeleg in Ecuador (to mention two extremes), have similar objectives in the development of the economies of the countries.

La Villette, in relation to the size and development of Paris, is helping to serve young professionals of the industrial and business enterprises, thus aiding the economic development of the country. The Rural Museum of Chordeleg produces crafts of the small town of Chordeleg, so craftsmen work the silver and gold of the mines. They are also helping their country in another way. Indeed, both museums, because of their role in the community, must be involved in a lot of public decisions and themes of discussion in their own areas.

In the *World Federation of Friends of Museums Chronicle* it is stated of Canada that: 'Museums, historical sites and other cultural activities are in a prime position to attract large numbers of tourists. In a sense, we are the marketing "loss leaders" by providing low cost and universal accessibility' (*Museum* no. 152 (1986), p. 255).

If we analyse that statement, it is not totally true since culture generates foreign exchange and a museum generates culture, since it lives and enriches itself from the society. Mr Sylvio Mutal, Director of the UNDP Regional Project of the Natural and Cultural Patrimony in Latin America, said in 1986 (Sarquisimato, Venezuela, during the opening of the Course of Museum Administration in the Latin American Area) that the day when museums have people queuing for entry like in the banks, movies and buses, that day the museums will be performing 100 per cent of their role.

We know that a lot of museums have people queuing because they have good exhibitions and interesting and attractive activities for their community and foreign visitors. But others are far from having people queuing and if they want to enter the modern way of running museums, they must improve to have queues as soon as possible.

In this sense, the Costa Rica National Museum has been working to change the permanent exhibitions to show, as I stated, the historical process of Costa Rica, from our geological formation until our time, as a process of biological and cultural changes. Today 55 per cent of the tourists who reach Costa Rica visit the National Museum. With the new museum, including remodelling and expansion and the new exhibition, we expect that percentage to increase; and we also expect the tourists to stay, because of this, an extra day in our country. This is an important economic fact since in the last year tourism in Costa Rica earned 10 per cent of the total export income. So, with this, the museum will be closely related with the tourist industry and will reinforce even more our identity, as well as the economic development of the country.

In my opinion all the communities in the less developed countries must have a museum, not only presenting the history of the community, but also being the centre for discussion of the city itself, as well as a centre integrated into the tourist industry and other cultural activities. We need this so much in the rural areas of the Latin American countries, including my country.

Because of these important roles that the museums are beginning to play, we must think seriously about the legislation and status of the museums. They need to be dynamic centres of the community itself, and we must administer them like successful private enterprises, and protect them with the best laws in each country. Then the museums can continue to communicate the plurality of opinions of the country, as well as being one of the more important entities in the reinforcing and rescue of the national identity.

To quote Makaminan Makagiansar, Assistant Director-General of UNESCO in charge of the Sector of Culture, writing five years ago: 'Today, however, museums, everywhere are being gradually transformed. The museum ... has had to come to grips with the notion of service to contemporary society as a whole' (*Museum*, no. 141 (1984), p. 3).

In underdeveloped countries, the reinforcement of the cultural identity is one of the deepest popular aspirations – perhaps the most important after shelter and food – and museums need to assume wider responsibilities and change in order to serve all its communities, instead of just a small elite.

Finally, there must be a direct relation between the museum and the government ministries and agencies responsible for not only cultural action, but also other aspects of the daily life in the community, making possible the creation of the necessary understanding in order to receive help from these agencies, the necessary scientific and objective help. This will take us to a permanent feedback and dialogue between the museum and government, to the benefit of the community that we, in museums, are called to serve.

Discussion

LORD MONTAGU: We have examined of course the political position of museums throughout the world, and obviously must throw out the problem of the independence and objectivity of the directors of those museums and how they can themselves be independent of political control. Perhaps could I ask our two politicians here today to start off the discussion.

MARK FISHER: It is absolutely essential for their credibility and for the health and diversity of our culture that museums are very clearly independent of the state and of the government, and that they present a balanced and pluralist view of our society and of that particular area of our culture. Lorena stressed representing *minority* cultural views as well as the *majority* and I think that is a major problem for us. There has always been in Britain and indeed almost all cultures where there is an absolutist tendency, not just from political parties and government but inside cultures, for the dominant cultural view to prevail and to dominate the minority tendencies.

But there is no aspect of a museum's life or museums as a part of our culture which can possibly be neutral or objective politically (with a small 'p', not party politically). Everything that a museum does from the appearance and position, location and type of its building, its relationship with its community, whether its direct community or the national community, its choice of objects, the way those objects are presented, how it relates to the question of widening access – all these inevitably are politically non-neutral, politically loaded questions from whatever section of the political spectrum you come from. And these present major problems.

I think that in the UK we have tended to ignore that or slide away from it and assume that it is easy to find a politically balanced or objective view of those things – through the two areas where there is a direct interface between government and museums, i.e. funding, and the appointment of trustees or boards, how do we preserve the independence and give museums the confidence to make those key political decisions? Just as historians when writing our history (as museums write our history through objects and artefacts) cannot be politically unbiased, how do we give you in museums the independence to pursue a clear view as you see it of our culture while retaining a diverse position?

I think the key areas of that, as I say, are the appointment of boards. We know something about that in this country at the moment with the grave concern about the balance of one or two of our national boards, and I am thinking particularly of the Victoria and Albert Museum which hasn't got any museum professionals on that board at all. That is a worry when government, I think perhaps inadvertently, perhaps deliberately, has appointed boards which have not got the balance or expertise to preserve that independence. The second thing is of course funding and I think that is a much more difficult thing because I don't think that even pluralist funding in itself preserves independence. I think the relationship of independence to funding is a very very much more complicated thing.

KENNETH HUDSON: What Mrs San Roman has said to us is the most important talk on a museum subject that I have heard for many, many years.

As I was listening to her, I realized more and more what a museum backwater the United Kingdom is becoming. We are extremely good on technical matters. But on philosophical and theoretical matters, very bad, and becoming worse. Now there is, as far as I know, only one museum in Britain which has made an attempt to do what Mrs San Roman is talking about and that museum is the People's Palace in Glasgow where the immensely courageous curator, Elspeth King, has been steadily crucified by her own local authority. That is something that makes me bitterly ashamed because this is a museum which when people come from abroad to look at it, they see it as one of the shining lights in what is happening in this country. So far as her own country people are concerned she is treated like a minnow instead of as the whale that she actually is.

The other point I would like to make is this. I don't spend a lot of my time in England nowadays: I spend most of it abroad and I see experiments in other countries along the lines that Mrs San Roman was talking about of a very very interesting nature. Those experiments are not having the influence in this country which I would like to see. This country is becoming exceedingly smug from a museum point of view.

DONALD HORNE: Museums are essentially a part of the political life of a country but there are certain mechanical difficulties in ensuring that they act in that kind of way deliberately instead of, as it were, by accident. No comparison can be made with books: it is very easy to produce a number of different books. There are some problems in it, you don't shoot authors, or if there is a monopoly the government intervenes to provide a market wherever it may be, but it is quite easy to produce a new book. But it is also within a book possible to produce different approaches.

Discussion

Museums introduce extraordinary mechanical difficulties in providing a pluralistic approach. You've got this great building in which the government is going to say: You've got your objects. There is a limited number of objects and there are difficulties about putting up ten different museums to experience ten different views, whereas that difficulty doesn't exist with books, and within museums there are difficulties as well.

TOMISLAV SOLA: I have no wish to speak about politics. I feel so much detached from it, and actually, I do object to it very much as well. I think it should be stressed that the role of museums may indeed lie in opposing politicians in many ways and many occasions.

The quotation from a speech of Sylvio Mutal, UNESCO/UNDP representative for South America, caught my attention. I think he is oversimplifying things by saying that queues in front of museums are their goal, and the final accomplishment of their role. To put it better, it is part of their role or part of their possible accomplishment, but only if we add quality to it does it partly make some sense. But in the context of this theme, politics and museums, I should point out that it is curious that the numbers game – the more the better – actually functions best in totalitarian regimes. Certainly during Hitler's Germany and Stalin's USSR you had record numbers of museum visitors, and the museum system was functioning beautifully. So I would say it is not that really, but that what we are trying to impose is some other logic. I would say democracy is much more than this, and is finally a question of quality rather than quantity, while regarding quantity as a part of what we seek to induce in the quality all the time.

What I would like also to hear within the scope of this theme is some talk or thoughts about the entire world scene, in particular about the relationship between developed and underdeveloped countries, or the Third World as it is often put. I think this is also an area of reflection on this very same theme, politics and museums. What appears to me to be the case is that museums are very much following the patterns as set up by politicians and are actually going blindly behind them and helping politicians to conquer the world. I am sorry, but I am speaking about the developed world and its influence, sometimes a really dangerous influence, upon the underdeveloped world. I will try to put it a very simple way.

Museums are there to serve identity, and for the protection of it. They actually only come into existence where there is an identity to protect: in other words they stem or grow from an identity. One could also put in another way: in developing countries or underdeveloped countries, we need those wells dug into identity where you can always find the distinctive fresh water of that country for inspiration, as the source of self-respect, for the constant wisdom that we all need for our development. But instead of that fresh water from those wells that are dug into the identity of the country, we actually have an import of Coca-Cola and Fanta, and this is what I drink. Namely, they have imported our museums of the developed world and it does not function there. It does function in the sense that they actually become dependent again, not necessarily in the economic sense but what is worse, in the cultural sense. They are losing not their money but their souls. This is I think an important aspect that should be stressed when we are speaking about politics and museums.

CLAUDE LABOURET: We all agree that museums must be free of the political pressures but that objective is not that easy to reach. I have been in publishing all my life and it is difficult to say when you are objective and when you are not objective. By the end of this year (1989) we shall know whether the French, 200 years after the Revolution, have been able to give a well-balanced presentation of the Revolution and I would like to just state two facts.

Last year I visited a new museum in Caen. We all remember the terrible battle of Caen in 1944. Well, there is a splendid presentation of D-Day on two screens. One screen shows the Allied point of view of the landing and the other screen at the same time shows the landing as seen by the Germans. That would be typically the answer to the Hawaii case Lorena San Roman mentioned. But on the other hand Kenneth Hudson made me remember that in the Army Museum at the Invalides in Paris there is still no reference to Waterloo!

KENNETH HUDSON: Apparently 1814 was there and 1816 was there but 1815 is mysteriously missing! And the attendant in the museum said 'I have a lot of people asking me if we have anything about Waterloo and I don't think we have.' He said so many of them seem to be English.

PATRICK BOYLAN: 'Politics' are two things. One is the more subtle, indirect, political direction which is often financial pressure; and one of the things that the Association's Council will address next week is what evidence we put to the Select Committee of the House of Commons' inquiry about admission charges. The Association's view is that it should be, to a considerable degree, neutral as to whether there should be charges or not and that it should be a matter for the governing body of museums themselves to decide. What the Association does not accept is that museums should be subtly starved into submission and the introduction of charges by the pressures of underfunding and so on. This is one of the things that the Association will want to have a look at, as to whether museums making these decisions are doing so on a free basis or not. But of course indirect political influence and pressure goes very much wider

Discussion

than this. Staying with Latin America, what happened to museums under military dictatorships in Latin American countries, in countries like Uruguay or for that matter Brazil? The long-established regular museums were closed down completely or starved totally of funds while great new monuments to the military might and so on were created: they were the museums that received the money. But of course political pressure is much more subtle than this: it comes much closer to home, certainly into Europe. In my own research field, no one could deny the fact that French decisions in the last thirty years on early prehistoric archaeology research has been very much orientated towards proving that so far as Europe is concerned Adam was a Frenchman! The political implications of the pressure from President Giscard d'Estaing leading to the establishment of a site museum at Terra Amata (where one of the excavators was related to the President's wife – adding a further dimension) was apparently completely missed by the Committee which gave it a European Museum of the Year Award!

Possibly museums in this country are not so responsive as they ought to be, and I have got every sympathy with points made about the People's Palace Museum in Glasgow. I suspect Elspeth King is not here today because at the People's Palace (like virtually every museum in this country), funds for travel to meetings like this let alone travel abroad are not regarded as necessary. (I think the average Glasgow Museums department has £100 a year for the whole of its travel and research and everything else and certainly wouldn't bear the cost of two days at this meeting.) But the issue is much wider than that. I think the museums in this country are probably concerned too much with their visitors and not with the wider population they ought to be serving. René Rivard has caricatured certainly French museums and many others by saying that they are concerned solely with a building containing a collection and with the visitors that go to that building, whereas they ought to be concerned not with their museum building but with all of their defined geographical territory which might be a small village, or it might be a whole nation. It should not be concerned just with the objects preserved in that institution (although that is clearly one of the most important responsibilities) but they should be concerned with the total heritage that those collections represent. Above all, they should be concerned not just with the visitors who come through the door but with the total population of that area that they have defined as their territory or their sphere of influence. They should be just as concerned (or perhaps even more concerned) about the non-visitors. These are, I think, quite political issues, possibly with a capital 'P' instead of a small 'p'.

DAVID BEST: I want to take up the point about the relationship between museums and the private sector, and the politics issue. Clearly those of us who represent the private sector and who may be approached for funding have a delicate balance to strike in anything which has a political, with a small or large 'p', aspect to it. But before talking about how that might affect us, it does seem to me, following a point that Patrick Boylan has just made, that it is necessary for the museum or any institution of a similar type to decide what its role is in the community that it serves. We as private sector institutions provide a service to a territory which is very diverse and very wide and in seeking to find out how we can best support, and then further our interests and those of museums by providing funding or material support. We have to know how our partner, the museum, also relates to its territory and its catchment area and the population that it serves. It is only when that's clear and it's also clear to us what methods it will use for research, for presentation, for exposition, for education, that we can decide whether it is our philanthropic string which is being pulled or our commercial marketing string which is being pulled, or what the specific area is that we can use to address the needs that that museum presents to us.

So the question of balance in terms of the museum or institution presenting the full range of its artefacts in a balanced way, relating them to the community which it serves, is only achieved when the institution has set its stall out in a way that we as potential funding bodies and potential supporters are in a position to know how to respond, whether as charitable foundations, or as direct sponsors in order to gain marketing profile, or as service providers. And that seems to me to be an enormously important issue for museums to address over the next ten or fifteen years as government funding without strings comes under increasing pressure and as you turn increasingly to the private sector to provide it.

LORENA SAN ROMAN: Many museums at least in my region of the world, perhaps 80 per cent or more, don't have policies, don't have a planning system. They really don't know what they exist for, and so it makes it more difficult for them to obtain something. I agree with you that if you have the full range of possibilities so private enterprise can say 'I am more interested in this, this and this.' They already know more or less the way they should go because the museum leads the way. If not, then perhaps they are doing different things that perhaps may not be the best for the community.

DAVID BEST: Yes, if I could just top that up, with just one remark. That's also the situation in which the museum is most vulnerable to external pressure, because if it doesn't have its own plans and priorities

Discussion

and missions it is most amenable to having those of others imposed upon it.

BARRY LORD: As a museum planner working in very different parts of the world I see many of these issues in living colour. One of the contributions I want to make at this point has just come up at the end of the last contribution by David Best, which is that it is essential for the museum to have a plan: its own programme, its own agenda, is put into the arena of the private sector and the political pressures that it is subject to, recognizing clearly that it is a political player and has to have its own objective agenda. I think it is interesting that we probably all of us have agreed with two contradictory statements here this morning and this is not unusual. Mark Fisher stressed that there is virtually nothing a museum does that isn't essentially political, which I quite agree with, and on the other hand Claude Labouret's argument (that we would probably all agree with), that we should keep political viewpoints out of museums. It is very interesting that we probably all agree with both of those propositions and yet it could be suggested that they are essentially conflicting points of view.

Listening to Lorena San Roman, I remembered a Yukon Indian chief who told me during a planning exercise we were doing up in the Yukon, of his contention that every nation, every people, has its own museum, so my people (referring to his own very small Indian band in Yukon) must have their own museum too. And I was very struck by that. I thought we have come a very long way for me to be hearing that in the 1980s from a Yukon Indian chief. We have come a very long way from the Imperial museums that claimed universal knowledge in the nineteenth century that Donald Horne has written about so evocatively. We have come a very long way when that Yukon Indian chief can see the necessity for his people to have their own museum to express their point of view.

Just to finish, I wanted to point out that a number of us have touched on what I think is really critical. This is that when a museum does not have its own plan, its own agenda, and enters into this situation, what we must always look for is what is missing in what the museum presents. Whether it is an exhibition or an interpretation of facts – it is the missing components that are interesting to me. When we had a major exhibition of Mayan exhibits from Guatemala there was no reference to what is happening to the Mayan people today. As a result in a number of museums in North America we had demonstrations on the street, protest demonstrations, organized by people who were calling attention to the plight of the Mayan people today. What was missing from the exhibition was any reference to the living, breathing, reality of those people today. I think that in a great many of our exhibitions and a great deal of our treatment (and certainly we found this in Canada) of the native subject matter, it is absolutely critical in any ethnological, anthropological or historical exhibition to bring the story up to the present and to make sure that you do not present any culture as a dead issue, as a matter that is closed, or simply to ignore or to assume that everybody knows about the present situation of the people whom you are representing. Of course this is especially crucial when one is dealing with minority cultures.

I would just like to point out that it is very often in what isn't there that one really sees the museum not having its own clear directions in the political field.

PAUL PERROT: Are museums tending now to become much more tourist attractions, forgetting their role as educational institutions, particularly in further education, and is this not a danger which we should be very careful to watch because a very important role of the museum is to continue to sharpen the minds and the intellects of the people?

JOHN LAST (Conference participant, Member of Museums and Galleries Commission): I was very much affected by what Tomislav Sola said. If I got it right, he said 'Museums are to protect the identity of the nation.' In view of what Mark Fisher said and what Patrick Boylan endorsed, if we accept the mission of projecting the identity of a nation in a museum – do we feel that the mission is in any way threatened by the pressure today in this country particularly for museums to seek their resources from the non-public funding?

KENNETH HUDSON: I think the whole future of museums lies in a mixed economy. I think that's a matter of hope for me, not of gloom at all. I don't see heaven as lying in single funding from public funds and anything which is, if you like, a dilution of that as being a steady movement downwards to hell. That isn't how I see it at all. I think that independent funding is a means of getting what we want, not what we don't want, but I want to see a mixture of the two. I think that's where sanity lies.

It's very difficult to define what the mix should be. I'm not prepared to lay down percentages coming from one source or coming from another but all I know is that so far as new ideas are concerned, in this country the overwhelming majority in the last twenty years have come from the independent museums. They have been our great sources of new ideas and new thinking, and I can't believe that had we not had those we would have had more new ideas than in fact has happened. I think the reverse would have been true and I think other countries are exceedingly envious of us for having had this supply of independent funding. It's one of the treasures that we are perhaps not sufficiently grateful for.

Discussion

PATRICK BOYLAN: I don't think there's a disagreement on that one: That's what John Last's point was. Are you going to find it difficult to find private funding perhaps, not in the mainstream? I think the answer is that one case does not prove anything. I can say that the Boston Children's Museum struggled for eight years to get funding for an exhibition in the Museum on the one total unmentionable of modern society, which isn't sex or nuclear war – it is death. They struggled for eight years to get a commercial sponsor: they wouldn't touch it with a barge-pole. Death is impossible anyway in the States, and for children absolutely impossible. So I think that some areas are not going to be as acceptable as others to private funding.

MARK FISHER: I think all of us would agree with Kenneth Hudson about the importance of independent museums, but I think the most exciting things that have happened certainly in our culture in the last ten or twenty years in the museum service have been the whole development of industrial museums as a whole. We have Neil Cossons here as a living testament to that. Most of that has come from the independent sector, so of course you want plural funding but I think John Last's very key question was 'is it a threat?' and I think in two respects it could be. First, let's look at the question of sponsorship. As David Best very fairly recognized there is a danger that in order to attract the necessary sponsorship, museums, increasingly almost unconsciously, could be tempted into asking 'what exhibition do you want me to put on that will attract you?' And all of us would agree that certainly on the design side of the V&A the absolute key thing recently has been to see what the Sock Shop exhibit has been doing there. There are a lot of very important things happening in British design. We lead the world in cultural design but whether the Sock Shop absolutely gets to the nub of that, I somewhat doubt, but of course the money was there from the company to put it on.

The other major threat of course is in the area of charging. It is inevitable that once you get into charging the natural tendency is to entertain. Of course, museums must communicate and make attractive what they are saying, but the slide from being attractive and comprehensible and communicating well to simply entertaining is the key question. I think that what Kenneth said about Elspeth King and The People's Palace, Glasgow, is very important. Last year many of us in this room will know that Elspeth was very keen to put on an exhibition of the role of women in Glasgow society. Women in a very male chauvinist city like Glasgow have had a terrible time over the last 150 years and she had some amazing material to illustrate that. The competing concern for the Glasgow City Council was an exhibition from Glasgow Celtic Football Club which they were going to pay for, which, in the year of the Garden Festival, was very attractive and was going to pull in a lot of people. They had a difficult choice – do you do the popular thing (football is very important to the culture of Glasgow) – or do you do something that presents a rather ambiguous and worrying image of Glasgow culture and put on the exhibition on how women have been mistreated in Glasgow for the last 150 years. The Council chose Glasgow Celtic Football Club. So it is not just in the independent or commercial sector: there are dangers in the public sector as well.

LORENA SAN ROMAN: In Costa Rica we have been putting entertainment and education together very easily, trying to rescue our identity at this moment, because of our celebration of one hundred years of democracy. We take the kids and have a competition in which they draw democracy – quite difficult isn't it? But from 8–10 years old they are thinking how to make these drawings because the winner will have a trip abroad and it is very nice for them. Also, we are asking the high school students to write an essay on the subject, and really they are beginning to think towards something that will be in the end, entertainment, because the prize is travel. But in the middle they are thinking about their nation's identity, something they have, perhaps, never thought of before.

FRANS SCHOUTEN (Conference participant, Reinwart Academy, Leiden, Netherlands): There has been talk about politics, and about the museum being objective. For years museum professionals have been saying that museums should have objectives, but I think that having objectives makes it impossible being objective! And although I agree with Barry Lord about the Maya exhibition I wonder why there isn't an exhibition on Renaissance paintings that is stressing also what is happening with the Communist party in Italy nowadays!

LORD MONTAGU: Kenneth Hudson mentioned Heaven and I think it would perhaps be naïve of any of us to think that any politician is an angel at any time, and I think it would be naïve of us to think that any state or government-funded museum is going to be free from political influence. The discussion has been a wonderful advertisement for the argument that the only truly independent and objective museum is going to be a museum that is independently funded. That is what independent museums are in this country.

4 | *Politics and museums 2*

Art and politics

Eric Moody

I have been commissioned by the Conference Organizers to talk about 'art politics', about whether politicians are likely to continue funding the arts and what politicians will expect in return for their investment in the arts. Indeed is funding likely to be redirected or cut off and how are governments likely to interact with the private sector? My answer to these questions is based upon my own experience which is mainly in the area of galleries, rather than museums in general.

I have heard some museum professionals, usually in private, bemoan the linking of museums and the arts and actually this is an attitude with which, despite my background and commitment to the visual arts, I fully sympathize.

The association, I think, in the British context, probably stems, apart from the human habit of collecting and sorting every kind of object from our material culture, from the source of government support for museums and galleries at local and national level.

The contemporary conception of Art with its capital 'A', hangs like the albatross of the Ancient Mariner around the neck of artists, arts managers and those condemned by association, museums. It might be more efficient, I want to argue, to divest ourselves of such an encumbrance and to argue a case for museums in general, some of which contain works of art.

Art in the so-called West and increasingly elsewhere in the world has become associated with the individualistic self-expression of some contemporary practitioners. This egocentric art is, in a strictly utilitarian sense, useless to anyone except the artist and connoisseur. Even the art of the past, offered in the present, can all too often have no apparent function, even though its meaning and function in its original socio-economic context was explicit. We need not, I think, rehearse here the many previous uses of art save to note that most do not apply today. All contemporary governments of whatever political colour have, I think, a very ambivalent attitude towards the arts, which derives from this very contemporary definition of art.

Some so-called totalitarian states ban useless or degenerate art while employing those arts and those artists who are prepared to express the state's rather than their own ambitions. So-called democratic states, while protesting the importance of the arts in general, can create environments where the generality of art increasingly finds it difficult to survive, especially, and paradoxically, those arts which seek to apply themselves.

Art's contemporary value, apart from a market value which I want to touch upon in a minute, resides precisely and strangely in its non-utilitarian condition. Societies like our own which say that they cherish the individual and the individual entrepreneur have, I think, inadvertently found a function of sorts for art as a non-functional symbol of individualism. These societies are usually secular with concomitant elaborate market economies. They have, in other words, I think found a new religion – Art.

Art, like its predecessor in this respect – religion – is now custodian of an other-worldly, spiritual dimension, different from the workaday, different from going and getting, ducking and diving, profit and loss. In fact the paradox of this situation, familiar to many clerics, is that art, the new religion, is required to achieve all sorts of impossible goals, goals like helping to revitalize economies and regions. If I might interject just a passing personal note, I don't think I can take another conference on the arts and urban regeneration!

In countries with a welfare or residual welfare tradition where there is government provision for art, health, etc. we see a decrease, gradual in the case of Britain, or sudden in the case of a country like The People's Republic of China, of financial support for the arts even, again paradoxically, as politicians of one colour or another protest personal devotion to the arts. The words of our own Prime Minister, Margaret Thatcher, are not atypical of the words of many politicians, again of whatever colour.

Closer scrutiny of these government or quasi non-governmental support systems reveals support for the art that these systems themselves define. The medium of subvention becomes the message, if I might borrow Marshall McLuhan's expression, and the message to us all is loud and clear and echoes down the decades in Britain from Maynard Keynes to present day pronouncements about the arts. If I might just quote from Lord Keynes, this part of a radio broadcast made in 1945 anticipating the birth of the Arts Council of Great Britain, 'The work of the artist is individual, free, undisciplined, unregimented, uncontrolled. The artist walks where the breath of the spirit blows him. He cannot be told his direction because he does not know it himself.' This caricature of the artist and his relationship or lack of relationship to society persists to this day. It is a caricature on which the marketing of the arts is based.

Art, to use the words of younger commentators Andrew Brighton and Nicholas Pearson, is a very 'special' sort of activity perpetrated by very special sorts of persons. This perception of art (again I note the paradox) is, I think, an interesting one but actually it does help, in a paradoxical sort of way, the development of a diverse system of funding for that which we call art, or which we associate with art by special pleading for art as an object of charity.

I want to come on now to the subject of sponsorship – corporate sponsorship as we have learned to call it, following the American example. Increasingly the arts encouraged by governments are looking for business sponsorship to remedy the shortfall between their ambitions and public subsidy. Brian Appleyard recently provided the figures for Britain. To use his words, since they are most apposite, 'the new heady cocktail of altruism, advertising and highbrow kudos lures companies to part with around £30 million a year, increasing at the rate (according to Appleyard) of £5 million annually.' The figure, he says, is disputed. The British Labour Party thinks the correct total is more in the region of £25 million and our Arts Minister thinks that the total is more in the region of £45 million. But interestingly enough these figures fall far short of countries like the United States, even if you work it out on a per capita basis.

The best response, according to many on this subject, including Appleyard, is that governments should create the conditions under which corporate patronage of this sort, sponsorship, can be best achieved. The jargon is that governments can perhaps best provide 'tax breaks' to improve the situation. I would like to suggest that the United States, and perhaps others to a lesser degree, are very secular societies who understand perhaps better than we do the new religion – Art – and its role as a provider of corporate salvation.

We in Britain have managed corporate sponsorship for individual galleries within museums but the United States has whole museums, not to mention collections, owned by corporations which is a completely different scale and sort of patronage. British habits are, I can see, reflected in countries which have been influenced by Britain one way or another. British habits of subsidy, and what tax breaks there are, encourage a particularly British notion in a completely new interpretation of the 'arm's length principle' – an arm's length principle which applies specifically to sponsors. The result is the preservation of precious artistic integrity, but often precious little patronage. When a corporation merely guarantees against loss and when an exhibition, say, is very successful, that corporation can have completely free advertising without parting with any money at all. You can all think of, and perhaps you have been involved in, examples of this kind. In our effort to preserve artistic integrity we may jeopardize greater corporate patronage.

Alongside this business of trying to raise money for museums there is the art market. Museums stand in a very peculiar relationship to the world of the market and particularly, since I am drawing my examples from the visual arts, the art market.

We must remember the nature of this business. If I might quote very quickly from Karl E. Meyer, 'A bit of canvas with a few dollars' worth of paint, provided that the brush was wielded by a Cézanne or a Rembrandt, can bring greater capital gains than glamorous stock or a corner lot on Wall Street.' That truth, of course, has been confirmed over and over again. I think the record at the moment stands at £30.2 million for that very famous 'Irises' by Van Gogh. The art market is a business that can be reduced to a very simple equation – reputation equals price. The part played by museums and galleries in the market reputation of all sorts of objects, not necessarily art, has to be addressed in the context of funding for the arts and funding for museums and galleries. I think the relationship between some institutions is, to say the least, problematic and the art market gets a very good deal.

There is, of course, and I am moving on to present, an alternative, another business which goes on alongside our business. It is the business of advertising, and it is of course quite closely related to the world of sponsorship.

Here we have, I would like to contend, a different sort of art. An art which is essentially an applied art. Something which is far more prosaic but no less glamourous than that art which we have come to expect. The art, as some have called it, of persuasion, is rapidly becoming the largest cultural component in our western society and, incidentally, in the British economy. For this industry the tax breaks, as we have come to call them, are in place but more importantly in my view, this industry stands in a very positive relationship to government whether the government be local or national and whatever political colour.

Advertising agencies and their agents, the advertising artists, are *commissioned* by governments and industry to persuade, inform and to improve their image. This is something, incidentally, that art as we traditionally defined it did with alacrity before it and others considered it to be above such things. The advertising industry with tight deadlines and big money to be made – we might just pause and consider how much money is being spent on the privatization of British industries: and we all are familiar with the role that advertising plays in that process. Advertising is constantly on the look-out for inspiration by exploiting the art of the past and the present with little if any recompense for the artists and the institutions that house them – museums and galleries. Art for them is a national resource, not a component of a tourist industry or an inner city regeneration project. Here we have in paradigm an industry which has largely divested itself of that notion of art which I outlined to begin with, but is sustained by a sympathetic government, subsidy and tax breaks and, like the art market, exploits the content of our museums and galleries. Who then is being subsidized?

The 'greening' of governments may ultimately lead to a broader understanding of resources and resource management, and the financial and other implications of such an awareness, but as part of this process we as professionals in the museum and gallery sector must argue a case for the unique role of museums as repositories of inspiration. Successful advocacy of museums to business corporations, to governments of whatever colour and whatever level, does not require special pleading by association with art, even though there are substantial, including market, vested interests in such conceptions. We must, I would argue, using words which perhaps you might think are more appropriate to the nineteenth century, consider art, craft and design as part of an integrated, material, cultural major national resource, closely associated with education, which is to be managed and exploited. The word 'exploit' is perhaps an unfortunate one to end with, but that is what I mean quite literally. Exploitation does not necessarily have to have a pejorative overtone if it is carefully managed and controlled.

If we can get politicians to appreciate the arts as a resource rather than as an area of special pleading then we will have achieved a great deal. Our relationship with business will be far more business-like too – less a charity, more a service to be paid for by those that profit from it.

Discussion

LORENA SAN ROMAN: I want to mention something quite interesting about what Eric Moody has said. What is the relation of the politics and the art in the essence of creation and of inspiration that you mention? For example in our area of Central America the art is an interpretation in many ways of what is happening there. There we ran a joint exhibition last year of artists of Salvador and Costa Rica during the last ten years, and it was quite impressive to see the inspiration these artists have derived from the different political situations. The artists in my country paint a big variety of things ranging from personal sorrow or illness to the beautiful, but 80 per cent of the pictures of the artists of Salvador were of war. So really for us it was a big point of discussion of what they were feeling and thinking. The Salvador artists were not supported by anybody, but those in my country had support from private enterprise and also the government, so I think that this is an interesting link that you may perhaps have had in the times of war here in Europe. Artists really are so linked with what is happening around them for their inspiration or expression.

ERIC MOODY: I go back to this very special position which we have in Europe and I think in other countries like North America, Canada and Australia. Because of all sorts of reasons but mainly the dominance of a particular perception of art as a commodity to be exchanged in a commodity market, this interrogative role of artists in relationship to their society has to a large extent, I think, disappeared. We don't see this sort of direct response to cultural, political and social phenomena that you have just described.

SIR PHILIP GOODHART, MP: I think that it is inevitable, regardless of what happens in any general election and between now and the end of the century, that public support, the support of the taxpayer for museums, will not only go on but will probably increase in real value. But I think that there is likely to be some rechannelling in the way in which support is given. And to which aspect of museum life support is given. Acquisition of collections of course is one of the items and inevitably hits the headlines. In recent weeks there has been a lot of publicity in the press of yet another Turner possibly going overseas because possibly the valuation of that particular Turner was made incorrectly. The total present acquisition grant from central government is £9 million a year and I don't see that increasing dramatically in the future under any government.

Discussion

Of course there has to be some support from public funds for some acquisitions but what I would like to see, and what I think this government intends to do, is to see more money switched to the problems of conservation, and the Museums Association in the course of the last year has of course underlined the problem of conservation. The £9 million grant for acquisitions could perhaps be diverted perhaps to conservation and do rather more good.

I must say my enthusiasm for spending yet more public money to acquire more Turners would be rather enhanced if we did exhibit the Turners we had adequately. I like the Clore Gallery. I think it is exceptionally well done, but in the Reserve Galleries upstairs, there are about fifteen major Turner paintings which one cannot see adequately at all because the lighting is all wrong. I would rather see more emphasis on showing what we've got than on the question of greater acquisition.

The question of admission charges is inevitably at the moment at the centre of the political argument and this government has said that it will leave the matter largely to the Trustees and Boards, but I think that inevitably there is going to be an element of helping those who help themselves. This Sunday, I went to the Ashmolean Museum which has just launched a massive appeal for more than £2 million. I arrived at 3.55 p.m. and was very nearly pushed out of the door because it shuts at 4 o'clock in the afternoon. The Ashmolean is only open for two hours on Sunday which seems to me to be the worst of all worlds as far as both visitors and indeed staff are concerned. No admission charge is made but there is a bowl for contributions and on that particular Sunday £14 had been put in the bowl. It does seem to me that perhaps the public would be better served if the museum had been open rather longer on Sundays and if some charge to visitors had been made. If there was rather more evidence that the Ashmolean had been prepared to help itself, then perhaps both the public through its appeal and the public and the taxpayer through the Universities Funding Council might be more generous.

DONALD HORNE: I have some difficulties with the narrowness of Eric Moody's approach and I'd just like to clear those up before making a contribution to his approach. I take it that when you are talking about art you are really talking about fine art, the visual arts. It seemed to me that the kinds of statement you made about those simply do not apply to people who write or produce plays etc., who can become much more directly related to society than fine artists are, so I don't have to disagree with you about that. You were also speaking about art museums. It seems to me that what you were saying about art museums has nothing at all to do with the kinds of discussions we were having earlier this morning about, say, The People's Palace Museum in Glasgow which is very directly related to intellectual and moral, and if you like, political processes.

Now I just have two observations. One is: it is always possible, you know, we imagine that art was only invented a couple of hundred years ago and we imagine that art was part of a ceremony which served religious life. It could also be the other way round. It may be that not only art museums are the cathedrals of the present but also that the cathedrals were the art museums of the past. Some of the concerns that we now think of as art may have appeared to be serving religion, but they were engaged in particular types of processes which themselves should not be dismissed as not having a validity of their own.

As to tourism, I really think in a place like London which is still among the top five destinations in the world, there are other questions like providing litter bins. (I was interested to see that the reconstructed Eros is now guarded by twenty-four litter bins which are surrounded by rubbish.) Being thoroughly businesslike about this, when you go to some of the major art museums or the West End theatres to opera or a play 75 per cent of the audience may sometimes be tourists, so you might as well treat the tourist industry with every kind of care and delicacy about maintaining standards. But it seems very odd with Britain having a flourishing tourist industry at the same time it should be cutting down one of the reasons why people come here and leave all that rubbish in Piccadilly Circus. And I am expressing this view because I share your despair about art museums.

A different kind of view is Le Grand Louvre, which you can now enter via that excellent pyramid and engage in the ultimate subway experience without really experiencing the museum itself at all. If you are in a hurry you can buy your postcard and your relics and so forth and move on without getting in the way of the kinds of people who want to go and look at the art and other things.

My last observation is however a more hopeful kind. It is something we have become interested in in Australia. We have very largely given away the metropolitan art museums – I mean the art museums in our metropolises except for the one exception in Brisbane, where the collection is so second or third or fourth rate that they have no alternative really to getting rid of the chronological hang and presenting the paintings in a way that can make them quite interesting. Instead we have our eyes on the regional galleries. In Australia we have a great number of regional galleries which have in the past been devoted to presenting the town's treasures so that nobody need look at them.

Discussion

The tourists may come and look at them. The younger regional gallery directors are dissatisfied with this process and we – and when I say 'we', I mean this Australia Council of mine and a number of other bodies – are concerned with encouraging the younger gallery directors still to have the kind of art you describe, but to work out some way in which the people in those towns can be brought into some kind of collaboration with it and possibly negotiate some meaning with it. Secondly they should also be looking at other types of arts activity, so that even if some of the things are rubbish, these regional galleries, which sometimes have quite interesting collections, can be given an entirely different kind of function from that of being citadels of higher art in a philistine community, which is the kind of way in which they are currently presented. Ultimately of course they may have developed such specialities that they will then be taken over by the tourists.

MARK FISHER, MP: Can I take up the point that Philip Goodhart was making when he doubted whether any government between now and the end of the century would actually have any commitment. He might be not surprised to know that I have a slightly different view. But I would say that ultimately it is up to us, you, me, as the electorate, to determine both the atmosphere and mood in which those decisions are made by whoever is in government, and indeed to elect a government that is committed to that. Undoubtedly I think Philip is wrong when he says that it's not going to matter much who is in power over the next ten years. There is a choice, and it is a choice we have always ducked in this country and we failed. We in the UK are out of step with the rest of the world, hopelessly out of step: we have not had the confidence about our culture and its importance to demand of governments over the last twenty-five years, Labour and Conservative, really serious investment in taking our culture seriously.

You only have to look abroad and reference has already been made today to La Villette – £700 million worth of investment in just one science museum in Paris. I have just come back from the Soviet Union and looking at what *glasnost* and *perestroika* are doing there and to see the investment that they are putting in. For instance, in Leningrad, Gustav's Russian Museum is expanding to three extra sites and the whole thing is being restored and a huge international co-operative action is taking place there. And what they are doing is very diverse. They are recreating and restoring the Tsarist traditions and arts and looking at portraiture in the nineteenth century etc. Other countries are doing it – we are failing to do it.

I believe there is a good case that we should be making and it is a case that must prevail over the next ten years if we have any care in our society about our culture. First, whether we value our culture, we spend less as a society, whether through national or local government on the arts, than we spend on the licence fee for the BBC. The total expenditure of national and local government is £900 million on the arts, which works out at 50p a head a week. It really is nothing. We must as a society value our theatres, our concerts, our museums, at more than 50p a week. I believe that we do and I believe that society would respond very well to a government that had the confidence to say 'This is important' about our culture.

The other argument is of course the economic one and we shouldn't shy away from that. I was sorry to hear Eric Moody sneer (and some people laughed at it) at yet another conference on economic regeneration. I think that anybody living in Dundee would have a very different view of the way that the Blackness section of Dundee has helped both restore confidence and identity and pride in that city and of course has attracted in other investment because artists have come in and restored the built environment there. And I think that what is happening in Newcastle and Sheffield and Swansea and many of our major industrial cities shows that Eric Moody is totally out of touch with what is happening outside London. Indeed you only have to look at the very specific area of Bradford where that new Museum of Photography has transformed it. You can see there in microcosm the impact: there are now nearly 800,000 people a year visiting it and they are bringing money in to a local economy. That Museum alone contributes to the economy every time anybody comes and spends money in the car parks, the restaurants, hotels etc., quite apart from what the Museum has done in improving the environment, the culture of that community and the image of Bradford. So there is both direct and indirect impact that can be measured.

And whether we accept all the detailed points that John Myerscough was making in his report last year, the scale of what he was saying is undoubtedly true. So there are two reasons there: the importance of culture and the recognition that over 600,000 people work in the arts and culture in our society, and that it is one of the few areas of our life where we actually export more than we import, when you look at publishing and the film industry and broadcasting and the record industry as well. The attraction of tourists with foreign exchange is because of our culture – they don't come here for our weather, they come here because of our traditions and our language.

Discussion

So I think that on both those points, the economic and the cultural, the arts are of great importance, and this should be recognized by any sensible government of either party. It's ironic that as a Socialist party we have to be making these points to a Tory government about the free market economics of the arts. The government ought to understand it, but they don't. But either party over the next ten years ought to recognize that for those two reasons there should be, and there must be, a huge increase to bring us more in line with the rest of the world, and I believe that society wants this. The important question perhaps for today is what should governments properly expect in return. Should they expect anything and what should they expect in return for that increased investment? I think that inevitably any government will expect some return. It is important that a government has a strategic policy for what role museums and our culture play in our lives; who is it for, whose culture is it, who are we investing for, whether it should be a widening of access, and the place of minority voices and minority cultures to it – all the things that Lorena mentioned early on today.

I think that is right. What is I think sad and mistaken about the present situation is that apart from a flirtation with the free market this government alone hasn't got a policy about museums. It hasn't got any idea what it expects from museums, or what role museums are playing in our culture. It's because of that lack of strategic policy that they've got themselves into the nonsense over the V&A restructuring and indeed the nonsense of chronic under-investment. It is a nonsense that you have museums like the Tate needing £27 million worth of repairs, and galleries' roofs leaking, not being able to acquire things that they ought to acquire, and not being able to conserve things that they ought to be conserving. I repeat, this stems not from the meanness of government but the fact that this government actually hasn't got a cultural policy and certainly hasn't got any idea what they expect of museums. I think that the case for investment is overwhelmingly there and should be taken up by every political party. What is important is what we should expect in advance, but unless a government has a clear strategic policy then I don't believe that either we're going to get sufficient investment, or are we actually going to get our investment properly targeted into the areas of our culture that need to be supported.

ERIC MOODY: I feel obliged to respond on a number of accounts.

If I appeared to sneer perhaps I did, but it wasn't my intention to undervalue the contribution that the arts make. But the response to the argument that I presented by Mark Fisher, the passionate response, is typical of something that I think happens time and time again when we address this subject. People get on their political high-horse of one colour and another and passionately defend the arts or culture, and even though they might acknowledge that we are a heterogeneous rather than a homogeneous society there is no actual real discussion of which culture, or whose culture, and all those other very important arguments.

What I am trying to say and I hope I can say it more cogently here and now is that the argument 'we must support culture' is all very well and good, but governments of whatever political colour will always have higher priorities than the arts and the culture which has been so eloquently defended by my colleague here.

I think what we have to do, and this is where I hope I am making an original contribution to this debate, is to examine through the paradigm of the visual arts, visual culture, a reinterpretation of the traditional role of museums as a place that contains valuable resources. I would like to call them, if you like, the rainforests, our cultural rainforests in which there are all sorts of potential solutions to be had for those who have the wherewithal to go forth and use them. I am not therefore just talking about the arts; a technology museum that is full of redundant technology may well provide us with solutions that we thought were for all sorts of reasons unnecessary. What I am saying is that one industry in particular, advertising in the applied arts, uses that great collection of stuff, objects if you like, called the history of art, held in all sorts of places – some of them with roofs that are leaking – as a resource to be exploited. We should be in the business of enabling that exploitation and to benefit from the profits that are made directly and indirectly.

I think we have looked, for example, to corporate sponsorship as our salvation or a part of our financial salvation, but I think we will see that corporations, like governments, will sooner or later discover that they too have priorities when it comes to altruism. We have seen it where corporations like Exxon have withdrawn from corporate patronage of the arts, and perhaps for very good reasons which I don't need to rehearse, gone into altruistic giving in other areas like education or the environment. However, I don't know whether they have got enough money to save the environment!

KENNETH HUDSON: Two very brief points. The first is that I think there's far too much investment in the arts. I think it's high time an awful lot of air was let out of art museums. I resent the constant implication that art museums are in some way superior institutions to all other kinds of museums. I think this is in the first place arrant nonsense and in the second place socially very dangerous. I don't believe it's true. And in connection with that, may I say that I am not brainwashed by what the French or the Russians may say about investment in museums and art in their capital cities. To get a true viewpoint of that, you want to go into the French provinces for example and hear what they say about the grotesque over-representation of Paris, and you will find that in order to finance this ludicrous nonsense at the Musée du Louvre that the provinces have been starved to an extent that is totally shameful, and you will find exactly the same thing in the Soviet Union. So I don't wear that one at all. These great places are put up for the greater glory of the current president or prime minister of each country. They are political symbols. They have nothing at all to do with culture, except that the greater glory of the prime minister is in itself a phenomenon which is interesting.

Now the other point that I want to make is this: I have been fascinated very much in recent years as to why modern non-representational art is so greatly favoured by many businessmen, particular successful businessmen. It's a phenomenon that deserves a much greater study than I can give you today. But I want to make a suggestion and that is that there is a very important psychology involved here which has a great deal to do with sponsorship, and I put this question to myself: why is modern non-representational art the only form of masturbation which has such a high social prestige and such a high market value – because that is what we're talking about. And then I realized that of course capitalism itself is a form of masturbation. It essentially depends on wasteful activity. And so capitalists are necessarily interested in sponsoring non-representational art because they are sponsoring the core of their own motive power. I don't find anything mysterious about this but what I am saying is that it's a slightly taboo subject and that's why I have broken it this morning and I am very pleased to have done so.

PAUL PERROT: I was inspired by Kenneth Hudson's remarks as I have published some years ago on that very subject, although I don't think it's too useful to introduce the term 'masturbation'. The basic point I would like to come back to is the one that Lorena San Roman made in reference to Eric Moody's comments, in which she referred to the difference in subject matter between the art of various countries. In her experience the contemporary Salvador artists were 80 per cent concerned with the subject of war for obvious reasons, and I found it interesting that everybody's response to that was to say, well in our own countries we just don't see that kind of subject matter as a response to actual experience.

But of course what Kenneth Hudson has just pointed to is that we do very well precisely that. I have been saying this for many years – that is precisely what one does see in our museums and art galleries. There is such a thing as corporate art: that is what one does see, whether there is corporate finance or not. I quite agree with Eric Moody that very often we hear a lot of talk about corporate patronage but very often the actual amount of money invested is miniscule in relation to the advertising value that is derived from it. The amount of talk and concern there is in the museum community about this corporate sponsorship is very often quite out of proportion to the actual cheques that have been signed.

But there is such a thing as corporate art and it does have to do of course, first and foremost, with the assertion of formal manners. I think the key factor when one is looking at any art museum or other museum phenomenon, history of science museum, is always to analyse what's missing, what isn't being said, and if merely formal manners are being presented then precisely those unpleasant subjects that are not brought up in polite formal society are not being addressed. Or, what is more typical is that unpleasant subjects are being addressed in irrelevant manners. They are being brought up in such a way that they are merely the subject of individual personal experience, essentially titillation, and not integrated with the overall social political fabric. I think it is an evasion of the fact that these subjects are very often missing in the art museum experience, and that is really the danger that one gets in the type of sponsorship we are speaking of. That is to say, one encourages the visual arts as a kind of corporate art in which social contexts, social relationships are either not stated or they are brought up in marginal ways that are not integrated with any kind of overall experience.

The art we see in our museums is just as much representative of the actual basis as in the case of the Salvador paintings. That is of course in the context of the individual expression which I think Kenneth Hudson was referring to, which is of course the culture of individualism, the culture of that whole capitalist viewpoint on the world, and the fundamental basis from which the art museum is derived.

KENNETH HUDSON: Can I just say here that there is a very large difference between individual expression and masturbation. I was talking about masturbation. Had I been talking about individual expression I would have put the matter quite differently. I don't know why you chose to tone down my remark because that turns it into something else which I wasn't trying to say.

PATRICK BOYLAN: Could I make three different points? One, I'll leave it to the party politicians to slog it out themselves more than adequately, but I would like to take up one of Sir Philip's points. That was the argument that there couldn't be any change within the remainder of this century in terms of attitudes. Well, we have within the last week been celebrating or at the very least marking, ten years of the present government, of massive change in political attitudes and so on, during which the unthinkable perhaps, and certainly the traditional, have not only been

Discussion

challenged but also have been very effectively changed. Also, join The Museums Association and read the current edition of the *Journal* and what I have said there about the Green Revolution. Who would have thought even three years ago that attitudes in every single party, with the government taking a major lead, could have changed so much towards the environmental issues that some of us have been crying about in the wilderness for so long. We are getting very little recognition at all for the fact that we have been fighting environmental issues for so long in museums and the voluntary sector. But change can take place, and regardless of what happens at party political level a change in attitude can take place if that is the mood of the country.

A second point I think perhaps worried me most about Eric's contribution. I know that he set his own parameters very clearly at the beginning, but I think that there has been too much consideration of the issue of art in the narrow sense. Art museums are important, and I would certainly defend them as a central part of our culture, but they have a very small minority of the museum issues and problems.

I suppose my final point is that possibly the debate about abstract expressionist art and that type of thing is past, and that artists themselves have moved on in the last 8–10 years, as other people have moved on. Perhaps the most memorable expression was that of Peter Fuller in the days when he was a Marxist critic – and before he followed Paul Johnson and David Owen and various other people into a very different political viewpoint. Peter Fuller castigated and said the unthinkable about contemporary abstract art just ten years ago at the ICA when he described American abstract expressionism and the followers of it in this country and Germany as presenting the 'Official State Art of the NATO capitalist powers'. I don't think Peter later followed that line but in any case I don't think we should destroy the art museums or the art trade simply because of one particular art style. We must have a catholic view looking at 800 years of European art and indeed beyond that. And what about our science museums? I hope these are issues we are going to come back to.

CONFERENCE PARTICIPANT (no name): I don't actually share Kenneth Hudson's hostility towards art museums but I do think, picking up from Eric Moody, there are ways in which the art trade in this country could finance the museums and thus allow for the flourishing of the science museums that Patrick [Boylan] has talked about. The art trade is a very very rich sector and it is also the least controlled, I think, in the world. There are problems with the illicit trade in antiquities which is allowed to go through the London auction rooms. It wouldn't happen in France – it doesn't happen in many countries because governments don't allow works of art that are known to be stolen from their countries of origin to be traded. If we do allow such trade in this country, the profit from this immensely lucrative trade ought in some way to go back to the museums. It is well known that the art trade uses the professional reputation and expertise of curators and in general gets a great deal from the museums, but they don't give back, so I think we should be urging greater support from the art trade in London for art museums. If the Tate was funded by Cork Street it would let everybody else off the hook.

I do also think, Sir Philip, one should say that the Ashmolean Museum which does have problems is a university museum and university museums have had a lot of special problems. It isn't necessarily free suddenly to change its policy towards admissions and so on. We are talking about the continued linking of museums to higher education so it would be a pity if the Ashmolean was divorced from the university system of which it has been a part for the last 300 years.

GEOFFREY LEWIS: I will gladly follow that point up. I think the issue of the illicit trafficking in art is perhaps slightly off the main issue. The real issue is whether the art trade should finance museums and galleries in this country. And I think that in itself raises certain ethical issues which would concern a number of professions, and maybe that's an area which could also be debated. Let's leave it at that at the moment if I may.

MARK SUGGITT (Conference participant, Yorkshire and Humberside Museums Council): If museums equal cultural rainforests, start worrying when you get a sponsorship offer from Macdonalds. Anyway, what I'd like to do is to draw together some threads. I think first of all we have heard from both sessions this morning that funding is very important. We have also been accused by Kenneth Hudson of a form of philosophical intellectual bankruptcy, something which I completely disagree with. I was rather amazed to hear both Kenneth and Lord Montagu bring forward the old myth of the independent museum as the way forward, which ties in with some points raised later on. We have to remember that we are in the country that was prepared to buy the Thyssen collection (for urban renewal in Docklands, I believe) but which at the same time is spending more on removal of graffiti than it gives to the Museum and Galleries Commission. This attitude does not allow the development of many other initiatives similar to the People's Palace, so we have to ask ourselves where do we go from here? My question, which leads on from this is: could the panel tell me of any truly independent museums that have never received a penny of public money?

KENNETH HUDSON: I think this question is a complete red herring because I have been pleading anyway for a mixed economy. By the mixed economy you may start from the base of a museum wholly funded by public funds or you may start from one wholly funded from private funds. One is trying to get the other kinds of funds all the time and that's a process which is going on and I think that's the way that the future lies. I am not out for purism on this at all. As far as I am concerned an independent museum is not a museum that never gets a scrap of public money. I truthfully don't know of any of which, in the last resort, that is true – 100% privately funded, never a penny, directly or indirectly from public funds. I know of no such museum, and it is becoming increasingly difficult to find a public museum that gets not one single penny from any private source. That is equally a myth. Some of them like to cover it up in some countries more than others. In France, for example, where private funding is obscene in the museum world, or in Sweden where it is similarly obscene. They are jolly good at covering up the fact that they do in fact get money from private sources. It's not 100 per centism that I am arguing for.

LORD MONTAGU: I suggest the questioner might go down to the excellent stand of the Association of Independent Museums downstairs and they'll give you a long list. Go and ask them.

KATHY ZEDDE (Conference participant): I represent one of the provincial museums associations in Canada. I notice that a lot has been said this morning about the extent to which museums are funded by governments. I would just like to say something about helping government to make informed decisions as to what they spend their money on. Quantity is one thing and quality is another, as Sir Philip said earlier about conservation. I think it is up to the museum community to assist government in making informed decisions about where they are spending the money. In Canada the definition and promotion of professional standards is one way this is happening, and in which we are trying to give the government something to go on in terms of decisions that they are making. We are also looking to Britain with great interest about the new Registration Scheme and the kinds of standards that this is going to promote in terms of maintaining professional standards in museums. So I would just like to make a plea that we don't just talk to governments about how much money they are giving us. I think it is up to us to help them make informed decisions about exactly where the money is going.

NICK BAKER (Conference participant): I am in fact the director of an advertising agency but I am here today out of personal interest. This is a day off. But as possibly the only representative in this room of the advertising industry I thought it would be worth while responding to Eric Moody's point about my industry as a potentially more important source of funds because of our desire to plunder the resources offered by art galleries and art museums. The reason that advertising agencies plunder this particular resource is not because we love art, much as we do, and particularly much as many creative directors do, but because it is believed that the sort of images that can be plundered from art, from the art of the past and even from contemporary fine art, have meaning for the public that we are trying to communicate to. And not only meaning, but they have a greater resonance, and can carry a greater emotional or intellectual conviction than the images that one can conjure up by phoning the latest glossy fashion photographer or whatever. And the reason why that is the case is because the public in this country have to a considerable extent been educated through museums and other means in the past to value that art, to look at that art, to take something out of that art, to be moved by it. So I don't think there can be a divorce between looking to the public in the educational role of the arts, and looking to the advertising industry to put money into the arts. The only reason that we will put money into the arts is because they do have that place in society which comes from the sort of investment and the sort of educational programmes that have been carried out in the past. I think the analogy with tropical rainforests is all too appropriate. As you cut down the trees you should be planting more, and if the emphasis switches too strongly towards reaping the benefits of what has been sown in the past then by the year 2000 or thereafter those benefits won't be there to such a great extent, because the public won't be so involved and won't be so responsive to the images you have in your museums and galleries.

ERIC MOODY: I am grateful for the opportunity to respond to that very quickly if I may. I did draw attention to the advertising industry but it wasn't necessarily to think of the advertising industry as yet another source of subsidy for museums. What I was trying to suggest was the fact that that industry benefits from a very creative balance of public subsidy, proper legislation and (to use the jargon) tax breaks, and also, perhaps more importantly, it has a very interesting and direct causal relationship to a source of patronage. The way our government and other governments use advertising is tantamount to commissioning artists to achieve their ambitions, which was the case in the Renaissance or whatever period you want to choose. What I am suggesting is that this is a paradigm which we could address more closely, a cultural paradigm, and it has been developed through a very subtle blend of all those things that we have mentioned this morning.

Another thing which I wanted to say in response to Patrick Boylan on my art museum focus today, is that I was set the brief by the person who invited me here, and I responded to it. The thing that I should just point out is that the visual arts aren't an insignificant component of this phenomenon that we are choosing to address. And perhaps we should just rehearse the fact that the visual arts has four national quangos

Discussion

working on its behalf, it also has in England twelve regional arts associations and it has national councils in Scotland, Northern Ireland and Wales; it benefits from the regional arts associations and the area museum services of one sort and another. In fact, if you take a slightly more catholic definition of the visual arts, it is one of the major components of state support for the arts in general.

CHARLES RYDER (Conference participant): We have been tantalizingly close at a number of points in this discussion to a critical unspoken word which is money. Quoting from the programme there is politics in bold face, identity in normal typeface and funding. The point that I'd like to raise is 'whose money is it?' We all go on at great lengths in discussing the difference between the private sector and public sector funding, but if I am not mistaken most of the private sector funding comes from profits. I don't believe it comes from directors' salaries, I don't believe it comes from wages, I don't believe it comes from union settlements. I believe it comes from profits which we essentially pay for as consumers. I am wondering if anyone on the panel or whether the panel collectively would like to suggest any way that we might, as a society, take some guidance from our own relentless association with the things that money can provide for us.

Just a quick anecdote – in the current copy of *Vogue* there is on the editorial pages, not the advertising pages, something on offer which is a bit of cotton net to be worn by women. You can only have this on special order. It costs £600.

ALAN JOHNSTON (Conference participant): I am a consultant for the Luxembourg Museum of Natural History. I have been travelling around in the course of my studies in Europe going to different conferences and I keep hearing all this talk about funding for the arts and art and history and this sort of thing and how important it is. I would just like to make the point that the voice of the natural history museum all over the world seems to be a very small one at the back of the room saying 'well, what about natural history funding?' And as we near the year 2000 with the real tropical rainforests being destroyed and a real danger of the polar icecaps melting, I think we are missing the real point that the most important question of the years to come and for the year 2000 is the ecological question and not man's self-adoration as seen by the arts. What is going to happen about the funding for the interpretation of this very, very important point. And I would just like to end with a short statement. If we don't recognize the value of ecological problems and therefore the interpretation of them in natural history museums, and follow this up with political and economic action, I can see in 20 or 30 years' time my descendants visiting the Tate Museum and before they go in they have got to rent a sub-aqua suit to get in because London has been flooded.

LORENA SAN ROMAN: We in Costa Rica are looking for a solution. Our museum has the third biggest aquarium in Latin America and so what we did was to create a Foundation for the National Museum that is totally independent. So we do the fund-raising through the Foundation. For example, we began with the membership and we said: Join us in our wonderful adventure spanning 10,000 years. So this way we obtain money for many of the areas that it is not so easy to fund publicly. Also we are a little freer to manage the money on the projects that we want.

LORD MONTAGU: There is no doubt that state-funded museums, and not only in this country, are under siege in some sense. Also the whole of their future role and their politics are obviously being questioned. But at the same time of course the independent museums have made an enormous contribution and I am sorry that there is any feeling that there is any competition between the two because, as Kenneth Hudson said very well, they together make up a whole contribution. The time may come when all the sponsorship money which at the moment goes to the independent museums will go to the national museums. The reason they haven't perhaps got it up to now is that they haven't been seeking it, and perhaps sometimes they haven't been attractive enough for donors to give to. Perhaps I'll just leave you with the thought that the new entrance to the Los Angeles Science Museum is actually through a Macdonalds hamburger joint. However, whether the Los Angeles Science Museum would have happened without this important sponsorship I don't know, but that is a question I'd like to ask.

5 | *People and museums 1*

'Reading' museums

Donald Horne

I am going to begin with an anecdote from Emile Zola's *L'Assommoir*. Those of you who have read the book will remember the calamitous marriage between Gervais and Coupeau. After getting this cheap wedding they decided that they would go for a walk before having the banquet, but then it rained, so some know-all says instead 'Let's go to the museum' – at that stage that meant the Louvre as there was no other – and off they go. They pass through the Assyrian Gallery and they think the stone carving is much better done by Parisians in the 1870s than it was by the Assyrians. Then they have a certain amount of respect for the gallery when they see a haughty attendant with a red waistcoat and gold-braided uniform. They walk respectfully through the French Gallery non-stop, but they are struck dumb and motionless when they get a small lecture from an old woman on 'The Raft of the Medusa'. In the gallery of the Apollo the polished floor particularly impresses them and of course they are, by this stage, beginning to snigger at the naked women. They go into the Long Gallery where, says Zola, centuries of art passed before their dazed ignorance.

Already weary but feeling less awestruck, they dragged their hobnail boots and clattered their heels on the noisy floors. They are lost through eight empty galleries and then a room of drawings, none of which they find funny. And suddenly they are in the Maritime Museum. After a quarter of an hour's tramp through the Maritime Museum in which they find no interest at all, they they are back among the drawings which they find even less funny. They wander aimlessly through the galleries; they are afraid they will never get out of the Louvre. When they are out in the courtyard they say: 'Oh yes, we are glad to have seen it all.'

I began with this anecdote because it illustrates five of the functions of the museum as an initiatory rite into the mysteries of scholarship at that time in the nineteenth century when the public cultures of the modern industrial society were forming.

First of all it shows awe from contact with a palatial building and from being in the presence of the costly and the mysterious objects within it. Secondly it shows baffled reverence for scholarship. Thirdly it can show baffled contempt for scholarship. Fourth, it also shows titillation from seeing, in this case, nudes, but it might equally well have been dinosaurs' bones, Egyptian mummies or some other oddity. And fifthly, it shows that the museum is extremely useful as somewhere you can go to get out of the wet!

However, in these initiatory rites there were two more serious functions, one of which was the pedagogic presentation of these museums which was encyclopaedic, taxonomic, specialist, authoritative and positivistic with, lastly, the arousing of a curiosity that could lead to a widening of the horizons of experience.

Now if you compare these two functions I am assuming that what is most useful about museums are not the encyclopaedic, taxonomic, specialist, authoritative and positivistic pedagogical programmes that have been their heavy legacy from the nineteenth century but in a phrase *the arousing of curiosity* of a kind that can lead to a widening of the horizons of experience. If there were no prospects of discovery, or at least no prospects for illuminating one's existing experience, why go to a museum?

Here I would like to point out that we are not 'the public'. We are many 'publics' – there is no 'the public' – and we are not passive. We are all participants, as these characters in the Zola book demonstrated, dragging their hobnail boots along the shining floors. When we go to a museum, all of us are negotiating meanings and those are the meanings that that museum has for us. And we are all of us, however ill-educated or highly educated, critics of existence and, as such, we approach a museum not on the terms of the museum, but on our terms. We can seek from it material for our general criticism of existence. Or, as I would put it, museums can mean most to us if we can learn to 'read' museums.

There are, of course, special problems: to what extent is curiosity aroused by contemplating objects and not just reading the labels, and in what ways is reading a museum different from reading a book?

Reading museums

The heavy legacy that can weigh down so many museums or has done so in the past, came from the way in which they emerged as part of the public culture of modern industrial societies. Despite the diversities and complexities of these societies (or perhaps because of them) there is projected in each of them, whether capitalist or communist, liberal-democratic, social-democratic, fascist, militarist, or whatever, an impression – a mirage, if you like – of a public and visible culture in which all citizens are made to appear to be common, if differentiated, participants.

In earlier periods there were no public cultures of this kind. There was a ruling class culture, and the bulk of the people followed a folk culture that was largely invisible. But with the industrialization of culture and the creation of modern industrial nation-states public cultures have been, as it were, invented in each nation-state. They purport to represent the national life of that state and they also purport to provide the national version of the mysteries of existence. A public culture is, of necessity, a form of limiting and organizing realities. By its very nature it must be representationally repressive and museums have necessarily played a part in this.

Through the inescapable fact of their very scarcity, museums have been prompted to present narrow and selective views of the national life and, in general terms, of existence. Given their traditions, how could they do otherwise? On the whole, among other things being such costly and visible objects, museums tended to attract only conservative backing, no matter what type of society it was. In any case, also, there weren't enough of them. I am trying to make the point that they tried to present a diversity of subjects – unlike books. Even if it had been museum policy to present a diversity of social approaches, diversity of approach within them is possible but it is difficult. In any case, it has been against the normal practice of museums as bodies of authority even to consider a diversity of approach.

I think there were three particular circumstances of the birth of modern museums at the time of the development of modern industrial societies with their public cultures, and I will just confirm my diagnosis and prognosis in looking for problems and opportunities.

One was the connection of many of them with modern ideas of progress and evolution. Museums could be linear, leading the visitor from rotative steam engines to rockets, from Byzantine to Renaissance, from Stone Age through the Bronze Age to Iron Age progress, from amoeba to man and from entrance to exit.

Another was the strong connection with nation-states at the very time when new nation-states were forming in Europe or the existing ones were strengthening some of their characteristics. Some of them were strengthening as empires: all, or almost all of them, held characteristically European views of the non-European world. Museums were both among the producers, and were subsequently the guardians, of the body of national knowledge and wisdom, in the presentation of national character and the national past.

Thirdly, was their connection with the modes of science and industrialism. Museums became part of the attempt to secure a rational control over existence by cognitive methods, in two ways. One of these was taxonomic: a systematic representation that museums were configurations of knowledge. It was only one configuration but they could tend to suggest that this was the only possible configuration. They systematized existence in the nineteenth-century pattern by dividing it up into subjects. Then they subdivided each of these subjects into its own classifications. The result could be that to move through a museum, genus to genus, from school to school, from age to age, was a declaration made with one's own body with tired feet, exhausted brain and aching back, but the existence was taxonomic.

A second was that as declarations of faith in positivism and objectivity, museums could summon an aura of authenticity, in particular what you might describe as the objectivity of objects. They became part of a highly material and positivistic culture of which another example was the idea that the camera cannot lie, whereas of course we now know through a selection of subjects and style and so forth that the camera can do nothing but lie. They also reflected that idea that history would be based on documents and that in some sense if it was based on documents it was therefore correct. There was also a kind of magic in them – one of the many ways in which they were placed in sacred and secular form. By being catalogued, bits and pieces of many kinds could be transformed into objects or, as the public calls them, exhibits, and that was an entirely new form of being. This became in fact, I think, a significant act of secular transubstantiation, which is the kind of reason why I suggested in *The Great Museum* that some of the objects in museums have become holy relics and that tourism is the modern form of pilgrimage.

In the manner of the times, with their concern for public enlightenment, all three of these were ways in which museums were related to the formation of public cultures providing systems of initiation for knowledge. And in the manner of *our* times, it is, I think, the legacy from that past that provides some of the current problems with museums.

Reading museums

Before moving into the main part of this discussion, I would like to point out, on a slightly optimistic note, that I think museums can have an extremely liberating role in the future, through the diversifications of more pluralistic approaches to knowledge, which is one of the points which was being made this morning, through a reconfiguration or a reshaping of knowledge into new ways of seeing the world and perhaps even, through all of the rubbish and litter that surrounds us in our looking at objects, to a rediscovery of the object itself. And so all of these museums provide an enormous potential for social and cultural and intellectual, and for that matter, moral, change.

Firstly, now I have moved on to the middle part of this, I will talk about *museums as a configuration of knowledge*, both as between them and within them.

First of all, as between them, there were the arbitrary divisions between different kinds of museums. There was a period early in the history or museum formation when there were some holistic approaches, in which it was assumed you didn't have to cut up things into different bits – you could put them all together in the one museum – just as there was a holistic period then of something called the political economy which, to our great detriment then split up into about five different social sciences. But then there were set firmly the rigid divisions of museums into particular subject areas – antiquities, art, natural history, ethnography, science and industry and (in one way and another, from museum houses to army museums), what you might describe as history.

Yet what was characteristic of all these divisions was that they militated against recognition of a complex society. They were, in fact, anti-social, which is to say that they left out of the museum experience what characterizes us as human beings and that is that we are the social animal. And even in relation to divisions of knowledge they were much more arbitrary and missed out on much more than was occurring at the same time in academic knowledge itself.

Let us consider a few examples of what other different territories might have been devised. If we learn to 'read' museums in my sense, in any case we can devise those territories for ourselves.

One example is this: if there was a point in an ethnographic approach of representing certain cultures by material artefacts as in the case of the natives or rural folk, why doesn't it also apply to the populations of the modern industrial societies?

A second example is why not, in historical treatments, have museums specializing in the culture of a particular period with the whole thing running together – military, industrial, art, or whatever it might be?

A third is why should the military or the industrial, for example, be separated out, when so much else could also be separated out: the Labour Movement, for example, women's work? You could go on for ever.

Lastly, why should art be separated from other visual design of the time and over the period before art was invented? Why should that kind of thing be separated from the social functions – in fact, why shouldn't art, for instance, be in history museums, or if we are going to go on having ethnographic museums, why not put European art in European ethnographic museums?

If there are to be new major museums – I don't want to take up the 'what's to be done' argument – they can be general museums with wide enough horizons to put on theme displays. We have in Sydney something called The Powerhouse. The architecture is deplorable – it is post-modernist stuff which guarantees that in ten years it will be out of date – but the other part of its museum policy that I thought was a good idea for a future museum is that it is a general museum. They have a very wide collection and within it you have six or seven different museums and, apart from the steam engines which I think are irrevocably fastened into the cement, the others can be replaced one after the other. There can also be smaller museums that bring out new holistic themes. The existing museums between them could arrange more multidisciplinary theme-directed presentations thereby helping to engage in their own demystification. And by these types of reconfigurations, as they call it in the United States where they are trying to re-do the humanities so that they look at them in different kinds of ways, the world can be turned upside-down within our imaginations and given a new meaning which may have more relation to our present condition.

I'll take one example of what reconfiguration might look like: this would be the reconfiguring of the ethnographic museum as we know it out of existence, at least in its traditional or existing forms.

Given the enormous changes in what used to be regarded as inferior peoples, might this not be expected? Is it not in some ways slightly odd that we should still lump into a single category of 'non-European' cultures so different as those of Japan and Africa, as if somehow they were more like each other than they were like European cultures simply because they weren't European. The basic idea in ethnographic museums has been, as they say now in Copenhagen (where they are spending I think $50 million refitting the ethnographic department of the National Museum), that the collections are 'other people's things', not that they are 'strange objects from other lands'. There are different kinds of ways one can typify this problem. One is to go through the Ethnological Missionary Museum in the Vatican. Yellow arrows quietly direct the visitor along white marble floors beside plate-glass walls and you can see superb artefacts from most of the world's 'other' civilizations. You move past it all with a sense of the varied colour and texture of human civilization. But there is something missing – it is meaning. No explanation is given: most of the objects are not even labelled. But there they are – they are colourful and beautiful and you can make what you like of them. That would seem to represent the problem of the ethnographic museum as something that merely presents the beautiful artefact.

On the other hand, in Amsterdam, with enormous sympathy and skill the Tropical Museum has tried to overcome the strongly colonial approach that is part of the traditional presentation of cultures, by adding oil-drums, bicycles, modern street-stalls, shanty houses, street noises and political posters to the traditional objects amidst old collections, which then have all the more meaning. One might think, yes, OK, they have done that with these objects and other lands – should they perhaps also have gone along to the Rijksmuseum and added to its art galleries, oil-drums, bicycles, modern street-stalls, shanty houses and street noises to remind us that Dutch people no longer have quite the beliefs that they did in many of those paintings.

I'll take one example of reconfiguration in the positive sense and that is of the Australian aborigines. The Australian aborigines, as in the United States and in Canada, were put into natural history museums. You have sticks, stones, minerals, aborigines and things of that kind, fossils etc., all put into the one natural history museum. Also, they tended to be concerned only with weapons, either hunting weapons or fighting weapons, which were often artistically arranged. Spears done in a fan so you could look at them and see a fan of spears, and you knew when you took your children there when you grew up, they would still be there. This represented aboriginal society as one concerned only with fighting and hunting, a sparse, almost non-cultural society as it were. At the beginning of the 1960s the art museums took up aboriginal artefacts and said: 'These are not ethnography at all, they are art.' For a while that was of enormous use because it reminded the visitor that the aborigines were real people, and they began to understand that in fact aborigines lived a more leisurely life than people did in modern industrial societies, and they spent more of their time talking to each other, gossiping, than we manage to do. In many art museums they have now developed their own mystique about it. If you go into an Australian art museum, you see a bit of aboriginal art, and it just gives you a little label and doesn't tell you anything else.

A possible final approach in a country which actually has its natives, as it were, still living within it, is that you should have aboriginal cultural centres which display these objects, but which go beyond normal museum inhibitions and point out that they are based in ceremony. It would be necessary to indicate also the ceremonies on which the objects are based, with illustrations of aboriginal dancing and so forth. It also must, surely, indicate how these motives, whether in dance or the visual arts, are now being developed by contemporary aborigines in modern art forms as well, and you might have a few of them around so that visiting American tourists can ask them some questions.

In countries which don't have their natives, I think you can by all means continue to have these wonderful collections of objects, but you could put them together under themes, and shove in some of your own civilization as well. If you want to indicate initiation rites, you can indicate initiation rites if you wish from Africa, South-East Asia, Oceania, Britain, Bulgaria or whatever it might be, and bring out some of the commonness of human activity. Try to believe that when God created the world he didn't really create a final encyclopaedic division between people of European background and all the others. That is the end of ethnographic museums.

As to classifications within museums, Linnaeus, of course, had already begun developing taxonomies in the eighteenth century but it was in the nineteenth century that the great typologies were to emerge – from the division of painting into four great 'Schools', to the division of pre-history into three great 'ages', as happened when the predecessor of the National Museum in Copenhagen by the 1820s had one room for the Stone Age, one for the Bronze Age, one for the Iron Age, and you moved through them and admired progress.

Decisions such as these determined that a visit to a museum became an ordered event in which the museum itself imposed a systematic pattern on the material the visitor was to see and in which the visitor was expected to celebrate progress by passing from room to room in a certain succession. Once a particular form of order had become familiar, the museum experience could become partly one of revision. In going to a museum, one reminded oneself of the particular classifications to be expected from that kind of museum, which is still one of the main functions, I think, of visits to art museums.

I worked in Sweden a couple of weeks ago and then indeed in Copenhagen, but in the refit of the Ethnographic Department of the National Museum

Reading museums

in Copenhagen they intend to provide new exhibitions, more or less of the kind I was describing, but they intend to put a lot of the rest of their stuff in what they describe as 'open storage'. It's there and you can look at it and if it happens to interest you, instead of the museum telling you in what context to see it, you can go off to an information system and find out something more about it.

Here I should also bring up, I think, the special case of art museums. It is in art museums that I think the rigidities of systematic presentation have perhaps had their worst effects. They become in effect art history museums, with the tradition of the chronological hang in national Schools determining museum presentation. Yet there was nothing in the material itself that demanded this particular emphasis. All these art objects could have been arranged and thought about in quite different ways. Art museums are configured on a historical framework but since they won't supplement the gaps left by the absence from the collection of other material, art museums are not the place in which to seek the meanings of paintings in the terms of those who painted them and those they were painted for. Not only are the paintings not put into a social or general cultural background, they are not put into a general design background either. You get no impression of the trash, for example. Usually what is offered is simply from the accidents of collecting, but the tradition of the chronological hang makes it seem more than that, it makes it look historical.

Imagine instead art museums produced in a different kind of way, related to themes and similarities. I recall when I was here a couple of years ago, the National Gallery had done a thing like that called 'Body Lines' and some of the people belonging to the curatorial sub-culture were appalled that a Gothic woodcarving crucifixion should be in the same room as a Baroque painting of a crucifixion.

Secondly, *museums as guardians of the national past*. They were to begin with, in some cases, grandiose declarations of imperial power. The unparalled collections in the British Museum and the South Kensington enterprises were a declaration that Britain occupied a large part of the world and was now busy classifying it.

There were the grandiose establishment of the Museum Island in Berlin and the museums that put forward the Austro-Hungarian view of existence in the Ring in Vienna when they knocked down the fortifications. The creation of a system of national museums in Tokyo, Kyoto and Nara show that Japan was also modernizing in the nineteenth century.

In the Red Square itself they put up a national museum of 300,000 exhibits and in Washington there was the presentation of museums as part of the history of the display of civil religion at the heart of the nation's capital. So the museum palaces now take their place along with the White House, the Capitol of the Supreme Court and the temples that enshrine the Constitution and the spirits of Lincoln and Jefferson.

There were also the conquest halls, such as the National Maritime Museum, trophy halls such as the ethnographic departments, national museums within countries ranging from the present Czechoslovakia to the present Norway: the national museums where even the laboratories have a nationality. There was the development of the idea of a 'golden age' for a society the Irish founded in Celtic carving, the Norwegians in study of medieval churches and of Viking ships, the Serbs in gallery frescos, and the Germans in the National Museum at Nurenberg.

National character was discovered in declining peasantry, to begin with in Sweden and then all over the place. There were collections of national art displaying the national past, the national character, the national landscape. There were liberation museums, whether it is the Independence National Park in Philadelphia or Guanzhou, China, where there are nine museums celebrating the departure of the imperial bandits, including one which is called The Museum of Anti-British Struggle.

Along with the liberation museums are the revolutionary museums of the communist countries and the V.I. Lenin Museums. There are the military museums, beginning in 1905 and then an enormous batch of them after the First World War, and there are the on-site history museums, some of which are complete old towns. In Singapore for the moment they have decided to have old towns and the only way which they can now create old towns is to destroy what remains of the old towns that exist so that tourists can understand that they are old towns. There are also the museum houses of great men, whether it is Jefferson in Montebello or Deponegerro in Yugoslavia.

There is also the development of aristocratic tourism, whether it is the palazzo, or the country house or the chateau, in which you saw the aristocracy of the past cleaned up for art lovers without some of its other characteristics, and the transformation of religious sites into tourist spectacles. My example of the latter would be at Kyoto, where in the Temple of Ryanji, once relatively undisturbed, was the famous stone garden. You now have the tourist buses lining up and you are supposed to sit there and contemplate, but you've got about two minutes to contemplate before the next lot move in, and while you are contemplating a voice over the tape is telling you what you should be thinking.

Reading museums

Meanwhile, national definition continues. In Bangkok in Thailand they discovered that perhaps the Bronze Age began in Thailand rather than somewhere else, and immediately established an annexe to the history museum called a pre-history museum to establish the supremacy of Bangkok in that important period in civilization. Not only is the Louvre now 'Grand', it is also the 'greatest museum in the world', we are told, and I notice there is something called the Palazzo Pozzi which started in Venice a couple of years ago which is now celebrating, according to a description I have read, the way in which Italians invented modern painting.

I think here we have to listen to the silence of history in these things – look at museums and see what's missing. I have indicated what is missing in ethnographic museums and in art museums. One other example would be army museums, and what is missing there is the entire society in which the army existed. Not only that, but the society of the army itself, not to mention the fact that in wars people get killed and become rather unhappy in lots of other ways, and that they can be rather destructive of life.

The silence in industry museums can be equally instructive. As Kenneth Hudson put it in *Museums of Influence*, we have many museums of industry but we have yet to have a museum of industrialization.

Well, as was pointed out this morning, some of us can pride ourselves on living in a liberal-democratic pluralist society, so what are we going to do about it with museums? In the sense of locality we can do the kind of thing that, for example, I saw last week in the Glasgow area at Springburn where a community museum is helping people to define themselves. You can find similar kinds of things in Tokyo and you can find them certainly in the Scandinavian countries. Not only locality but ethnic similarity: the Pueblo-Indian Museum for example in Alberquerque, or the great number of African-American museums throughout the United States or the self-definition museums of the Mexican-Americans in California are also examples of this.

In other words, how do we offset bias in museums? Apart from the ordinary authoritative mystique of museums, one can nevertheless to some extent be positive, assuming that we are not one public but many. There should be the possibility for multiple readings, and if there are going to be readings we can assume that many different kinds of people come into museums and they all have a right to a certain kind of service about the stuff they are looking at. There can also be perhaps a more positive programme of encouraging alternative readings. Museums might give themselves the responsibility of reminding the people who visit them that the contents of a museum can be read in a number of different ways.

An example of that would be in Paris at the moment. There is a thing on Australian aborigines which is not too bad, but an alternative exhibition has been put up in the corner reminding people of what might be missing from the official exhibition.

When I was here last, a couple of years ago, the Manchester City Art Gallery had in its bookshop something called *A Feminist Looks Round the City Art Gallery*: an alternative handbook which could, for those people who hadn't read John Berger's *Ways of Seeing*, remind them of how one could see in an art gallery a certain type of projection of the female form and the female future as somewhat different from the kind normally presented. Whether labels can allow for differences of opinion I don't know. Can one set off objects against each other or even look at the same objects? Shouldn't perhaps all museums have in their entrance spaces a little display area in which they say to people: 'You are entering here something that has been put together by us. We could have chosen quite different objects and these objects might have been put together in different kinds of ways. Please have a look at them yourselves and if you feel like it go to the shop and buy a bit more about it.'

We need to promote *the* mystique of the object. I think that an overall principle of public funding for museums should be that physical access to museums is only a beginning. Expositions should be arranged so that there are possibilities for intellectual access as well. Normally, this requires the provision of some information and even if you have one of those lovely jumbles in which the thing is not organized in a linear fashion, you should be able to find out something about the stuff.

There are troublesome beliefs. One is that art needs no explanation, which I don't think I need enlarge on here. Another is a new one called 'the democracy of the object'. This was illustrated in a devastating failure in Australia last year in something about the Australian national identity. The organizers thought that there was no single Australian national identity, but a lot of different ones, so they shoved in a whole lot of objects which people didn't recognize. It was carried around in a tent and the technology of the tent was so great that people had a splendid time going to the museum and watching the technology of the tent.

There should perhaps be sometimes the signed exhibition, a simple state-ment as you do with a book, a poem or whatever it might be, that this is an exhibition by somebody but that there could have been other presentations.

I shall conclude with just four anecdotes.

Reading museums

One is, I remember being here a couple of years ago when somebody was talking about Woolmer Castle. Apparently the Duke of Wellington died there in a chair. Now this chair was one of the most revered objects in the castle but the chintz was wearing out. They discovered a little bit of un-worn-out chintz at the bottom of the chair and persuaded the manufacturers to copy it. They had redone the chair and you can buy the chintz at the shop, I am told, but it suddenly occurred to me that the Duke of Wellington was allowed to die but not his chair.

Another memory is of going to the Athens Museum of Popular Art, done in the most tasteful form like a jeweller's shop of eighteenth-century folk art, with no reference whatsoever to the conditions in which eighteenth-century folk art was produced in Athens. One might as well have given up in Athens, and simply looked on it as a jeweller's shop with an element of design. On the other hand, in the Shanghai Museum is what may be one of the world's greatest collections of Bronze Age instruments but ordered entirely in terms of motif (done very splendidly) and manufacture, with no reference whatsoever to Shanghai or to the social conditions under which these emerged.

And finally, in the Santa Fe Museum of International Folk Art, an eccentric architect had collected 100,000 toys, dolls and things of that kind. Hating linear and rational and categorizing presentation in museums he put them together so that they simply told stories. They were in situations and you found that you go into a museum which tells you nothing – no linear progress, no categorization, nothing of that kind. Consequently, you have no alternative but to look at the objects, and to have that very rare and memorable experience of a museum visitor: seeing nothing but the objects.

Discussion

TOMISLAV SOLA: It seems to me we have heard an absolutely brilliant exposé on the diversity of the museum world – the richness of resources that we have, and the consequence of that seems to me to lead to the conservation and the communication aspect of museums. If we are the databanks of the tactile which explains the evolution of our species as well as natural evolution, then this presents a totally new responsibility. If the museum movement is going to continue to develop then museums must develop, must change, must be responsive to local conditions and to the needs of the moment, but always with a sense of respect for the past and transmission to the future. And it seems to me this is the core of what we are about. If we could come back to this morning's discussion, if that is really hammered in and explained to the public and our trustees and staff who may sometimes be exposed to this or that temporary allurement, that then some of the difficulties that we have in funding may be not overcome but certainly will be reduced.

BARRY LORD: I'd just like to comment on the paradigm and marvellous description you began with, because it reminded me of the discussion about what business museums are really in. I think it is something we really need to be careful about. In many management studies it has been found in private corporations that it is crucially important for the corporation to get a very clear and concise grasp of exactly what it's actually offering: whether in the case of the railways, for example, it's really offering transportation or whether it's really in the hospitality industry.

In the museum field I was struck recently by reading an evaluation of exhibits at the Royal British Columbia Museum where at I think the cost of about £1 million there has been a replacement of some conventional case exhibits on the ecology of the Pacific Coast. These conventional cases had been taken away and replaced by walk-in dioramas which surrounded the viewer and the visitor walked through these dioramas which recreated the ecology of the coast (which indeed you can walk through as the real thing, a couple of miles away from the Museum just outside the city of Victoria). They had taken the care in this case to monitor the case displays before dismantling them. As to their education value let us say they had tested visitors before and after entering the exhibit, and then they administered the same tests after they had spent this £1 million and installed their walk-in dioramas, and the bottom line was that of course there was minimal difference in the test results after the dioramas had been put in than before. The education value of these

Discussion

exhibit changes had been relatively minimal, so that one might say that from a purely educational point of view (if the museum is in the education business), it had been largely wasting its money and time by making this significant change. The reporter on the staff of the Museum in reporting this study concluded by saying that nevertheless as museum professionals we feel much happier with the new exhibits. But what struck me was that when you get that kind of result you have to conclude that you are asking the wrong questions. Essentially we like to say that museums are educational institutions, but I think we are slightly wrong on that. As educational institutions surely they are less efficient than universities, schools and so on.

Similarly we like to say that museums are entertainment institutions, and again I think we are slightly wrong. There are more efficient places to go to if you are merely seeking entertainment. I was casting around in a speech recently trying to put my finger on what it is that museums are about. I think this was well described in the example that you led off with, and I came up with the nineteenth-century term 'edification', which I think is a somewhat discredited term now but one which we ought to dust off and look at again, as I think that's precisely the business we're in – edification means the broadening of one's perspective, the sharpening of one's interests, the loosening of one's prejudices and beginning to see the relationship between things that one didn't see before. I think that is really precisely the exciting thing, the satisfaction that one gets from a museum experience. If we start defining ourselves as institutions of edification rather than trying to be institutions of education or entertainment we would perhaps identify what it is that museums do rather well. We might also identify the reason why we have been so successful in the twentieth century and presumably will be more so in the twenty-first century if we get a clear fix on precisely what it is that we have to offer.

SIR PHILIP GOODHART, MP: In the course of the last couple of months I have taken two visitors to Neil Cossons' excellent Science Museum. One was a distinguished American professor and the other was my 8-year-old grandson and I think that one of the most hopeful developments in the whole museum world in the last 10–20 years is that the edification of young people has been enormously enhanced by the new technological displays in most new museums. Can I just correct an impression of Patrick Boylan, who I think perhaps misunderstood me. What I was trying to say was that between now and the end of this century any government was bound to increase the amount of public spending on museums, just as I think that it is inevitable between now and the end of the century that there should continue to be an increase in the number of museums and the extraordinary diversity of museums we have seen in the last ten years or so, and I think it is inevitable that we will continue to see an enormous increase in the number of people who visit those museums whether they be private or public.

FRANS SCHOUTEN: I don't want to ask a question but I would like to make a statement. I would like to start with an anecdote. As a young child I used to visit the Museum of Antiquities in Leiden where I live, and I found it a very intriguing museum although it was in nowadays terms a rather old-fashioned and dusty place. I think we need to look at other resources as well. There recently has been an investigation in the United States on why people love video games and they find three important issues, which are: (1) there has to be challenge, (2) they have to raise curiosity and (3) there must be something of discovery in it. If you take these three elements: challenge, discovery and curiosity I sometimes find nineteenth-century museums offering more of these three than modern museums.

NEIL COSSONS: I would just like to welcome what Philip [Goodhart] has just said about expansion. I think what we need to say through Philip to the government is: 'Please now', and not wait till the end of the century. It isn't only the British Museum that is falling down – an awful lot of our museums are. But it is not just a matter of funding, it's a matter of policy development. I'd have thought that was coming through very clearly and in that respect I think we have been enormously privileged to hear Donald's [Horne] views. If only the British government would employ him as a policy adviser we would be in a much better state! Somebody said this morning that we in this country as a museum profession are very good at professionalism and technique but we pay less attention to theory and policy. It's certainly true of the government and I think it is equally true of the profession as a whole and in that sense Donald really has addressed some very fundamental issues.

Barry [Lord] has stressed the word edification. I think everything Donald says provokes us into thinking about what we should be doing and what the essence of a public service obligation and definition is. Edification I think is a very interesting word, but it cannot by itself carry the full range of responsibilities. Neither can the public service broadcasting definition (which has a lot of relevance to museums), to inform, educate and entertain, but obviously the museum service must go beyond that to include preservation, collection of evidence, and providing of evidence for the future. I would suggest that our responsibility goes beyond that one step further and that our museums are failing if in addition to all those things they aren't sending people out of those museums provoked to ask questions. In that sense scrutiny and stimulus was implicit in

Discussion

everything that Donald was saying about how we should present our material.

It has to be said that we are very good at one-off shows, and in the standard of catalogues. Both the erudition and the explanation to the public are awfully good in specific exhibitions but there are still a number of very major galleries and museums that don't present and tell the story of their total collections: the Tate is a classic example. They are superb at one-offs, and yet it isn't possible to come away with any grasp of what story about our visual arts and culture the Tate is telling. I gather that Nick Serota is going to be rehanging the whole collection this autumn and that should be very exciting indeed as a way of forcing him and his curators to tell the story of what the Tate is and what our visual culture is. But I think we have to ask ourselves very specific questions and I would have thought that Donald has helped us enormously.

The one question I'd like to ask him is what role has broadcasting in the new technologies to play in helping museums communicate, not just with the people who come in, but with the whole of our community?

DONALD HORNE: I think Kenneth [Hudson] actually answered that in his *Museums of Influence* when he pointed out there are some things which it is possible that videos and television can do better. He mentioned specifically the question of the old style ethnographic department. What I was trying to do was to find an answer when all these wonderful objects can still have a use which broadcasting can't do. In other words broadcasting is already there providing all kinds of activities and ways of looking at things that in some of the traditional kinds of museums are no longer necessary. But that means that museums themselves can do things that broadcasting can't do. I think that would be my answer, but maybe the other way round.

LORD MONTAGU: Have you heard of the idea of the new electronic zoo without any animals, which I think is rather an attractive idea!

EVELYN SILBER (Conference participant, Birmingham Museums and Art Gallery): We've heard quite a lot about the need to make our museums much more stimulating, to present challenges and to allow our visitors to interact far more with what we are showing. Something which I would like to question is whether what we are asking for (with all the implications that it has either at strictly school or college level or at a much wider public level), doesn't itself presuppose a lot more self-critical questions, for example, about the nature of museum training and the opportunities for curators, designers and others to step aside from many of their daily jobs in order to reconsider how they are presenting their collections.

It is my impression that the predominantly straight line of development from academic training into traditional demarcations between disciplines tends to reinforce rather traditional methods of presentation. I would like to suggest that it is in this area that consistent and really generous political support and funding is really essential, together with action on behalf of museum staff by The Museums Association and the Museums and Galleries Commission.

GEOFFREY LEWIS: Perhaps I should come in on this issue. It is a profound issue, and it's a very proper question which goes right to the root of much of the debate that's going on at the moment about training. Clearly there is a whole area of theory which has not been developed in the museum context, and we at Leicester certainly and I know others as well, are now conscious of this and developing some theoretical aspects of museums by applying theory from other disciplines to museums. This is vitally important for the better understanding of museums and for the creation of better museums as well.

Now I would say on this point that there is a dire need for recognition of the need for research and for the funding of it. Museums so far have tended not to have funding for research into their fundamental aspects. I believe this is an area which we must look at, and it is an area that has not so far really come out in any of the discussions on training. It affects us also (and I am saying this as an aside) as a University Department of Museum Studies. One of the yardsticks, I am sure, people are aware more and more, is the research aspect of our Department and the extent of the money (and we have to come down again to the issue of money), that the department is attracting for research purposes. There is no tradition of funding research in museology and this, I suggest, is an area that we must develop as we look towards the year 2000.

It follows then from this that training for curatorship, and I purposely emphasize curatorship and the interdisciplinarity that that implies, should be broad-based. We are talking about an old word which has been much confused, but we are talking about museology. We are talking about an understanding of the museum operation in a truly interdisciplinary context and, with one plug for Leicester, may I say that that has been the theory behind Leicester's approach since it started long before my time in 1976.

Discussion

PATRICK BOYLAN: Obviously I would like to echo all of Geoffrey Lewis's remarks but perhaps take things even much further, particularly in relation to Evelyn Silber's point, and indeed to echo something that Kenneth [Hudson] said at the very first discussion. We are, I am afraid, extremely insular in the UK. We do not, in the profession or the governing bodies, really know what is happening outside the country. We do not have access to foreign museum literature, we don't travel; we don't have money for such literature, we don't have money for travel. We're going to become an increasingly isolated backwater if we're not careful.

I have just come to the end of twelve years of close involvement in training at international level with the International Committee for the Training of Personnel of ICOM, and we have two other Board Members of that Committee here today. There is no doubt at all that in some respects the UK still leads the world in the standard of what it provides in the museum training field. On the other hand the take-up of professional training by the members of the profession is really very small. It doesn't matter if we set up a Museum Training Institute for which, after sixty-five years' hammering at the door of the government, we have now got government support to launch it – substantial funding for an initial period of five years – but this initiative is not going to work unless individuals and employers come forward to use the training opportunities. Looking towards 1992, I think we have to look at European standards of training, and within the next four or five years we have got to build up our museum expenditure on training in the broadest sense, in which I include travel and sabbaticals for further reflection and research. We have got to get budgets up to the minimum standard of the best continental practice in the European Community, that is 2 per cent of the payroll budget for the training etc., and revitalization of the existing staff.

Our national expenditure on training in UK museums is absolutely abysmal – I would guess under 0.2 per cent of payroll. And I think this is primarily the responsibility of museum employers. I don't think we can go back and say 'Right, we've been doing things wrong up to now, therefore central government has got to pay everything.' Central government is actually putting substantial amounts of money into the Museum Training Institute initiative and it is now up to the profession and the employers to contribute their share – it is a matter of rearranging priorities within our museums and we have got to get down to that.

PETER CANNON-BROOKES (Conference participant, Editor, *International Journal of Museum Management*): Can I adopt a slight devil's advocate attitude because there are many of us who are curators by background who feel that museums have seriously lost their way.

Museums are concerned with objects and the intellectual structure of the museum is the collecting of objects, the assembly of knowledge about objects, the conservation of objects, assembling that knowledge into a rational structure and the provision of access for the rest of the community to it. We are concerned with the relationship between people and objects. That is what museums are about.

Museums are archives: I think that this is a word that has not been used today and it is a word that can be used to very considerable advantage. There are archives of documents which we are very familiar with, and the community set up those archives to preserve documents. Museums were set up by the community as archives to preserve objects. We in the western world, and this is by no means true of all cultures, convey an immense amount of information through objects. We can transmit information from generation to generation. That is why we are the world collectors of objects. We thus have a responsibility to collect and maintain and to pass on to future generations and our function is an object-based one.

Accessibility is very important and display is in fact a very efficient means of providing access to objects, but for God's sake do not misunderstand this. Putting things on display is an efficient means of providing access to the objects in the collections. It does not have a virtue on its own and this should not blind us to the fact that in the function of collections display is secondary, as is education. These are secondary elements that are erected on top of the primary core functions.

This raises fundamental problems. There are different criteria for judging the efficiency with which you conduct your core activities, from those with which you conduct your secondary functions. The management of museums requires a clear understanding of both the core functions and the desirable secondary functions that are erected on them. I would suggest that we should give very careful consideration to the idea of splitting the funding in the museums between core functions and highly desirable secondary functions so that both can be assessed according to their own criteria, because we should not kid ourselves that one single set of criteria is equally applicable to both because it is not.

SAROJ GHOSE: I am tempted to differ from the last speaker. In the museums of the present generation not only in the third world but in already developed countries like the United States and this country, we have started feeling that the object is of primary importance and display and education is of secondary importance. We don't agree to that one. We feel that with the democratization of society museums have to be people-minded. Who are funding the museums? It is the people, not the government, not the corporate bodies, but the people through the taxes and through the prices of the commodities, who are funding the museums. And museums have to be very effective in contributing to people's education, and in some cases maybe for formal school education. These should be the primary duties and responsibilities of museums. If education is the primary goal of schools and colleges the medium is different, so education should be our primary goal and the object is only a medium, nothing more than that.

CONFERENCE PARTICIPANT (no name): Our colleague Saroj Ghose is putting his finger very firmly on it. The contrast we are facing at the moment is between people-centred activities and object-centred activities. I have nothing against people-centred activities. This is the fundamental contrast between for example, science museums and science centres: they are both honourable professional activities but they are not the same thing. We are concerned with museums: I wish you the greatest success in India in creating science centres but that is what you are creating – they are not museums.

SAROJ GHOSE: The difference between science centres and science museums is fast vanishing. There are lots and lots of institutions of a combined nature. The greatest example is represented by Neil Cossons here in South Kensington with Launch Pad in the traditional Science Museum existing side by side.

TOMISLAV SOLA: We were actually talking about museums and people and I think this is a good thing. Museums are on the second wave of civilization, like ancient Egyptian scribes, who would respond immediately to the command 'Let it be written and documented' and they did it. Now we need something else to move us along this second wave, not after a lag in time but very much in the present. And this is a rather uncomfortable position that implies risks that we have to take. This also means that the role of museums will be a counter-active one, which means that the public will identify its own needs in museums, regarding them really as their own. Goethe said in 1825, 'You only learn from those whom you love.' Museums should achieve that position, otherwise there won't be communication or any sort of real understanding between the public and museums, because museums are viewed by the greater part of the public as a part of the establishment itself, whether we admit this or not.

CONFERENCE PARTICIPANT (no name): The responsibility to the past can only be met if the present is properly served and if we can, as Tomislav just said, generate a the sense of affection and involvement among the public, making them see that the objects and collections of our museums were all made by our fellow countrymen or by our predecessors, they were made by our species. If we are going to understand our collections and services better, we need to also invoke the interest of all of those whose ancestors created them: our resources are not part of this or that social class or group, they are part of a total society. I also think society has the privilege of having contact with and of exploiting these objects not only for themselves, but for what these objects may do in the future for their grandchildren.

I would hate to see us dismiss the potential of new technology and not only of television but videodisc and computers. I think we have the means enormously to enlarge the penetration of museums. Our vast resources are of both individual value and of great variety: that smorgasbord of the museum that was described earlier can perhaps begin to be linked together, not only for the specialist but also for the general visitor. Why not relate pieces from different cultures, and see what was happening at the same moment in time historically, but without denying the primacy of each object? I agree with Peter Cannon-Brookes totally on that primacy, but there is a parallel primacy to be considered. There is no point having blood if you don't have a heart to propel it, and I see the object and its primacy, and the educational function within the museum having very much that relationship.

LORD MONTAGU: There is no doubt in any of our minds I think that museums are, in a sense, going through a revolution, and I hope this is a revolution that most people welcome. Our successors facing those challenges in the twenty-first century, as has so ably been said by Geoffrey Lewis, and also by Patrick Boylan, are going to see as central the question of training both our young curators and current and future directors to face these challenges. Also, I couldn't agree more about the need for museum people to travel and find out what else is going on in the world. I would however say that whenever I go to conferences overseas they are already always packed full of English people. I think the real problem in relation to travel for study is for the Third World countries: they are the people who find it most difficult, and equally they need most to come to conferences such as this one or ICOM conferences and meetings and so on. And I think you would be interested to know that the profits from the London ICOM General Conference six years ago were put into a charitable fund and are used to send people to ICOM conferences and meetings, particularly from this country. That was a good way to use our surplus from that conference.

6 | *People and museums 2*

People's participation in science museums

Saroj Ghose

Man has seen the agricultural revolution, the Renaissance, the Industrial Revolution and is now on the threshold of an information revolution which is likely to shape his mind in the next century. Massive assimilation of information, systematic storage, quick retrieval and unobtrusive dissemination of knowledge may lead man to a new understanding of life and values that may mark the beginning of a new era in human civilization in AD 2000.

Museums, like computers or any other information tool, teach man to look back at his past heritage, to assimilate information in a systematic mode, to analyse gathered experience in the context of present understanding, and ideally to predict the future based on such assimilated information. Like any other information tool, museums store massive amounts of information contained in its collection and disseminates such information through its presentation. Richness of museum collections symbolizes richness of data storage in an information system, and it is the speed of retrieval system that distinguishes one museum from another. How quickly a visitor can get access to or retrieve the stored information from an artefact depends on how interactive is the object or its presentation in a museum.

The mode of presentation in science museums has undergone considerable change since the Crystal Palace Exhibition. Science museums, primarily a legacy of the Industrial Revolution, and a much younger concept compared to art collections, were mostly developed as people's institutions right from their inception. Such institutions, funded by a democratic government, even if under Royal patronage, had more accountability to the people. The concept of informal education for the people was therefore implicit in the very format of science museums right from the beginning.

Side by side with the artefacts came up a new brand of exhibits to explain the basic function of artefacts and to demonstrate scientific principles. Animations were devised to simulate a particular situation which cannot be created in a museum setting. Push-button demonstrations were introduced to bring the concept of experimentation out of laboratories into museums. Audio-visual techniques were presented to create a particular atmosphere. Scaled down and sometimes scaled up models, sectioned artefacts or models, life-size dioramas, meticulously created period rooms and many other different modes of presentation were introduced into science museums to compact more information into a given space and to attract and induce people to retrieve information as quickly as possible. With new inventions and innovations in laser, video, microprocessor and computer technology, science museums went through a radical change. All this came in an evolutionary process spanning over half a century and reflecting a shift in basic objectives and functions of a science museum.

The level of interaction in science museum exhibits changed as well. The first change came in visual presentation when standard glass cases and continuous wall cabinets were replaced by aesthetically designed colourful and functional displays which had a popular appeal. Audio effects were used to simulate a real-life situation. Dramatic situations were created through multi-media presentations, even through to animated dinosaurs. Tactile perception was brought in by allowing visitors to touch and handle more and more exhibits. From the 1970s a whole new generation of participatory exhibits infiltrated (I use this word very deliberately) the science museums to change their character. The use of muscles and the motor action of the brain brought in an emotional involvement of visitors with inanimate exhibits or objects, so much so that science museums, or for that matter science centres, became vibrant with visitors' interaction.

Interactive exhibits are those which throw a challenge to the visitors – I was very happy when one member of the audience raised this in the afternoon session – and adjust into different situations like a chess player. The objects behave like a chess player, and visitors must derive information through a discovery process by a systematic analysis of the database, which is again inbued in the exhibit. The level of interaction in a science museum rises high with more and more interactive participation of visitors, and the effectiveness of the science museum as an information medium is greatly enhanced.

People's participation in science museums

If exhibits are one piece of basic hardware in the information system, the other hardware lies in activity-orientated programmes in which visitors must participate interactively. Making museums more people-minded has become a new trend with the emergence of nationalism, particularly in the Third World countries. Science and technology are used as powerful tools for a radical socio-economic transformation in developing countries, where science museums are viewed as a very cost-effective platform for the popularization of science, creating a scientific temper in that society and inculcating creative faculties in the young minds of the nation. Museums in developed countries where accountability towards the clientele assumes a dominant form have also joined in this movement of involving people in museums' programmes and taking museums out to the community.

The operators of the science museum information system can be grouped in two: schools and the non-school-going community. Science museums all over the world are a favourite place for schoolchildren for interactive games, dramatic presentations and a free-for-all atmosphere that is so much different from a regimented school situation. Many science museums have devised ingenious activities to 'catch them young'.

Discovery rooms with touch-and-manipulate objects and kits have sprung up in many museums, but more remarkable are those where the entire museum, and not an isolated discovery room alone, provides the opportunity to the children to manipulate kits and teaching aids, as done in some US children's museums like Boston or Indianapolis.

Teachers' orientation courses for understanding museum exhibits are not so uncommon in museums of today, but noteworthy are those where teachers are trained regularly in the development of teaching aids and kits with the help of a workforce of students as is done in India. Science writing, debates, elocution contests, science fairs, and nature camps are some of the variations in museum activities organized in different countries for school children. Classes are organized in museums for inducting young children in hobbies relating to computers, amateur astronomy, biosciences, mathematics, chemistry, rocketry, aero-modelling and environmental studies. Camp activities of Sweden, India and USA, particularly by OMSI of Portland and BITM of Calcutta, deserve a special mention. All these programmes are meant to develop a broad-based general understanding of science, which is termed non-formal science education, so necessary for strengthening the base of the society.

In India, museum programmes for schools have transgressed into the domain of formal education as well. Curriculum-based activities are organized to give support to classroom science teaching. Teachers are trained to develop teaching aids with the purpose of building up their own school laboratories. The programme is intended to instil a culture of self-reliance in educational technology through a joint effort of teachers and students.

[At this point Dr Ghose showed a short excerpt from a video of recent work by members of the National Council of Science Museums of India.]

This is just a small cross-section of the activities of science museums in India but we know that this is, to a greater or lesser extent, a general picture of good science museums all over the world.

So much has been said and done on school programmes because of the homogeneity in the composition of the target groups. Specific programmes aimed at specific age groups and level of understanding are comparatively easy to organize. A far more difficult situation arises when the science museum attempts to address the non-school-going community with heterogeneous audiences. When the age varies from 8 to 80, the level of educational attainment varies from illiteracy to the highest academic degree, and the gap in socio-economic status is as wide as the ocean, it is hard to design exhibits and software which would be equally acceptable to all. The risk of having problems of communication gaps, resulting in big information gaps, cannot be ruled out in community-orientated programmes, no matter how well these are organized.

A method for taking out interactive exhibits to the community was ably demonstrated by Ontario Science Centre through its Science Circus. A comparable example, though differing in concept as well as contents, is the Discovery Dome approach supported by the Nuffield Foundation in this country. The Polytechnic Museum in Moscow has been running about twenty travelling exhibitions, not much interactive but of great social relevance, throughout the USSR.

Science museums in India started its first Museobus twenty-four years ago and by now the fleet contains twenty large buses criss-crossing the length and breadth of the country. Two other examples of regular travelling exhibitions are those organized in the USA by the Smithsonian Institution and Association of Science Technology Centers. Two examples of bilateral travelling exhibitions of a very large size are the ones organized by China in the USA and the other organized by India both in the USA and USSR. All these reflect an attempt to reach out to the community outside the four walls of the museum. A smaller but much more interactive programme for reaching the community is being organized by some US museums in the form of 'Community Math' programmes or 'Shopping Mall Exhibits'.

People's participation in science museums

Science museums in India have taken up a host of people-minded programmes. Science drama, the annual science march, programmes for fighting superstition, and regular television programmes by science museums have become essential components of a nation-wide people's science movement. The most important of this kind of activity is the adoption of some villages in remote interior areas of the interaction of science and technology to improve the lifestyle of the common man. Rural developmental programmes have never been thought of as a basic or even subsidiary objective of a science museum, but this is the kind of programme that has brought out science museums in India to the focal point of attention in the eyes of planners, financiers, politicians and finally the people at large.

Jawarharlal Nehru, the architect of modern India, used the term 'scientific temper' quite frequently as a goal to achieve through the science and technology planning of the country. This is something like generating a new line of thinking, a new culture, a new ethos. Will museums succeed in becoming a generator of new cultures rather than projectors of old heritage? That is the question which has been thrown open to participants in the next ICOM General Conference in The Hague later this year, and I think this will be a burning question for 2000 AD.

Discussion

PATRICK BOYLAN: I would not like to challenge anything that Dr Ghose has said. I would just like to reinforce the enormous strides that have been made in India in looking forwards and making museums centres for science education, for social development and so on. Our two politicians have now had to leave, but it is a pity they weren't here to hear and see this presentation because in fact the science museums are seen as an absolutely central part of India's national economic and social development, as well as the country's educational development programme. This is in no small measure due to the efforts of Dr Ghose and his amazing colleagues. I would like to take this opportunity to thank him personally and most warmly for the fact that the Indians did in fact invite out a number of people from the UK last December, and as one of them I can say we have seen only a tiny fraction of what the potential is under the National Council of Science Museums' agenda.

I am sure this is a very important area which we need to look at in all countries in relation to the future. Perhaps the most important thing of all though, I think, if we are talking about new approaches to museums, is the need to integrate these sorts of technologies into the mainstream museums. I think what we need are not 'Launch Pads' (looking as though they are things that have landed *from* outer space not going towards outer space). Instead those approaches which have been used so imaginatively in the introduction to engineering in Launch Pad in the Science Museum should be integrated with the real collections, the real thing, the historic technology and the present-day technology of the science museums them-selves. On the whole I think this has not been done. Places which have established science centres within traditional science museums have mainly kept these separate, and I think that is true for example even in Bangalore and Bombay.

I am sure that the way forward with the great scientific objects and industrial heritage objects that we have in our industrial museums and science museums is to actually bring them to life, and not have them sitting there as pieces of industrial sculpture. It is probably not practicable to run this machinery all the time and in some cases modern safety requirements will not allow it to be run. Also, if you did it would wear out. But we need to bring it to life in an interactive way in order to understand what is actually going on in terms of the basic science or technology behind it. And of course we can use modern approaches of audio-visual communication, film, video, etc., to show what the thing was like when it was really working. I am sure this is the way forward.

Discussion

I would like to see, finally, much greater emphasis on contemporary and future science issues. In the UK a marvellous job has been done in fairly sanitized 'Industrial Heritage' presentation in the last twenty years, appealing to our concern about nostalgia, but if we look to the new century, the century we have got to look at will be the twenty-first century and not the eighteenth and nineteenth centuries.

LORD MONTAGU: Could I ask Dr Ghose a question? Having stimulated these children, which you have obviously done very well, into an interest in science, what opportunities are there for them to go on to further education? How many science places are there available in universities in India to absorb this new wakening of the interest, because I think this is enormously important.

SAROJ GHOSE: I would like to say here in this connection that the opportunities now being offered to today's children are enormous – in my generation we didn't have this kind of opportunity in India. And I am happy to note that the children who are going out who at one time or other have been very much active in the museum still maintain – though they are scattered in different professions through science and technology – very close links with the museums where they had their first exposure to science, and I am tempted to mention one very short anecdote.

When I was working in an interior village some time back about four years ago the Divisional Commissioner of that village – that is an Indian administrative official – came and introduced himself to me and said 'I have a certificate signed by you very nicely preserved in my house. I want you to go to my house and have a look at it in the evening.' I said 'What kind of certificate is that?' He said 'In 1967 when I was at Class 10 of a local school in Calcutta I participated in the science seminar organized by your museum and I got the third place.' Now that's the kind of attachment all these students still have to the museums. Probably, that would be our greatest success if we are able to hold them to that kind of interest.

BARRY LORD: Thank you very much, Dr Ghose, for that really fascinating look into the extension of the science revolution into India which I found really delightful. I think it is important to see what is happening in this field worldwide is not merely a technological change in the way in which we are doing things, but rather in looking to the twenty-first century we need to see what's happening as a change in the nature of knowledge and a change in the nature of learning, education or edification (or whatever we call it).

When I started in the museum field about twenty-eight years ago I remember being told that it was extremely important in the art history field (where I started) that I should learn where paintings were held, who owned them, because the large part of the knowledge of a curator consisted in knowing where things were so that you could put them together for exhibitions etc. Nowadays if that isn't already on computer it is going on computer, so it is really irrelevant today for a curator to have that kind of knowledge.

The whole nature of museums is going to change. In many fields, especially in the museum field, as we see the impact now of the videodisc on top of the existing computerization, on the nature of knowledge in the museum itself, let alone in the sciences that you are discussing. The nature of the learning process is changing. What blackboard teaching has in common with the older type of museum exhibit is that it is highly edited to present one type of experience. When you go into the museum, as when you sit in the classroom row, either the curator in the museum or the teacher in the classroom is saying: 'This is the one way I can communicate this to you.'

The difference for people who have grown up with computers, with word processors, with electronic communications etc., is that they expect to have open-ended experiences, not a 'one to many' situation. They want to enter into the learning experience and have a 'many to many' type of communication experience. You see this in science centres and it is really exciting to see the kinds of practical applications, too, in relation to the Indian social and economic conditions that you are pointing to.

But, coming back to the point that was made at the end of the preceding session, I think that we also see invisible storage turning into visible storage or open storage type of exhibits, because again they give a 'many to many' possibility for the visitor instead of the highly edited exhibition which is a 'one to many' type of communication. You have the visitor going into visible storage and being able to assemble in his or her own mind the exhibition the visitor wants if he or she cares to use their imagination or takes an interest in specific objects. And of course there is the possibility through computers of obtaining far more information about each object in the visible storage than you could ever have in labels on a conventional one-to-many type of exhibit.

We have looked at Dr Ghose's video of science demonstrations, and I think one of the significant issues that's going to cross over from science museums and industrial museums in the twenty-first century is the growing concern to preserve the skills and processes, the traditional processes that are getting lost even when we are preserving the objects.

Discussion

The way to do that is surely through the continual training of new generations to be able to keep alive the processes that otherwise we are losing. That is I think an important extension of our work: we need to continue to take the focus off the viewing of the physical object and change over to the experience of the process. Therefore, of course, we need to concentrate on the retention of the process, not just through videotaping people who now know how to do things and recording skills that are being lost, but also through training, and giving the experience to our visitors.

Can I refer to one specific application of this approach? I find it rather curious that even in 1989 we still don't have very much application in the UK of the children's museum. We see science museums much more on a national basis, and children's museums are starting to appear in Asia, Australia but so far they seem to be primarily concentrated in the US and we have a handful in Canada. I am referring specifically to the children's museum as an experience centre which is based not only on science but also on arts and other aspects. This is something which I know the Eureka project in the UK is planning to pioneer, and we have in Britain got bits and pieces of children's museums, but we still haven't yet seen a children's museum as such. I wonder if in the year 2000 we will not be seeing a much more generalized children's museum movement as well as the continuing spread of these science interactive experiences.

PAUL PERROT: I think the kind of integration that Dr Ghose mentioned is absolutely essential. We heard earlier about the blind visitors struggling from one gallery to the other, not really understanding what it is all about. It happens of course to sighted young and old, and it happens particularly with school visits. We need to infiltrate the educational system so that within the standards of learning there is a place given to the kinds of things that only museums can do, such as learning from objects, so that museums can then start developing special programmes and special exhibits that are tied in to the curriculum that is given at certain times of the year. The museum visit will then become extremely meaningful and leave a lasting impression, rather than, as so often is the case at the moment, the school visit consisting of military marching through by adults who may be tired and not interested. In fact, the teacher may not even be there and may stay in the coffee room, and certainly most often has not prepared herself/himself for the kind of experience that could be derived from such a visit.

The other aspect that Dr Ghose of course has mentioned, their twenty Museum Buses providing a touring exhibition and education service. My museum in Virginia has had automobile exhibitions for the last thirty-five years and when I first became director I wondered very much about the advisability of such vehicles, particularly because of the risks to works of art, but I soon found that the risks could be taken care of by just changing the nature of the objects that were shown. The important thing was to have the real thing, whatever it was, and to have it interpreted and integrated in whatever way possible within the kind of environment to which the automobile was going, which were generally very rural. And this has worked very well in stimulating an interest in giving a museum presence to communities that have no museum and will never a museum because they will never have the sufficient base to support it.

So this kind of outreach, the kind of outreach at the V&A, which they used to have in their travelling exhibitions which I believe are now defunct, provides not only a means of education, enlightenment, entertainment – whatever you want to call it (I believe it is education in the very highest sense of the word because it suggests a continuing process through the years), but it also has a political effect. These communities benefit from this and the political figures in these communities learn to appreciate these kinds of services. Then if they do appreciate it they are more willing to not only support the activity itself but to support the headquarters that makes the activity possible in the first place. So I think that this notion of outreach, of preparing the visitor for the museum visit, rather than expect him to be struck by lightning the minute he walks in and understand everything, is a very important dimension. It has political and economic ramifications as well.

HAZEL MOFFAT, HMI (Conference participant): Perhaps I could say first of all in connection with what has just been said that for maintained schools in England and Wales from the beginning of the September term, all the schools have had to follow a programme of science which has been laid down and agreed by Parliament, the National Curriculum for Science. I would hope that in helping children to learn according to those programmes of study that teachers would see the relevance of using museum visits.

Later this year, Dr Elizabeth Goodhew of the Horniman Museum is going to edit a series of documents and produce them together as a booklet on the use of museums in primary science, and I hope this will bring together good practice showing how school science can benefit from museum visits and the use of the museum loans. You mentioned that sometimes teachers do not prepare their children very well for museum visits, and I won't go into a long talk about teacher training. Clearly it is important that teachers of primary and secondary school children are trained to know how to use museums effectively, but the initial teacher training curriculum is so full at the moment that there is little time to build this in, but it should be there in some form. This is obviously my personal opinion, but

Discussion

it means that we very much also need in-service training for teachers. We can open the door to them during initial training but we must make sure that there are plenty of in-service programmes as well. These will not only be initiated by the local authorities, sometimes the museums themselves initiate teachers' courses; above all both need to work in collaboration to put on courses for teachers so that they do the best possible for their children.

MARK SUGGITT (Conference participant, Yorkshire and Humberside Museums Council): What we have been doing is talking about taking museums and museums activities out to the community but I have been wondering what the museum professional thinks – what we are taking out is what the professional thinks the community should be having. So you could say in some respects that the curator, to quote Peter Jenkinson in an article which was published by the University of Leicester, the curator is still the gatekeeper: we know what we want and we know what is good for the people out there.

I think that if we are starting to think seriously about what has been called people's history, and the fact that we want museums to be relevant to the societies they serve, I want to move the argument a little further. As Donald Horne has said there are many publics and therefore there are equally as many histories: I was wondering if the panel could suggest ways in which the public can have a real input into what the museum does for them. I know this has been tried in America and certainly in places like New York where I think it was an art museum that actually held a meeting with the general public in New York and said 'What do you actually want?' So this initiative wasn't just for schools, it was for the adult population of that area.

So the question really is, are there any practical ways in which the public, those many publics, can actually have access to the policy of a museum? Also as a rider to this does this potential de-professionalization of the museum worker worry them at all?

BARRY LORD: Our own Cultural Resources group has been involved in a number of management and planning reviews like those in North America referred to, where we have consulted with people. I think my most exciting single experience was with Cree Indians in Northern Quebec. I discovered five minutes before starting the session that I was speaking through an interpreter because they were non-English speaking and I don't speak Cree. I also discovered five minutes before the session that they had no word for museum in their language – it was a very interesting discussion! We actually found common ground because it occurred to me to use the concept of the cache, which is something valuable hidden away in the woods – hunting and gathering groups hide away things of value so they will know where they are, usually in trees or caves. And when I suggested that a museum was like a public cache, a permanent cache, that brought smiles to faces and people seemed to understand what we were talking about.

I think true professionalism in our field will involve constant ongoing input from the community and whether that is a local community, if you are a community museum, or whether that's a community of interest of people concerned with a particular area or discipline, both types I think are going to be very much involved. If it's an art gallery the consultation must definitely include artists, and their input as well as that of the community simply will be a criterion used in professional planning and management of museums in the coming century.

PATRICK BOYLAN: Obviously Mark Suggitt has picked up an extremely important point. I suppose traditionally we have looked to the governing bodies to provide that lay or consumers' view, although in fact many of the governing bodies and so on have obviously become very remote at least in the sense that they have become bigger and more complex. So I think we've got to look at new areas for consultation and feedback. I think if a museum has a good Friends organization, one which is not extremely biased in its class structure (that is obviously another challenge), it could be used in this way. But I think the most important thing is actually to listen and talk to 'real' people. I have enormous respect for almost everything that has come out of Leicester University Department of Museum Studies since 1966 but the one thing that I have got frankly no time for at all is the current application of Foucault's disciplinary society theories, which tells me that I have enormous power over the 890,000 people in Leicestershire. I don't in fact have a Foucault-style disciplinary power over my own deputy or my secretary, so how am I supposed to be exercising this Svengali-like power and manipulation over people living in remote parts of Ashby-de-la-Zouch and in some way moulding their lives?

And on the final point that Mark [Suggitt] made, the risk of some sort of de-professionalizing, I think we as professionals should be grown up enough to actually welcome this feedback and genuine participation. There are some things we have got to be prepared to go to the stake for, the real bottom line of our responsibilities. I support very much many of the things that Peter Cannon-Brookes was saying in response to the first half of the day is that the archival role of the collection and of the museum is a vitally important one. We must be prepared to keep the collections that have a long-term value because they are vitally important. So there is that central role that we must defend. But short of actually destroying

Discussion

the institution, its collections and its basic purposes, I think we should welcome any feedback we get and positively embrace the help and support and advice that we get in that way. The only people who are afraid of the truth or even unpalatable untruths are people who are in themselves weak and insecure.

LORD MONTAGU: Perhaps I could add something myself because there is the dilemma between the questions of do you give people what they want or what you think they should have? Now if you are actually going to ask people what they want you've got to do some research and this is actually not difficult to do. A certain museum in the South which I am not unconnected with does a major survey every year asking visitors which exhibits they like best, which exhibits they find the most interesting and so on, and that does help us plan the future displays and activities in the museum. I think that many museums have been backward in being bold enough to do research and ask their customers what they want. They may not always be right but at least it does give you a guideline.

CAMILLA BOODLE (Conference participant, Museums Association's Museums Year Co-ordinator): I was really interested in asking Dr Ghose if he'd applied these science centres to children with perhaps special needs. When I was with Patrick Boylan in Cardiff we visited Techniquest and what interested me was the Director said that science centres could be used by children with learning difficulties, maybe autistic children and children who don't respond at all to conventional learning. If museums were to prove that they could fill needs in that way that perhaps they hadn't done before, they might have new sources of money: this sounds cynical but I think they might. I also think that it brings into question the whole social role of museums. If you are talking about the public there is a side of the museum-visiting community, the handicapped and those with special needs, who we haven't really mentioned. It was particularly pointed out to me at Techniquest that these interactive science centres could be used particularly by those in wheelchairs because the exhibits could be put at an appropriate height, and also by children to whom conventional education is not really very suited.

SAROJ GHOSE: I would mention here that we started with two museums in Calcutta and Bangalore where the buildings were already existing when we started setting up modern science museums, but after that everywhere we plan our new building and then set up the science centre. Today, this is our first consideration at the architectural planning stage, how the centre should cater to the requirements of physically handicapped visitors. Now I am starting with the building and then we go on to the exhibits. For example, in Bombay the science centre is located almost adjacent to a blind school and we considered that they would be our frequent visitors to the science centre, so we had to devise a lot of exhibits specially keeping them in mind. A lot of exhibits have audio effects and we have a braille system of labelling so that they can come again and again and enjoy the exhibits.

It's definitely a very special consideration as far as the exhibits are concerned but apart from that, as I say, 50 per cent of our attention is towards the exhibits and the remaining 50 per cent towards activities and we have plenty of activities for the physically disabled people. Over almost all of India in different science centres, the year round, our special programmes are taken up: various kinds of training programmes, exposure-orientated programmes and various kinds of programmes which simply they enjoy, not that they are all the time vocational, and they are specially designed for physically disabled people.

PAUL PERROT: I think that when one gets to a certain age it is not as easy to do anything and it is certainly not as easy to find museums with readable labels, in terms of type-size, height and so on.

LORD MONTAGU: Perhaps designers might bear in mind that older people cannot read captions which are in a dark corner of size 16 type which is becoming an absolutely appalling trend in museum design.

SANDRA MARTIN, Conference participant, Manchester City Art Gallery): The speaker, I think, was going to talk about the ways to involve the community in museums. While he has talked about his communities in India, in this country especially in large cities like Manchester we have a very mixed community, mixed racially. I think we need to look at the ways in which we cater for all sections of the community, and I was hoping that the panel would talk about different ways of involving different groups and how we cater for all those different minorities as well as the majority. Can some members of the panel address that?

DONALD HORNE: I think you have to face up to the fact that you can't necessarily cover the needs of the very last minority Latvian. This is very difficult in any museum. When I was making the statement earlier about many publics, I was actually thinking of many publics within a certain degree of ethnicity and perhaps even of class variation. Once you have moved beyond that you may find yourself in that kind of situation which has a difficulty, and then you may decide not to use any words at all. The same kind of problem of course arises in illiterate communities. Leaving out the information in such a way would affect in different ways at least one of the two most important groups of people who go to museums. Children on guided tours would need to have things explained to them, but the middle-class people who are capable of doing quite a lot of reading

Discussion

don't get any service because the museum has been arranged in such a way that it won't offend people who can't do any reading.

What I am suggesting is that there is no very easy answer to that question except in quantitative terms. You may decide that there are some ethnic groups that demand a special type of consideration, but perhaps the only way of doing it is through providing a conducted tour as with children. In Australia we have got 120 or so languages but you can't have every label in 120 languages. Even more important may be the need to encourage ethnic groups to establish their own collections, and by that means not only continue to identify themselves but to proclaim themselves to others in the society, and to encourage other communities to come along and see what it might mean.

BARRY LORD: Very briefly our experience as planners working in multi-racial communities in ethnic groups and meeting with each one of sometimes 20–25 ethnic groups making up communities in North America, is that the solution lies with those groups themselves. You really have only to ask, that is to say you have to meet with them and ask and listen, and then creatively try to put their own solutions forward. For example, you can have 15 or 20 languages available on tape with multi-channels. Those groups themselves will provide the translators who will give you rarer languages that you couldn't possibly otherwise provide. They will be happy to volunteer and sit down and read the copy and translate it into their languages.

They will also stimulate exhibition ideas and they very often are the sources of collections for temporary exhibitions and that kind of thing. It is a very great mistake to assume that they only want exhibitions on their own culture: they do of course want to see those reflected but they also want to have inroads into the broad general culture, and on both scores the best way to find out is to ask and to listen. Again I think this is going to be increasingly the hallmark of professionalism in the museum field.

PATRICK BOYLAN: Coming from the city which has the largest percentage of racial minorities in the UK I want to say it can be done and it must be done. I think what is particularly important is that very frequently the indiginous population themselves are very interested in, and want to learn more about, the local cultural minorities as well. Perhaps it is time for the Association to have another conference on this theme to show what is being done in places like Leicester, Bradford, Coventry and so on, because it is now several years since we had the last one. But you mustn't forget about the museum staff either. We do need special staff resources and we need to do something about the profession as well in order to attract people from minorities to come in and undertake training.

ALAN JOHNSTON (from Luxembourg): I just want to share some thoughts, and pose some questions. Is the way forward in fact to look back to our roots, because if we all remember that the first museums arose out of collections? Why did collectors collect? They collected mostly because of the aesthetic value of the object. The object turned them on and that's why it was collected. Why did they expose these objects to the public? Because they wanted to share that enthusiasm for their aesthetic values. I think through our progress we have lost our sensibility, in the literal sense of our senses, to our environment. Not just our natural environment, but also our human environment around us. How many people in London who work in banks stop to look at the architecture or the structure of the roofs, or how many people outside wonder why a seagull is grey above and white below? I think the way ahead is going to be to take the object as a very important aspect and explore its sensual aspects: the hands-on games, touching sculptures because they feel good, going back to these roots. We have to move forward: museums in the year 2000 must break the metaphorical security glass around the objects by showing people the true values of these objects and therefore through these objects the true value of life.

LORD MONTAGU: Many thanks to all the speakers. Very briefly to sum up the day, I think that everybody agrees that museums should be politically aware with a small 'p' but I think they will find it more difficult to be politically objective with a big 'P'. However, everybody wants more money from the politicians, but they also want more independence from the politicians, and I think that is an irreconcilable conflict. Of course, all governments defend their record when they are in office and all parties in the opposition promise everything, but that is true in every area of life. But what is true is that when one gets into government unfortunately priorities do come to the fore, and it is quite impossible I believe for any government to – say – not build a new hospital or ask all the pensioners to give up their £10 bonuses at Christmas in order to buy a Turner. However, that is a question of politics.

We have also had some discussion on sponsorship. For some, sponsorship is a happy marriage, for some it is rape, but all of us know that all marriages have their problems. Perhaps Paul Perrot tomorrow will give some marriage guidance on this when he speaks.

This afternoon we have had a very interesting discussion on people's museums and there's no doubt that in the world of museums there is a great reappraisal going on. Some people want to go back to basics: maybe

Discussion

they're right. Many others believe there is a new way forward. What is true is that the old nineteenth-century idea that it was a privilege for people to come to museums, and they were really private research establishments for the curators, is at least dying, and in fact I think the last death has possibly just happened. People now do matter, and I think people feel they have a right to go to museums so long as they do not mind actually paying for that right. But whatever happens museums must remain centres of excellence. They must have academic, research and conservation experts; ensuring that these are provided is very much the job of the directors and curators. But generally speaking I believe that probably the way forward lies in participation and involvement by people in what they see in the museum, which will give them education, enlightenment, elucidation, and above all entertainment.

Professionals and museums 1 | 7

Museum professionals – the endangered species

Tomislav Sola

When I was a curator, some people (though sincere enough) would ask me: 'What on earth are you doing all day long in your museum?' Most of them have learned that we do exhibitions, although they wonder why it takes so long to do one. That was misunderstanding on the part of our users. Recently I have put myself in a situation that I have to say: 'I am a museologist and I lecture on it at the University.' It is a happy circumstance if they catch 'musicology' instead, and they just think that I am not good enough as a musician to play an instrument correctly. Most museum professionals do know, however, that museology has nothing to do with music, but they think museology is some kind of fiddling anyhow. That misunderstanding certainly comes from sections of our profession.

To tell you the truth, I often claim in the international museological community, to the utter astonishment of my brothers and sisters, that museology does not exist. But do not applaud if you are a hard-working practitioner, a pragmatist who denies anything like theory and who never learned Russell's joke about pragmatism. I suppose you do know the joke – it says 'Pragmatism is like a warm bath – it is getting warmer and warmer so imperceptibly that you are never quite sure when to scream.' I am exposing myself to criticism of misunderstanding both orthodoxy and fundamentalism, and hence of heresy. Our *'religio curatoris'* is still non-existent because we worship the wrong God – because the basic principles are still not clearly and firmly there.

But let us say briefly why do we suddenly talk about museology. If it is not just another trendy 'scientism', why is it that we are taught that our

Museum professionals – the endangered species

job cannot be done any more without undergraduate or postgraduate museological training? What is it about our jobs that has changed so much? In short indeed, everything. Museums have such a paradoxical situation: they were founded upon the wish to document the past to keep it as a productive experience, though instead of serving the present they serve the very same past as a continuation of it. This way, in a highly conditioned environment, they were expected to act as a secure shelter from the 'third wave civilization' that is sweeping away many eternal values.

But the drama of constant change that produces another 'great anxiety era', as Irwin Toffler would put it, grew into a deluge, so who is sure about anything any more? I only hope that our theories are not in fact some hasty prayers offered to an unknown God. Anyhow, museums resisted change as even they misunderstood the nature of the only eternity that is given to humans.

I will not risk getting myself an attribute of a 'catastrophologist', but instead I ought to offer you some minutes of silence to contemplate the poor state of our world. I am sure you know all the alarming data, but if you look at it, framed only by the limits of your own existence and, alas, by your own institution, you are right to get mad at all greens, not to mention that terrible creature, the 'green' museologist. But it is certainly not only greenery and what lives in it that we are talking about. If five hundred animal species a year disappear from this planet for ever (which is true), how many human cultures are exterminated and how many are being prostituted and devoured by expansive acculturation?

Now, why do I mix museums with this process? I always feel sorry that Orwell did not say anything about museums, because they really are part of this process: they are used and manipulated, they obey their bosses, and because they are, for the most part, like them: being concerned with power, profit and conquest.

What we are talking about, especially when it is about some critical analysis, is that prevailing, dominant, nineteenth-century museum model, now very often disguised within its modern buildings and heaps of modern technology. The museum concept is a derivation of the ruling power structure because of its conditions and its public on one side and its curators on the other. Knowing how many new museums appear weekly or even daily in the world, we surely cannot speak about the crisis of quantity. But there is a serious crisis of institutional identity and a crisis of concept. It is true that museums do correspond well with the shadowy side of human nature as well. However, extremely modern in historical terms – existing for some two hundred odd years at the most in their present form – museums are so well planted in society that they receive surprisingly little criticism. If they are sunk so deeply in the sin of possession and that of material values, how can they represent the spirit? When they try hard they do so by trying to compete with the reality itself. Reality is like dry sand in the first – the firmer the grip, the more fugitive and elusive it becomes. But museums are not able to get rid of the cult of the three-dimensional object and its representativeness. Museums are about ideas and concepts and the methods to achieve their purposes are necessarily many.

But we are in a ridiculous situation in many ways anyhow. We ask people to memorize – that is what we teach them in schools – but we invest millions to teach machines to think creatively. Why should it, therefore, surprise anybody to realize that museums are desperately trying to make their map out of reality as Frans Schouten has said, quoting Lewis Carroll: 'the map of reality on the scale of a mile to a mile'. It appears to me sometimes that we as harmless patients are allowed to play this absurd game in the courtyard of this madhouse of our world, guided by an insane arbiter. Our teams are divided into, probably, some Movable Objects, Buildings, Pictures, Papers 1, Papers 2, Free Animals, Imprisoned Animals, Killed Animals, Plants, Tools, Vehicles, Utensils, Performers ... those exposed to the rain and those under the roof. The rules say that we all play the game at the same time. There is only one goal and this is circular in shape: the playground is not limited.

You can just imagine what an effort it costs our museum public to make some sense and joy out of it. As our research shows, they are as mad as we are, but since they are conditioned to our crazy game from their childhood, they cannot afford to behave like Malraux's Indians that bring fresh tubers to their idols in Mexico's Museo de Antropología or like the bonzas in Bangkok that visit museums to praise their gods there. Even our nuns find it, alas, inappropriate to cross themselves in front of Lippi's Madonna when they see it in our museums.

Besides, putting museums at the centre of the heritage – still the prevailing spiritual pattern – puts us in comparison to astronomy in some Ptolemaic era, with the Earth at the centre of the universe. We in museums still need our Copernicus to write for us a paper, which would probably be named 'de Revolutionibus Orbium Hereditatum', establishing a system of heritage care in which the heritage itself would be at the centre, and with museum institution as just one among equal planets around. Only then we would need in turn our Keppler and our Newton to finish the discovery.

Museum professionals – the endangered species

I will not burden you with detailed schemes and I purposely wanted to shorten my lecture to show you this galaxy of ours. But since I was promised that these papers would be published, I see no harm in that and we may proceed more quickly – and it is quite a galaxy I can assure you.

The big lie of our museums is incurable unless they cease to claim eternity, immortality and infinity. They should know better than anybody else how inconstant and unstable everything physical is. What do they think in the conservation laboratories, as they cure dying objects, about the nature of things and people? If the right to die is guaranteed to people, should not objects have the same privilege. Or, if this is too provocative, do they think that the canvas from which they destroy a square millimetre of paint for the sake of scientific analysis will indeed endure forever? How far into the future in fact and at what cost? Can that cost be ethically justifiable?

Are there boundaries to the keeping things alive by constant restorations? Many museums already look like intensive care hospital departments, and I fear we shall soon install instruments that will clearly show to what extent the vibration from visitors' voices shortens the life of museum objects.

Life is birth and death in constant exchange, both of them justified and necessary. That short-term fear of death, if we continue to express it and demonstrate it in our museums the way we do, will bring only frivolity, affliction and frustration.

Saul Bellow gave an interview recently to one of our journalists in Yugoslavia and said: 'Fear of death is distorting us while we deny it. During this process we are desperately trying to achieve immortality and we shall really be always in great trouble.'

In the space between the two doubled infinities, that of physics (which is atom and universe) and that of spirit (which is individual conscience and spiritual system of universe), we are trying to attain eternity. We do it in our temples of vanity: quite a touching human ambition, but hardly acceptable within the concept of historical time, and ridiculous in terms of absolute.

If an orchestra fails you cannot blame the concert hall: it is always musicians, sometimes the conductor and rarely acoustics. If a museum fails it is, in most cases, because curators got it wrong. Industrial civilization is inclined to value quantity as often as quality. It has invented the man of action and the good curator is supposed to be of that breed, with big collections, huge museums, unique values, crowds of visitors, and many activities under any condition. But the future and its developments will reaffirm the importance of that contemplative man among curators as well as among the public. The curator will have difficulty in finding the proper balance between these two extremes.

Museum curators share very much the destiny of other European intellectuals. They feel themselves rather useless in the world that lives by different rules. While they are praying in their museum temples, the chivalry of modern professions is thundering outside their doors in growing crescendo. It may easily be a battle, judging by the noise, but that is how they fight for their future. Subdued by the 'fetishism of speciality', again a typical intellectual disease, they do not venture into things and situations that are not of their concern. The obligation is, as we should know, just the contrary.

And one thing more, known though to all and everybody: even in the UK which can be regarded as very advanced in theory and practice of museum work, more than half of junior professional curatorial staff have entered museums without any previous formal museum-orientated training, sitting next to Nellie, as Patrick Boylan calls it – the method of learning the job used in the textile industry a hundred years ago, if I am not wrong.

Next, I would like to say some words on something which I have entitled 'The Search for Resonance'.

The taxonomic division of knowledge, growing specialities, conquering and laborious spirit and ideals of quantity and speed made us, European barbarians and their descendants, the rulers of the world. But the victorious alley is leading nowhere: there is a solid wall of an opposing logic built into the triumphal arch. We will *not* pass through it.

Museums, and not only them, were (and still are) parts of the puzzle that nobody ever made to fit. We have been analysing the world for some centuries and as our needs are finding their way through the barriers, we perceive that the time of synthesis has come. We need clear vision, panoramic view, synoptic insight, and a holistic approach – we need to answer time again the questions, who are we, where are we from and where are we going. If you say this to a museum curator with all his practical worries on his mind, he would call you an irresponsible and unoriginal poet. The lack of professional theory is one reason, while the other is the professional solitude: his message is still formed at the level of his professional speciality; he does not see much further from his institution and that is the point of defeat or the point of departure for some reforming thoughts.

Museum professionals – the endangered species

In a museologist's collection of definitions you find such a diversity of attempts to define the museum institution that one should know immediately that something is, besides being wrong, going on: except for the traditional museum institution all other similar forms become evasive. Among the existing definitions the best are those that are the longest and that are the most poetical in their attempt. The truth is, we do not know any more what a museum institution is. This fact may drive legislators crazy and traditional curators unhappy but it should be faced. All the former limits are blurred, all the boundaries with adjacent areas are insecure or crossed already.

Museums do have libraries but libraries started to behave like museums, making exhibitions and establishing educational services. The same happens with archives. Ecomuseums opened the curatorial fortress from within. Georges-Henri Rivière, helped by others, played the role of Ulysses: no category of museum working process was left as it was. I have heard and seen curators trying to close the Pandora's box of ecomuseums, claiming that we have nothing but a version of the old 'heimat' museums, as they also ignored parallel changes that were happening in the last twenty to thirty years. Now we can speak easily about museums without objects, about museums of the future, that some forms of irregular heritage action have a museum character. The third wave civilization is giving birth, though a long and dramatically delayed one, to the 'third wave museums'.

As a profession we are still under formation and the least we can do for our future is to be aware of the processes that we are either part of or witnesses to. Wiser than ever we shall let things happen: we shall analyse the processes and try to get ahead of it, for the first time in the history of our profession. This will serve as a measure of our survival ability, of our fitness (as naturalists would put it) to adapt and to continue. So, what is going on? What are the novelties widening that area of ours beyond recognizable features?

I have a little list to propose to you, though it is very abbreviated compared with my full list:

- new, custom-tailored, museums, such as the fourth generation of ecomuseums;
- exhibition centres (changing, temporary, museums);
- science centres (museums without objects);
- 'entertainment enterprises' – as they described it in some articles – very much heritage-based;
- heritage industry facilities, like Beamish or theme parks;
- museums of the future (Futuroscope, Epcot);

- new, big national museums, which are still being created;
- synthesized museums;
- new heritage-concerned organizations;

and still more things:

- the tendency of convergence in the cultural and commercial sector;
- cultural investment to encourage development and economic growth;
- the tendency to conceptualization;
- cultural marketing that leads to individualization of institutions and respective image making;
- the tendency to integrative processes of the institutional sector;
- growth of the complementary sector (such as museum centres, documentation centres, orientation centres, services, travelling exhibition centres, etc.);
- the tendency towards integrated preservation;
- the tendency towards preservation *in situ*;
- the tendency towards integration in information sciences;
- the tendency towards total interpretation and communication;
- the tendency towards the planned and studied usage of technology;
- the tendency towards multidisciplinarity, direct and creative uses of museums, with the curator being only the focal point on which the activities are based.

There is also a growing tendency of inevitable change in all museum institutions, but this pressure is often just a swing from one extreme to another. And there is no sound, authoritative theory that can guide these processes. What we need is to change incrementally in a dual process of creating new and different museum professionals and new and different museum institutions.

Twenty years ago McLuhan was telling us all this, announcing the changes by his, so rarely understood, syntagma: 'The medium is the message'; or what even Romans in their way certainly would say: '*Tempora mutantur et nos mutamur in illis*'. The current problems of our profession, therefore, is due to the fact that we did not change together with the times. And we should have known better. We have had our prophets, our pioneering institutions, our innovative precedents: we had everything. Why has it happened that the museum boom of the early seventies still leaves us unprepared? Since then, the number of museums in the UK, for instance, has nearly doubled.

Some two or three decades ago we should have recognized and prepared for the creation of new types of museums concerned with technology, transport, social and industrial history and not least art. We should have done it differently but our profession was conditioned by the past models in the very same way as our public. The New York Metropolitan Museum of Art, to give one example, was doing exhibitions of a 'commercial' nature already in 1920. John Cotton Dana knew, seventy years ago, more of our future, I can assure you, than most of us do still today.

As the growing number of museums is not a guarantee of their monopolistic position, the increasing number of curators working in them does not guarantee the continuation of their professional identity either. If you just take the issue of the obvious shifts from institution to action, from product to process, from object to information, concept and idea, from education to communication – it may appear to you that we are facing professional transformation, as though we had allowed ourselves the luxury of hibernating the curatorial larva when it should have emerged as an interesting butterfly quite long ago.

Scientific and professional concepts always improved and progressed every time when seemingly different phenomena would, in the end, emerge as just different aspects of the same thing. That is true for physics, to take one example, but it should also be true for the entire configuration of heritage care. When in physics the field was widened to infinity, it only required the search for the common area of resonances. At the wavelength that all are able to receive we shall have the emission of collective experience happening.

One of the best but also very impractical definitions of a museum institution comes from Georges-Henri Rivière – a page long and of an excellent literary quality. It compares very well with the relativity that Niels Bohr, to continue this parallel, allowed for physics: 'When it is about atoms, we can use language only the way it is used in poetry. It is not that crucial to a poet to define facts as to create images.' I have, nevertheless, tried to define this common area of heritage resonances, going as far as possible in provoking disagreement. The museum, therefore, is any creative effort of cybernetic action upon the basis of complex experience of heritage.

Now for some few words about emerging theory, and, as I named it, on how to help the future happen.

Trying to argue that our profession, together with the philosophy of it is in a great transition, I often draw parallels from other areas of human interests. Don't you think, for instance, that our museums are functioning somewhat like medieval Dominican monasteries? There is a pressure, as I have mentioned in some other occasions, that we all become poor Franciscans, just taking care of our own existence and going out to the people. This is true if you analyse the example of ecomuseums or neighbourhood museums but it is true even if we speak generally about the finances. Our bosses demand that we live from begging, using donors and sponsors and so on, or from our own garden, which is actually our museum shop. There is nothing bad in that, provided that our mission is flourishing and our religion devoutedly practised. But so far we are in a worse position than the fourteenth-century Catholic Church was with all its Popes and schisms. We have some canon law and liturgical rules (i.e. museography and that we ambitiously call museology), but we do not have '*religio curatoris*', some theology of ours – I use the parallel rather freely!

Whether our God is the museum object or the museum itself, it is still a Golden Calf – nothing else. Imagine how far we are from the protestant congregationalism that some expect from us. We have some considerable epiphanic messages but we still lack our Bible. We are a different pro-fession with its substantial mission but yet in the '*status nascendi*'. It will be formed out of the area of resonances where the informatics will make possible the final appearance of that science of ours. Formed upon a phenomenon and not upon an institution our science has got a right to claim that status. It would be some kind of philosophy of heritage, some 'love for wisdom' (as its basic meaning suggests), that would be a systematic research of basic principles, laws and categories of reality, that of the character of identity and continuation of it, as well as of complex relation of man to his environment. This may function as a usable 'theology', shall we say, to establish our multi-faceted relations with the heritage. Putting it in a centre of our professional '*Weltanshaung*' – our professional philosophy – we are opening our windows wide: we are attaining the conceptual level not necessarily linked with the physical and three-dimensional. Any considerable religion, if we still accept this parallel, has allowed different liturgies and local languages. As to our language – if physics, as the mother of many sciences, has been forced to use metaphor whenever dealing with the unknown, we may also use it.

Whenever I dealt with theory, I always understood that my task is one of some counter-active nature, that I have to expose myself to a risk so as to be able to contribute. Proposing this science seven years ago I announced it by the provocative name of 'heritology'. Since then, I had the pleasure of counting those who have stopped laughing at me. I continued to play with conventions, naming it this time 'mnemosophy' and signalling that it is actually new contents that we are after, not the name. Again, resisting the poet that we all hide in our bosoms, I have tried to set up the shortest possible definition of that science of ours that I call simply the cybernetic philosophy of heritage. As the common goal of the entire area of heritage care is not knowledge but wisdom as it represents a system to be guided independently, I find those points actually hit home.

The main task of our theory is to force us into radical questioning of standpoints and the insistence upon the confrontation of the collective experience and present needs. Its method must also be of some problem-solving approach so that it is able to bring the feeling, intuition and knowledge of how to form and run the institution according to inner and outer circumstances. Serving as a mental opening, this theory should teach us the philosophy of our profession, teach us the future of it, enable the effective transfer of professional experience, teach us creatively to help us react in every new situation, and to give arguments supporting our professional self-respect and self-appreciation.

If applied to inner working processes, it should help the homogenization of the staff, it should give advice, instruction, support, impulse and serve as a basis of professional strategy. As the philosophy of our professions, it should provide us with criticism, it should serve as a constructive interpreter of them and finally, it is expected to research the future of them. Whether we speak about the single profession of heritage care, which I would strongly support, or several professions, the idea is that our vehicle gets finally its headlights.

So far as professional training is concerned, which I cannot venture into very much this time, I see already some Trojan horses being wheeled in – heritage interpretation and concepts like that one, for instance, that I know very well at Zagreb University being good examples.

Now we are approaching the end of my time, so I will say a few words about future professionals.

The brave prophet, Jules Verne, expected television to happen only in the twenty-ninth century. He was thinking logically but according to his own time. It is like breaking the sound barrier in aviation – aerodynamics change, optics changes, logic is different. As we in our profession seem to be breaking the very same limits of our dreams already, nothing seems to be too brave to foresee. The curious thing is that museum professionals have their minds dragged behind their actual practice. This also explains why we have to analyse institutions in order to make assertions concerning their professional staffs. The entire heritage care field may soon be facing these developments. Allow me the liberty to offer another list and which, I think, really needs several more pages:

- museums as the measure of their own environment;
- identity centres;
- a network of total museum units;
- heritage orientation centres (as a missing first information circle);
- regional, national and international heritage information networks;
- regional and national heritage media centres
- territorial (and/or national) stores of heritage objects;
- heritage data banks;
- heritage action *in situ* – supporting and amplifying living traditions;
- inclusion and treatment of heritage data and objects that are kept outside institutionalized care;
- the claim of museums and kindred institutions for independent status (much like that of universities).

Future shifts will be profound and numerous as we shall be facing the future without clear patterns and obvious rules. Besides art, in the usual sense, art museums (for instance) will contain technology, applied arts, performing arts – transforming themselves into 'cultural happening areas' or centres for creative communication.

As all this will happen due to an invested effort, it is logical to assume that all this will not be done by some traditional museum curator. One should be careful to avoid a vision of a future professional as some kind of supernatural being, a temptation that hardly any profession can resist. Driving a car is a serious business but running a metaphorical machine, like a museum, may require an alert spiritual eye, some feeling for commands and performances and – I should cry it out – love. There is, however, one qualification much more important – talent. When it is about creative communication, science is very much approaching art.

I will take the liberty of giving you one little parallel. As I say, our job is so much linked with art, especially the communications part and indeed, if you analyse both, you may see this. They have the same art and museum communication, the same source of inspiration, the same starting-point, and that's the concept of identity. They have the same capacity which is really creativity. They have the same goal, the same aim, communication, and they use the same method, that is interpretation.

Conservation and communication are quite opposed, 'fundamentally different' functions of museums, a dramatic dichotomy across the entire heritage area. A future professional will have to be able to bridge the wide span of the differences. The interpreter/communicator will have to be able to understand the researcher and vice versa. But the latent disunity will cause permanent breaches of the sector: this destiny we cannot avoid but we have to adjust to.

Curators are necessarily a breed of wide concern, 'witnesses of truth or injustice but neither of nation nor of a class, but justice for all times and all places' – as Bernard Henri Levy describes the class of intellectuals. They are not there to join the effort of preponderant forces of society – just the contrary. Curators and other kindred professionals are necessarily reconsidering usual concepts and given truths. When John Cotton Dana was speculating about his 'committed' sort of museum in his booklet *Plan for New Museums* in 1920 he said that it would be necessary 'to engage persons whose opinions of what a museum should be are quite loosely held, and whose susceptibility to new ideas and powers of initiation are quite marked'. It is therefore a suspiciousness towards the environment but also constant re-examination of what their own role is and what they have to fulfil.

In connection with this broad task, Alma Wittlin was, as always, beautifully clear, claiming that we must not allow 'man to remain in his present state of spiritual and emotional incompetence with regard to human affairs – to the control of his own mind and human relationships'. This huge task for museums and the like is asking for more than plain knowledge, meaning that it should be used to make a collage of information – a montage of spiritual attractions that resembles the art of cinema. Curators, or simply heritage carers, are supposed to widen the concept of their profession by the obvious circumstances, following thus the widening of definition of institutions and that of theory. In the past confused curators have given away their true role to architects, designers and insensitive managers, abusing thus their vocational commitment and showing an apparent lack of aptitude. Reprogramming their professional standards and acquiring a responsive professional philosophy will gain them an indispensable vitality.

As a dignified part of a broad heritage-preservation profession museum curators, although somewhat changed, will continue their existence. We have to offer to the endangered museum curator a compact basis for feeling secure as well as to the others from the field. Somewhat poetically, their transformation will cover the span from technicians of prestige to the priests of wisdom. That new breed (or at least new variety) able to cover and spread over the fruitful differences of the dramatic field of collective experience, from researchers to communicators, may one day be recognized as a profession of heritage engineers – a big and prosperous profession. Their education will be always an appropriate mixture of their basic academic discipline, of museography (or archives work or librarianship, etc.), of general theory and information science. Their final product will aspire to a status of an applied art of heritage communication. Their long travel started from Vanity and will end in Wisdom: then, they will search for the only Eternity that is actually given to us – that of human kind.

Discussion

CLAUDE LABOURET: Tomislav Sola has mentioned museum professionals as an endangered species: if that is so we obviously are facing a conservation problem. As a retired businessman and since I am interested in museums I wonder what non-profit organizations such as museums expect from business. My point is that they can expect more than money and more, in my mind, means learning from business culture and particularly with the management of human resources in a changing world. Businessmen have learned to their own expense that it takes time and pain to bring about change. In most businesses no real change occurs until the bottom line on the balance sheet has gone into the red. The fact is that it is impossible to impose any kind of change on anyone and if there is no change in the hearts and minds, so an endless battle starts between external pressures and inner resistance. Changes come from people rather than from systems.

My first remark is how many museum managers, if I may use the word, have to face an experience of time and pain comparable to that of business to implement change. We have entered an open world, open to competition, and we have heard yesterday that museums belong to a competitive world. The saying in my country, France, is 'les hommes font la différence': men make the difference. That means, again I am referring to business, that with the same technology available to all the parties competing there is still a winner and a loser. The difference between them is a matter of human skills, motivation and ethics. That is the reason why business has to make a top priority of management of human resources.

Very precisely, that means the responsibility for personnel which some time ago was at a very low level in the organization chart has now gone up to the top. Whoever is in charge of managing human resources is really at the head of the business now. The management of museums for the year 2000 requires new qualifications and attitudes to achieve a greater number of more complex tasks. Where the right people to perform the job are in office, don't they deserve as much understanding and support as the organization they are serving?

Secondly, business has put top priority on the management of human resources. Are museums ready to do the same? The two questions seem to be tied. If change means pain and time, management of human resources has to be a priority.

SIR PHILIP GOODHART, MP: There seems to be general agreement that scholarship is under threat in our museums at all levels and there seems also to be widespread agreement that our university museums are particular orphans in the storm. Paradoxically this leads me to ask the question: should there not be improved links between universities and polytechnics and the local museums where this is appropriate? And how can this be brought about if it is thought to be appropriate?

Can I as a consumer rather than a producer also flog once again my favourite hobby horse which is that in all museum training there should be a substantial display lighting component. It does seem to me to be inexcusable that there are black spots in such great institutions as the Tate or the National Gallery.

VICTOR MIDDLETON: I wanted to, in a sense, make a very pragmatic point and I think I respond to what Claude [Labouret] said here from a business viewpoint. Clearly there may be a cybernetic philosophy of heritage management and there may be somewhere out in the ether an elegant holistic theory for museum professionals, but the context of how people will deal with current pressures and how they will resolve the dilemmas with the available people (and I like your stress on change comes from people and not from systems), these are people with fairly limited backgrounds in a period of change.

So my view on a new professionalism in the era of change is that there are several strands, and they need to be brought together, and I'll comment on that at the end. There is clearly the traditional curatorial professional role which is to care for collections, be concerned with interpretation and display and associated elements with research and scholarship, and given the nature of collections that is going to remain fundamental.

There is a quite different pressure which has its own elements of professionalism. People who deal with the revenue side, be it managing admissions, be it trading or be it sponsorship: each of these has a claim to professionalism.

There is, thirdly, and perhaps I should have put it firstly following your point but I think in this context maybe it is third, the personnel or human resource issue which is the way in which new forms of relationship between managers and staff in museums will actually be handled in the light of rather different sorts of people, and that, too, of course is a profession. I think that comes together and my projection is that museums will need someone in a general manager role (and that after all is a form of administrative professionalism too), who can actually clarify achievable overall missions and goals and practical targets, and who can

Discussion

actually resolve the conflicts in priorities that are always going to exist, people who can motivate staff, who can actually manage business information flows as they get more complex and so on.

I think general managers for museums may or may not have curatorial expertise and they may or they may not need it, but my prediction is that more people will actually end up controlling museums from a general management professional background. Curators and the other elements play an important role which has to be co-ordinated, and these general managers may or they may not come from a traditional curatorial route.

PATRICK BOYLAN: I think perhaps we have national cultural differences coming out here. What Victor has outlined is certainly the UK system. You can't see a major British manufacturing business these days that is actually run by a skilled engineer or similar specialist, but just cross the Channel to, say, West Germany, and you find it would be almost unthinkable for a major engineering concern not to have someone with a doctorate in an engineering specialism at the top. What I would certainly insist we have today is outstanding management by people with a high professional standing across the whole of the cultural heritage and arts field in the UK. John Pick commented on this just a couple of months ago in *Arts Management* magazine, asking what on earth is government doing trying to persuade the Arts, which is probably the best-managed and most successful sector of the whole economy today, to adopt the practices of the UK business world which has been in solid and regular decline for most of the last thirty years, and has got us to the stage where we've now gone beyond the international telephone numbers level of balance-of-payments deficit. I think that's an interesting point, and I think possibly that national cultural differences come in here as well.

LORENA SAN ROMAN: Tomislav Sola gave us a good lecture in the great diversity of our world and even of one country. But I think that we must really analyse the staff of the museums that we have. We have been putting a lot of attention on the professional aspects, but when we manage the staff I truly believe that beside the specific discipline (which they must learn and know very well), the staff must know the society in which they develop and in which the museum is, and also how to work modern equipment. Clearly if they do not do this, the museums cannot have an open attitude towards the changes that Mr Sola was discussing.

If we want to be in time with the changes we need to have these kind of people, so we really need to analyse and select our staff well because in a museum we can never be an island. All of us working in museums have faced for many years the islands inside the museums. In almost all of the countries of Latin America we recruit pure scientists in the museums, and really only a very low percentage of these people who get into the world of museums understand what we mean by the rescue of the heritage, or the new museum philosophy that he mentioned.

DONALD HORNE: If we are talking about the training of museum people we must see the problem as part of the more general over-specialization of intellectual labour that has been such a characteristic of the whole modern industrial world. As I mentioned yesterday, people in the eighteenth-century were quite happy to talk about a political economy but also wanted to discuss everything: history, industry, about half a dozen subjects. I was also suggesting that in museums there has occurred an even harsher and more eccentric division which was not as comprehensive as that which occurred in these other areas. And within the museum business itself you have the division between the view of museums as archives which in theory could just mean nobody came in at all, you'd just look after the stuff and maybe scholars would look at it, and at the other end the view of expositions which finally might not include any objects at all.

There seems to be a need to provide people who have received something of a general education as well as a specialist education. I like the idea that British business has scarcely shown its capacity to lead business, let alone museums. But why should people give themselves the task of deciding museum policy, if they have not given some profound and systematic consideration of the kind of speculation that has been raised about the human condition generally?

PAUL PERROT: I view with some alarm the impression that museums are so different from other civic apparatus. What is the difference between a museum and a hospital? A hospital, if it is to operate effectively, must have different levels of specialities ranging from the surgeon to the assistant nurse to the cleaner to the supplier. We accept that and we accept that there is a medical profession. When we talk about museums we seem to concentrate on the role of the curator which is, of course, essential, but we lose sight of the fact that in many museums, *de facto*, there is a whole congregation of professions that work together, that are concerned with conservation, with preservation, with transmission, with education, with public affairs, with publication, with creation of exhibitions, with lighting. And so it seems to me this already is happening and I do not feel the sense that the museum profession is totally floundering. We perhaps have a crisis of confidence, but to have it projected to the extent that it seems to be projected at the moment is going very, very far.

Secondly, I view with profound alarm the notion that bankers, lawyers and former ambassadors can be better versed in interpreting and guiding museums than people who have made a life surrounding themselves by and studying and understanding those elements in past objects that are relevant to the future, and that can be helpful to the present. It seems to me an admission of an inferiority complex which as a professional, if I am one, I find totally unacceptable. In fact, I think that perhaps many of our multinational industries eventually will come to discover that to have manipulators at the head rather than producers and conceptualizers may not be the best way either to serve their stockholders or serve their customers.

BARRY LORD: I think the US auto industry in particular has had a number of studies done that show that one of their serious problems, globally speaking, over the last fifty years was the replacement of people who were passionate about the auto industry by general managers who don't really understand what the industry was about: I think that has been a general conclusion now about the cause of the malaise of the American auto industry. We have a directly parallel situation as you described, and it is extremely important that someone who teaches the courses on organization, management and planning in museum training should have the essential prerequisite for any person responsible for museums of a passion for objects. That kind of peculiar passion is a kind of sensuality, a grasp of the world that believes that there is knowledge, there is value, there is quality, that life has some meaning through the objective world.

There are many people who actually are not of that persuasion and they are best pursuing careers in universities, or in other businesses, but the person who is a museum director is a person who must have that kind of passionate belief in the 'objective world', convinced that it is worth showing and demonstrating and seeing the real thing. If you have that basic passion then I think potentially you can then learn the organization and management skills needed.

The assumption that because a person is a good curator then he or she is therefore necessarily a good museum director is an assumption that I think we all know to be false. It is not necessarily true at all. On the other hand the good curator can learn organization and management techniques, but so can an educator, so can a person who has been involved in museum development, but what they must all have in common is that passion for the object, which is the real mark of a museum director.

GRAEME FARNELL: I think that point is very encouraging. However, coming back to Claude's point earlier on, it seems to me that there are curators all over the country who are involved in the time and pain of initiating change and that's not just in the big museums, it is in the small and medium sized museums as well. I think this is a very encouraging development. But the problem is they are involved in this in a pretty isolated way with very little support in terms of professional training. Of course the Museums Association very recently has been involved in the Training Needs Analysis and again, I think it is encouraging and not surprising that management issues have focused very highly in people's perception of their own training needs.

I would hope that it will be possible to develop very positive models of the changes that have successfully taken place in large museums and small, and I would like to couple this with a plea for the development of positive models along with those of Tom's paper which it seems to me was a very interesting and very challenging one. But in practical terms it would be helpful to know from him where these new ideas and practices are currently being put into place and are working. If no museums are using them in the ideal form, then which museums are at least going in that direction?

TOMISLAV SOLA: What is the problem in applying these theoretical approaches in practice?

PATRICK BOYLAN: What Graeme was actually asking was are there examples of these new structures or approaches actually being implemented? One obvious thing is the ecomusée concept.

TOMISLAV SOLA: What I was telling you about was really a mixture that I have reached by analysing many experiences: you don't find quantities of new practices that will impress you always. You find certainly ecomuseums but you find the ecomuseum principles applies in many other museums: it is a matter of practice. I would say we are reaching that point of ripeness where we are able to orientate ourselves within the museum practice without having always models in our heads. Ecomuseums OK – this is one, this is not. I don't accept the logic, though I like their far-ahead way of thinking, so the future is already here, if that is the point you are trying to reach. It can be found in many museums.

Now my role, as I see it, is to assemble these parts and bits into some structural whole that may serve as a quite secure guess for our future. I understand that many of us would have trouble being confronted with these future visions of ours, because there is energy inbuilt in all of us that is resistant to change. But I believe the key turning point in our profession will be from the new professionals coming from undergraduate museological training and they will think differently. Not always, but as the time goes by it will be that way and we have to adjust to it.

Let me just add: even in the training courses there are also some places in the world where the new approach I have outlined happens. I wouldn't like to mention names because we might then have the wrong kind of discussion but they are there. I wouldn't also like to promote my own institution at Zagreb University, but we try hard to do it. Mind you, the future curators who come out of our courses will be really very wide in their approach, will not regard their job as limited to that Dominican monastery or this museum institution. I have nothing against traditional museums, and this is one of the points I would like to stress in my discussion. If you wish, I can expose myself to risk, and say that in 80 per cent of cases I would leave these museums as they are, because they are part of our cultural configuration. They should stay there: change, certainly; but not drastically. Such change might be quite harmful to do it. But we can do this in new museums: it is simply not possible to do it the way it was before. What I am speaking about is the other way of thinking: you may like it or not but it is there, and it will be presenting itself to you as a problem in the future.

KATE THAXTON (Conference participant, Museum of Richmond): I wanted really just to point out a very big difference between large museums and small museums which I do not really think has been brought up very much today, because the role of curator is very different in these institutions. What museums are being called upon to perform are many different roles, particularly in education, better displays and interpretation, etc. In larger museums increasing numbers of other professionals are being brought in and in this situation there is a danger that the curator becomes extremely specialized and returns to the old nineteenth-century form of curator, which was basically as a custodian and a researcher, pure and simple. In a small museum that is not the case. And we are being called upon to perform all these additional roles without the back-up of all these other professionals. I would like to hear the panel's ideas on the different way curators could then be trained and whether in fact we have two professions of curators rather than just a curator.

GEOFFREY LEWIS: There is only one profession. I believe there is a profession of curatorship. Whether it is a sub-set of heritology is a matter of much more deep discussion. So the first fundamental point I would make is that there is this curatorship. The point has been made that one should be passionate about objects. There is another aspect of this as well, i.e. that one must be passionate about people. This is coming out in a management context, and it must also come out in one's clientele context. Because time is short I will say in the Leicester Museum Studies Department management was introduced (resource management including professional management), in 1977, and it is well established there. Because of the issue of objects material culture was in fact introduced in 1978 to look at some of the theoretical aspects of it. Of the theoretical aspects overall on which Tom has dwelt, there is a desperate need for this work, and I would not like us to lose sight of the main theme of his paper. We do need to know more about the fundamentals: the whos, the whats, the hows and so on. This work should be being undertaken in our universities, particularly in our departments of museology or museum studies, and that was a point I was referring to yesterday – the lack of any identified funding source for this type of work at the moment.

FRANS SCHOUTEN (Conference participant, Reinwart Academy, Leiden, Netherlands): Those who know me well won't be surprised to find that I stand beside Tomislav Sola in all his points. But first of all I would like to refer to Paul Perrot's comparison of medical care and the museum profession. I do use that metaphor often myself but I do think there is one point missing in it, when you try to relate a museum and a hospital. In a hospital we are dealing with medical care. If you make the same point to museums we are not in museums of museology – we are dealing with museology. Should we argue that in the case of hospitals the object is not medical care but hospitalology or something like that? So all the time we are mixing up museums with our profession, and in the process we are not dealing with museums. Museums are only a vehicle: we are dealing with heritage and in that respect I would stress the point of Tomislav Sola that we are really dealing with what he calls 'heritology', and as long as we see the curator of the museum as a cornerstone of museology we will mix up the aims and the means.

PATRICK BOYLAN: I must say as one of two scientists if not more on the platform, I get very twitchy when people seem to think museums are solely about past heritage (hence heritology) because I think they are equally about contemporary issues, not least of course contemporary art, or for that matter contemporary science.

EVELYN SILBER (Conference participant, Birmingham Museums and Art Gallery): We have heard an awful lot from Tomislav and from other members of the panel about the new roles that museums are going to be called upon to play, and the new skills both of presentation and of content, and in terms of concept of the kind of issues we're going to have to take on board and present. My colleague from Richmond has pointed out the curator of a small museum is expected to be all things to each audience.

Discussion

I don't think this is a problem exclusive to the small museum – I think it affects all museums and I fear I am going to come back to that dreadful word money again. If curators and others working in museums are going to take on more expertise themselves, or more people who are specialists in interpretation, all are going to have to undertake a lot more training in order to be able to respond to changing needs. They need to be trained to be able to manage staff, technicians will need new skills in terms of presenting exhibits more interactively, all will need more contact with their communities, and possibly more external consultants. These are a whole lot of new and increasingly demanding, time consuming, reflective tasks, all of which require an awful lot of money and time for preparation.

I don't think any of these things actually take away from the fundamentals from which most curators have started and which have been emphasized several times: that need to be passionate about the objects and the presentation of the objects and ultimately that expertise, historical/geographical, according to the material or culture one is dealing with. One is still going to need that fundamental expertise though it obviously needs a lot more openness with it.

I don't see any functions that the current curator undertakes that they are going to stop undertaking in the next century, but perhaps the panel can think of some that curators should stop doing. Otherwise I think we are genuinely confronted with the fact that we must have more resources of all kinds. Most of us are not in the position of a business where we can simply say: we are earning a net profit, we can always change for the future. How are we going to cope with that?

Professionals and museums 2 | 8

Rambling reflections of a museum man

Neil Cossons

At this stage in the proceedings, everything worthwhile has already been said by people with much more expertise than mine, so all I offer are the rambling reflections of a museum man, and as somebody, however, with a deep suspicion of professions but an overwhelming admiration for professionalism.

Those of you who were at the 1982 Annual Conference of the Museums Association in Nottingham may remember that I devoted most of my Presidential Address (*Museums Journal*, December 1982) to a diatribe about professions, professionals and professionalism. But it does seem to me that the question of 'what we are', as people who work in museums, in particular how we are able to 'deliver', and what particular qualities we need in order to 'deliver', is central to the whole business of museums, particularly in a time of change, and when people want what we have to offer more, perhaps, than they ever have before.

This business of collections, it seems to me, is at the root of a lot of what we should be talking about. It does seem to me that the collection is the characteristic which is a common factor and a common thread to museums, and which does distinguish them from other types of cultural, scientific, and educational and entertainment institutions.

We can interpret the word 'collection' in a very broad sense because it can relate, of course, to site and buildings, and to whole areas of preserved and interpreted landscape. It is a heritage component that is common to the work that most of us do, and it seems to me that it has been the dilemma of how we approach the idea of collections that has been frightening us as a group of people – I am not going to use the word 'profession' – in recent years, particularly as new types of collection have been recognized and valued by the public, and as, conversely, traditional long-established museums have found the problem of how to handle their collections increasingly intractable.

We have, I think, a really quite alarming situation in which large museums of long standing now tend to see their collections almost as liabilities rather than assets, despite the fact that the reason for the museum's existence is to have and hold collections, and indeed, to do things with those collections. Also, it seems to me that those museums, with a larger and larger proportion of their resources being absorbed by the business of having and holding their collections, are increasingly aware of the conservation issues that those collections present. The science and technology of preservation of collections and objects has advanced rapidly in recent years, the net result being, of course, to make us more aware of how our collections are in danger, whether in store or on display. Collections and their care consume a larger and larger proportion of the museum's resources; collections in museums only get bigger. And so, with a large proportion of our staff resources and cash resources sucked into the business of looking after our collections, big museums tend to find themselves less and less able to do things with those collections – to do creative things with them, to respond to the new needs that a public has for them.

We see ourselves in the perpetuity business. The collection is immutable. The object in the museum is there, it is there for ever and it is our job to pass it on to our successors in a state no worse than that in which we found it.

There is a horrifying parallel, perhaps, with the way that we look at health care, in either a preventative or a remedial sense, in the way we have perhaps tended to look at museum collections over the last twenty years. We have invested a lot of intellectual effort and financial effort, rightly I believe, in creating conservation laboratories, and in the training of conservators to carry out remedial treatment of museum collections. What we now, I believe, have to invest in, in a strategic sense, is long-term preventative care. This will include the provision of environmental conditions necessary for collections in big stores, big culture dumps, where collections can be pushed in at one end in the knowledge that, other things being equal, they will come out when you want them, at any time in the future, no worse off than when you put them there. It seems to me that understanding the enormous cost-benefits of preventative, as opposed to remedial, laboratory conservation, is one of the things that can release us from 'this tyranny of the object', as one of the other speakers has called it.

So, it seems to me that large museums are lacking in confidence because of the fear they have of their collections. Their staff are frightened by their collections, but it is the same collections which are used as the stick to beat governments who don't look after our roofs properly or don't provide us with the sorts of resources which we believe we need to look after these collections. It is reasonable, it seems to me, for a government, in response, to look at the present state of our collections and say: 'why haven't you done a better job?'

We are certainly in this perpetuity business, but I think at the root of a form of conservatism which pervades the museum business, is a confusion between the fact that the collections are immutable and have to be looked after for ever, and the systems by which we do those jobs, regarding these also as immutable. That confusion, it seems to me, is something which we have to break out of. There are many, many, ways of funding and running museums. There are many, many, ways of employing people, whether on our payrolls, or as consultants or contractors to do both the basic housekeeping jobs and also much of the scholarly work which relates to those collections in a wide variety of different ways. It also seems to me that many of the people inside the museum business don't understand that, and are more interested in determining, if you like, when they are going to fly the aeroplane, rather than committing themselves to making sure they have the best possible qualifications and expertise to fly the aeroplane as their justification for being employed as pilots.

We are, in the UK at least, in a period, are we not, of deregulation, when traditional professions are under threat from consumers? We have seen architects and planners disappear in the abyss, not so much as a result of legislative pressure upon them, but because the population at large just didn't like what they had done to us. And we see, as the fingernails of the architect emerge on the edge of the other side of the chasm, the architect coming out again with renewed self-confidence, as perhaps other professionals, our teachers for example, disappear down the hole that they have just vacated, although we may see teachers again towards the end of the century as professionals again in some reasonably integrated form. And you can say exactly the same about lawyers and coal-miners. The people who have got some special skill and believe they can use that skill as a means of regulating how they deliver it are, I believe, doomed. On the other hand, there is a glowing tomorrow for people who have special skills and can demonstrate by the application of that skill that they can deliver something that people want.

Rambling reflections of a museum man

If we can shed the fear of our collections, and demonstrate that these are of significant value to the people who own them – because despite what Claude Blair (Co-Chairman of the 'Save the V&A Campaign') might say: 'they are taking our collections from us' – we are not the owners of those collections. We are only the trustees, the caretakers, for those collections and it is our job to make sure that we hand them on to our successors in good order. It seems to me that if we can demonstrate a renewed confidence in those collections and an ability to do things with them, in terms of looking after them on the one hand and using them in a manner that means something to people on the other, then we do really have an opportunity, as a group of people and a 'profession', to have a future.

I also believe that these long-established museums, with these great collections, are really in the most bizarre state, partly because of their fear of those collections – a sort of headless chicken trying to do all sorts of other things. You can look at many large museums with great collections in which most of their efforts go on non-collection-based activities. Just the other day, I was reflecting on the three museums based in South Kensington. There are three shows going on. I don't know what the current one in the V&A is – socks or knitting or something. At the Natural History Museum you have animated plastic dinosaurs, and if you go to the Science Museum you have Launch Pad, which is a whole range of interactive exhibits which relate to the principles of science and technology. But in none of them *are* the museum's objects actually being presented. Now many would argue, rightly I think, that the animated dinosaurs or Launch Pad are a significant aid to the understanding of geology and palaeontology and of science and technology or whatever it might be, and indeed to a broader understanding of the collections themselves, but isn't it interesting that museums put in an enormous amount of effort into such projects, and a lot of what is being used to try to stimulate visitors to come to museums is not actually those unique collections that the staff have made all the noise about, spent all the money on, and moaned and groaned about for so many years.

We have to turn things inside out. The 'core market', if you will accept this term, for the permanent galleries of the V&A is, I suspect, about half a million people with specialized interests relevant to the Museum's present form. The rest of the visitors go for whatever the V&A currently happens to be showing and a special exhibition. That is very much the case with other museums of that type.

But what we have failed to do in all of these kinds of museum has been to invest properly in our faith and our belief in the collections, and in particular in our ability to deliver them in a manner that the public want and will continue to want in our permanent galleries.

Now, because we in museums are not coping, we have got ourselves into the sort of state – a lack of confidence – in which the public too are losing faith in our ability to do the job that they believe we should be doing, so why should they give us any money, either directly or through taxation?

If museums are to be effective instruments of the societies that own them, they must reflect and react to the fundamental, social and economic facts of that society. That doesn't mean they should bend in the wind of every passing fashion – that's probably one of the problems we suffer from now. But it does mean recognizing that the society which gave birth to many of these great museums for its own reasons at that time no longer exists and that today's society has very different needs and requirements, though they need the same collections. In other words the immutability, the sanctity, of the object is the continuing thread, and it is a remarkably strong thread if you think about it. Of all the things that people do in their leisure time, the use of museums and their collections is one of the things that has a strong element of longevity built into it. The support for museums is extraordinarily resistant to changes in fashion, but museums are equally becoming more and more expensive to look after, and people are demanding higher and higher standards of them.

If we think of the newly industrialized society that gave rise to most of our largest provincial museums, it gave us, too, large scale urbanization, mass production, mass transport, mass housing, mass health, mass culture, civic pride and the tradition of public service, local government, capitalism, socialism, and professionals too. Professions are an essential element of the middle-class evolution of the middle years in the nineteenth century. In today's society we have the relics of all these around us, but today we also have different pressures and different opportunities: for example, we tend to be obsessed with the way in which wealth is distributed and assume that that is the most significant factor in society. We are overly obsessed with money, and have a belief that money is in some way in short supply. Money is never in short supply: it is just in different people's pockets at different times, and what we have to recognize is that we live in a society in which money is being transferred from one pocket to the other and we just aren't quick enough to get what we think should be our share of it.

Much more fundamental than cash and who is distributing it or whether we are operating in a market economy or a socialist type of economy, are the effects of the age of information which is just about to break upon us, the effects of the new age of leisure, and the fact that the individual will become the most powerful element in the community, rather than the community itself. But great museums were built to serve communities: they were a mass experience providing a very vital and valid insight – another speaker has used the term edification: an enlightening quality which was not available through any other medium. The museum is still a unique medium for education and communication if it relies upon its collection, but at the same time, it seems to me, we have the opportunity to deliver our services in a quite different manner and one that I think tomorrow's public are going to want.

It is not now too difficult for us to provide a product which is designed for individuals rather than a mass market. What industry can now do which it couldn't do a hundred years ago is use all the technology of mass production to produce an object which is specific, specified and tailored to the needs of one person using the power that information technology is giving us. And if we think of information technology as the information base on which our collections stand, we suddenly have available to us the means for placing a new form of value upon our collections, and our collections are only as valuable as the information that is associated with them.

This isn't to undermine the sanctity of the object or in any way deny this, but the object is something which carries vital information in historical museums; in scientific museums the information content is an essential element in making the object of value, although the criteria might be to a certain extent in art collections.

As an aside, I must raise the question of whether there is any point in using large sums of public money to bring expensive art into public ownership. 'Save the Titian' is an emotive slogan but the Titian actually isn't in any danger. The more expensive the Titian is, in market terms the less the likelihood of it being lost or destroyed in any physical sense. The only question is whose wall it hangs on or whose strongroom it lives in. 'Save the Rhinoceros' is a different issue altogether, because the rhinoceros might be extinct next week. Using the term 'Save the Titian' when what is meant is 'Let us have the Titian, here not there' is one of the serious confusions of our time. It seems to me almost irrelevant now for museums to spend large sums on buying things which have suddenly become very expensive, whether they are Bugatti Royales or Van Goghs.

In other words, if we have shortage of resources, shouldn't we then be directing those limited resources into the care of what we've already got, the careful acquisitions of tomorrow's collections, like laying down a good wine, and into the proper use and presentation of them? Once something becomes extremely expensive and collectable in comparison with the straightforward long-term care of it, we can almost forget it.

Trading in art is no longer very much to do with art – it is more like cocoa futures: art has become a commodity, and because it has become a commodity and has a cash price on it, the market will look after it, generally speaking, and won't need a museum to save it.

Now Kenneth Hudson isn't here today, so I don't want to pursue the analogy that he made yesterday about the respective values and reactions that people have towards art particularly and collections in general, but I do agree that large purchase funds are a questionable use of our limited resources. What is much less questionable I suspect, is the growing acceptance that we should have very clearly defined policies for the acquisition of the stuff. I suspect we should actually be collecting a lot more contemporary, perhaps ephemeral in the long term, material, having what I call a 'transit shed' approach to acquisition.

This is particularly relevant to a science museum which is attempting to document contemporary science and technology. We don't have either the natural selection of the past which has left us only a small portion of its relics from which to collect, nor do we have the perspective of time with which to determine what is, and is not, significant in the longer term.

What we have got is the real stuff, immediately available to us, and for virtually nothing. We could put it into a store for a very, very low cost per cubic foot and leave it there for as long as we like for very, very little cost. Then, at the end of twenty five years or fifty years or whenever we feel like it, we can get it out again, evaluate it and so on, and it is still new.

What we are contemplating in the Science Museum is to have a long shed into which we will push these objects. They won't cost us very much and at intervals of 25, 50 and 75 years we'll open the door at that point along the side of the shed and look at what we've got. And we'll throw some of it away: there is no other means of contemporary collecting, and we are all deluding ourselves if we think we can carry on adding the stuff at the rate we have been recently, without severely endangering the whole edifice.

All this requires a high quality of scholarship, and of intellectual understanding, together with the ability, in a housekeeping sense, to manage collections properly. But I believe that this approach is a much more responsible policy for ensuring that we have the relics of our past and our present available tomorrow than the much more vicarious and uncertain current processes of acquisition, that may depend upon what the curator feels like this morning, whether he got up in time, what university he went to, whether he read a degree in sociology or she read a degree in English or whatever it might be.

There is clearly more bias in the process of collecting as a result of the attitude, background and training of our staff. I'm not suggesting we'll get away from this by having a much more catholic and expansive collecting policy, and in searching out relics of the past and bringing them into our care when they are already worn out and therefore need a high degree of remedial attention. In fact, it seems to me that we currently indulge in a quite expensive hobby, which we can't continue to any very great extent. So from the Science Museum point of view, collecting new things is what we believe to be worthwhile. We think lots of people will be rather pleased to give us new things, but we will only take them on the basis that at some time in the future we might decide to throw them away again. Some of those new things, of course, will have enhanced enormously in value: even a 1958 Vauxhall Victor, still rust-free in its original wrapper, would be regarded as a very desirable object by many people who would buy one today for quite a lot of money.

So we have actually got the means, it seems to me, of turning over the stuff in a manner that will both enable us to build collections responsibly, and look after them on the basis of preventative care, rather than the never-ending remedial approach to looking after the stuff in which we currently invest an enormous amount of expertise. We can't get rid of that expertise: we cannot reduce our conservation laboratories: the current backlog is there to keep large numbers of conservators going for ever.

Who are going to be the people to do all this work? That core of scholarship and scholarly understanding which is going to enable us to acquire things and know about them is essential, and I am not sure that in many museums it has been there to the extent that it is needed. What I am absolutely certain of is that though the work should be done, it doesn't seem to me essential that it has to be done by people who call themselves curators employed in museums. I am strongly persuaded by Barry Lord's point that it is a 'passion for the object' which has been the root of the scholarship, and which leads to the ability to acquire and to have and to hold collections. I have no doubt about that whatsoever, and that imposes one special type of quality which must be at the root of however the museum scholar operates and works.

However, those scholars can have a much more varied relationship to the collection and therefore the museum. They can be in the museum in the form of research fellows, or they can move in and out. They can be employed by museums, or they work for the museum in a wide variety of different ways. It would be wrong, I think, and indeed rash, rather arrogant, and wrong of us to believe that the only scholarship of any worth relating to collections, is that which is carried out by people employed as curators in museums.

So, we are already in a plural society in the general sense. We are also, it seems to me, on the threshold of what you might call a new pluralism in the way that museums run themselves. I can see a museum with far fewer people directly on its payroll, but amalgamating the available professionalisms of wide varieties of different people brought in and out as they are needed and when they are needed. This operation would be manipulated by a core of people, perhaps much smaller in number than the present staff but significantly better paid because these will be very rare animals indeed, who have both the necesssary managerial qualities, and also have built those managerial qualities upon a foundation of scholarly understanding based upon museum objects. I am not at all persuaded that museums can be run by managers who haven't had their roots in a passion for the collections, and whether that passion is innate or if it derives from scholarship and training, it has to be there before the curator, or whatever we call him or her, moves on to become an effective manager. But the quality of management is nevertheless essential in order to manipulate the scarce and complex resources of the museum.

Finally, I want to focus on the rarest commodity of all in terms of the museum's people resources. This is not, I think, the scholarly understanding of the stuff. It is not the scientists who know more and more about less and less, to use the classic definition of the specialist. It is the storytellers. It is the people who can lubricate the collection, can fill the gap between the collection and the general public. And they are very, very rare indeed.

We are seeing increasingly the museum-like experience that doesn't derive from the object, but is based upon storytelling, and they can be highly popular. The Jorvik Centre, York, may be a museum or may not be a museum, but what it certainly offers is an ingeniously told story and a lot of people like it. What I find alarming is that museums with great collections now believe they have to become Jorviks because they see the crowds outside Jorvik. That, it seems to me, is largely irrelevant. What the museums have to do, it seems to me, is to acquire a skill which many don't have: the ability to weave stories around their collections. The stories which are relevant to the museum can be used to communicate with the public about their objects and to reveal truths about those objects which are not themselves necessarily self-revealing in the display of the objects themselves. That is why I come back to information being an essential element of having these collections. I think the idea of 'if you've got objectives you can't have objectivity' was a very nice little statement of yesterday. Objects can speak for themselves but increasingly if we are going to weave stories with them, and in particular weave stories that have some foundation, a form of scientific, historical or scholarly objectivity must be at its root.

I repeat that we need to have different types of people who are very rare indeed – we aren't growing them in museums – who are able to use objects as a means of communicating. And that, it seems to me, is a very specialized skill. That is why, in the case of the Science Museum, we are investing in a new Professorship in the Public Understanding of Science, because although we have these objects and we know a lot about them, we don't know how to talk about them or about the sciences and technologies from which they derive, to a non-science public.

What we have found out in the last five years is the size of the gap between what the scientific community actually does and what the general mass of the public believe about science. We are the first society which actually enjoys the fruits of science and technology without having any understanding of it. As a result of having no understanding of it society has a deep suspicion of it. Indeed we enjoy ourselves by paying subscriptions to societies which are inherently antipathetic to science, and a lot of that antipathy towards science is non-scientific. More than half the British population believe that astrology is a science. More than half the British population think organic food is fabulous but only 20 per cent of them actually know what organic food is, and so on and so on.

The popular media use science as a means of whipping governments, and certainly as a means of whipping scientists and technologists. Our belief is that what we have in the collections of the Science Museum is a record of science and technology, but we don't know how to use that record to communicate in a language which the non-scientific public will understand. That is at the root of what our initiative in the public understanding of science is about.

I think there are similar exercises to be undergone in the fields of the natural sciences and, to a lesser extent perhaps, in history and archaeology, though, perhaps because people with an arts background are more likely to have studied those sorts of collections and subjects, they are perhaps inherently more capable of talking about what they believe in, and revealing their passion through their objects. Scientists and engineers are perhaps less so and the already complex (and increasingly more complex) stories they have to tell are much more difficult to manipulate.

Now these, Chairman, are I think the random ramblings that I managed to read from the few notes I have. There may be many more. If there is one final message, it seems to me that it must be the need to achieve a renewal of faith in the collections we have, a much more open attitude to the way in which we manipulate them, and a very real ability to demonstrate to the public at large that we actually do a good job with them. All the moaning about stuff falling to bits in the basement does the basic cause of museums no good at all. We need to develop access to stored collections and the marketing of availability of collections. All of that sort of thing comes back to information technology and the power that information technology will offer in the future. It will enable people to spend their spare time, and they go there in the hope that they might find something which stimulates them. We hope that, too, and we hope that they might come back. (Museum-going is a spare-time activity: it always has been because people have done it in their spare time. They go largely because they like it, even though some people are dragged to museums, but most people go there voluntarily.)

But what we have to do, it seems to me, is to open the doors of our minds to the way in which the people we wish to influence with our collections perceive us. We must allow them to determine what we are, rather than sit here talking to ourselves and wondering precisely why we aren't getting anywhere.

Discussion

SAROJ GHOSE: Now Dr Cossons has raised a point which has been worrying us for some time in India. There are two very essential and vital points behind our strategy for collections. One of them is that the number of collection items is increasing in a logarithmic scale. Today, if a new museum wants to start its collection it will probably get ten items pertaining to the seventeenth century, 100 items for the eighteenth century and 10,000 items for the nineteenth century, and for the twentieth century definitely more than 100,000 items.

The real problem is that science and technology museums, when they collect contemporary items, because of the tremendous expansion of the horizon of knowledge and large number of inventions and innovations in science and technology nowadays the number of items are bound to be very high.

The second point which is connected to that one is that when we collect items relating to the eighteenth and nineteenth centuries, in retrospect we are able to judge the efficacy of that collection: what kind of item was it at that time and how would it fit in today in our museum concept of preservation and so on. But when collecting a contemporary item we do not know whether it will stand the test of time. Since we have to collect, it is something like that old saying, pointing a gun at the head, or publish or perish; in our case we have to collect or perish. In retrospect, for the older artefacts we are able to judge their effectiveness, but for contemporary artefacts we shall not be able to judge that one. In all probability we will be collecting lots and lots of things which ultimately may be considered as junk after 30–40 years and of no relevance at all. So this is going to be the second major issue for the collections, and I fully agree with Dr Cossons that a well-drafted acquisition policy or collection policy is necessary at least in the areas of science and technology museums.

I would mention one more point in brief, relating to the earlier lecture of Tomislav Sola. One thing that again bothers us in India – I am not raising the analogy of hospital and medical college with museums and museology department – but one point is the need to make sure that a large part of museology or museum training is practice-orientated. We find that the museology departments or museology training courses and the museums are yet to be properly integrated. This is not there, not only in India, but I know in many countries museology departments work in isolation, and not very closely with the best museums of the country. Theoretically, with this the people coming out from the museology department should be the best in the profession. Personally, I feel that the museology department and the best museum in the country should work together so that during the training programme everything that is best in museology: in display, in lighting, level and text is properly communicated. This idea has to be researched with and worked with, but would be an excellent example of the efficacy of museum training.

BARRY LORD: I want to just put in a word specifically for the discipline of museum planning – trying to differentiate museum planners from those other planners who are continually crawling out of the abyss. But specifically it seems to me that there is this emerging sub-discipline of museum planning which I think addresses precisely the realities he was describing.

Everybody is aware of things like corporate plans and business plans and so on – but there are two other specific components that seem to me more and more important in the kind of work we're doing in museum planning, both of which are really relevant to what Neil had to say. One is the collection development strategy. He outlined one very competent approach to a collection development strategy in terms of contemporary collecting of science and technology materials, or it could be in many other fields, domestic history and so on, with his strategy of the long shed, with a fifty-year lifespan. That is certainly one very graphic approach to contemporary collecting.

I think that one of the things which surely will emerge increasingly in the twenty-first century is that each museum will have as part of its corporate plan a collection development strategy. This will include a quantitative and qualitative analysis of its present collection, will include articulated objectives both in quantitative and qualitative terms, which will then be revised from time to time as the museum proceeds. That is something which we have not had in the past and is just now emerging. We are very excited about it. It seems to me there are very great possibilities for that as a management control device, something which will allow curators to get on with the job.

I think the issue of deaccessioning and disposal has to be examined and as in Neil's example of contemporary collecting leading to possibly even profitable disposals of what turn out to be non-museum bygones fifty years from now. Yes, I think that deaccessioning and disposal should be one of the questions to be considered. I am not urging it or arguing for it, I am simply saying that it is one of the things that must be on the agenda.

Discussion

But a collection development strategy for each museum clearly will lead us to an ability to control this role and to be able to speak to politicians and other funding sources in a much more coherent way about where we are going to be in 25, 50 or 100 years from now and be able to project our capital needs.

The other aspect which I am increasingly convinced is a crucial aspect of the planning components of the future is what I refer to as a research plan, by which I mean a plan for each institution that looks ahead probably 20 or 25 years and that says: this is the unique research that this institution can and should do whether it is with existing curatorial staff or whether it is with research scholars being brought in. I think it has to be 20 or 25 years because many of the jobs envisaged will be 8- and 10-year span jobs. If we have that kind of a plan and the results of research are linked to public activities, exhibitions and other public programmes, education programmes and so on, then we will be very clear that a museum is not a university, not a research institute. On the other hand we will then protect research and stop this business of jerking curators out of their research plans continually in order to meet programming objectives which vary with the wind. It seems to me that again a coherent articulated research plan can be the salvation, particularly in relation to the curator in the smaller institution. They can be a real solution, getting control of this through a culmination of research planning and collection development strategy, so I would just like to put in the potential contribution of museum planning in getting on top of these variables.

GEOFFREY LEWIS: Mine is really a question to Neil Cossons. What is the prognosis for information about the age about to break and the transference from the community to the individual? On the latter, could you go a little further as to say how you expect that to impact itself on the museum and particularly its interpretive aspect? Is that going to be profound or not?

NEIL COSSONS: I think it could be and just to give a simple example – visible storage in which you have publicly accessible spaces with very large volumes of objects and which you can interrogate through a keyboard and get large volumes of information which relate to those objects. This adds a whole new dimension of what the public perceive to be the mass of the stuff we have. Much of the public's perception is that there are these dark and dank cellars full of rotting, decaying objects and they are generally right! What they have to see is a wealth of stuff, visible to them – it is an enormous cosmetic value in this, in perception terms, of demonstrating the wealth of a museum's collection. A museum doing that now with conventional means, can't say very much about those objects. It isn't a very difficult technology.

PAUL PERROT: One of the things that plagues us I think is a territorial imperative. The fact that we tend to work in isolation from one another and particularly in terms of collection. It is perfectly clear that we cannot continue collecting in the future the way that we have in the past.

I often wondered why there was little progress with the Scandinavian proposal of some years ago of having a group of regional museums who each specialize in this or that one aspect of contemporary life for the whole group, and act as temporary deposits until the importance of the material becomes clearer, ensuring the preservation of a kind of example or rule of succession. I never understood why that very sensible model of the nineteenth-century contemporary collecting (e.g. from the major exhibitions of art and industry) died with the nineteenth century and wasn't picked up in the twentieth century, because it seems to me to provide a filter through which succeeding generations could make selections of things that had proved to be truly lasting, which could then go into more general museums, that tends to be panoramic and encyclopaedic of this or that subject.

One aspect of collecting that hasn't been mentioned is the role of the individual collector. Far be it for me to decry the importance of curators, but if curators only curated those things that they had collected themselves for the institution, our museums would be far less than what they are today. From that aspect I think the museum could minister to and co-operate with the individual collector so that he or she becomes co-opted to the task.

PATRICK BOYLAN: Of course, we must remember that there are some areas in which rate of collecting has massively reduced in recent times. One of the most obvious ones is natural history collections, where because of wildlife conservation considerations, e.g. the mass killing of every rare bird that flew over the UK which was the norm up to the 1940s has now ceased, and there are some other areas in which collections growth has almost ceased.

DONALD HORNE: I found myself in such agreement with the paper that for a moment I thought I might have nothing to say. I have overcome that embarrassment by raising a question that you are also now raising – collecting within the present configurations of museums which leaves a bit between gaps.

Discussion

And it seems to me that the suggestion raised by Neil Cossons is one of the ways in which that could happen. There are eccentricities of the future that we can't for the moment understand, but if we develop the idea of community museums of various kinds, not only regional but also community in the sense of ethnic museums or religious museums, etc., and there was a greater encouragement of collecting generally, then this would offset the possibility that the major museums are not collecting in your economically splendid manner for future reconfigurations of museums, as well as continuing in the present ones.

NEIL COSSONS: It seems to me that the process of acquisition is threatened from a wide variety of directions, and mature museums tend to be reluctant to acquire because they haven't got enough space. The size of the museum door has been one of the key criteria to determine what is or is not of cultural importance to society!

I went through about a dozen local history museums recently to just look at objects from the point of view of how big they are. I recommend this as a technique because there was no object in them larger than the domestic size of the front door to the museum. Larger museums have larger doors and therefore have larger objects. So our view of what is and what isn't important is determined much more by simple financial, pragmatic, storage factors and worries, or indeed if we can actually sell the idea to the chairman of the committee without being sacked or whatever it might be, than any ethics or philosophy of collections or anything of that sort.

And I think we have got to get out of this way of thinking. I suspect we can't afford to have lots of little museums collecting anyway, and that we're going to end up with some kind of new places that are sheds that suck stuff in on an almost random basis, and where the curators are going to be sifters and sorters and disposers of this wealth of stuff. After all, if you look at a lot of the collections that we really like they weren't put together by curators, they were put together by lunatics who had a total obsession with something like sweet-wrapping papers, so you create a National Museum of Sweet Papers, and people would flock to the thing because no curator would ever dream of collecting sweet papers! (On second thoughts, curators probably would collect them because they're small!)

But it does seem to me that what curators are, determines what curators do, and what curators are is determined to a great extent by what they are called. It's like people joining the Army and taking the King's shilling in the nineteenth century: they joined because they were attracted by glamorous uniforms, and I think people come into museums because they like the word curator. It's a dangerous word to have around because once you have been invested with this word there is no cure. It seems to me that the title actually constrains what we do, particularly in relation to these other professional specializations that have been referred to. It doesn't seem to me that the name 'curator' has necessarily any particular distinguishing characteristics, but just embraces a range of specialist activities which only work effectively when added to a lot of other specializations.

I can envisage the curator becoming the person who manages disposal rather than the person who is obsessed with acquisition, and I just throw that out despite the fact that I am quite convinced that the Science Museum collecting only 2,200 objects a year is not doing its job properly. It is just not a fast enough rate of acquisition or a responsible enough rate of acquisition. To document what we should be doing and to be able to have a faster rate of acquisition, we need therefore to link this to a very carefully manicured policy of disposal. My belief is that by the time we dispose of these objects they will have other cultural values, which will mean that people won't destroy them. They'll put them in their own private collections and look after them for us. So all that museums are doing, if you like, is tiding us over from the day the thing is made, through the period it is unfashionable, to the time that we can assess its importance and either keep it or not keep it. Even if we then throw it back into the pond, someone else will fish it out, polish it off and stick it on the mantelpiece.

GRAEME FARNELL: I had two points: the first one rather follows on from Neil Cossons' comments. I think that many people would probably agree with his persuasive argument for a plural approach to the provision of expertise, but I think again a lot of people wouldn't trust their boards and their committees to implement the kind of changes which Neil is suggesting in any sort of responsible way. It seems to me that the great fear is that this would be a way not so much of necessarily saving cash, but certainly of lowering standards. I wonder whether Neil would like to respond to that?

My second point is that in response to what Neil was saying about museums having a shortage of resources. I think it is important for us to remember that, yes, our museums have a shortage of resources undoubt-edly, and that leads us to have to take tough decisions about our priorities. Do we buy expensive paintings or do we do other things instead? So museums have a shortage of resources, but of course the UK as a whole at government level is not short of resources. In fact we are one of the very few European countries to have a very substantial government budget surplus. It seems to me that what follows logically from this is that another part of our professional expertise must be to develop cogent agreed and coherent arguments for museums to get a larger slice of this budget surplus.

NEIL COSSONS: It seems to me that what Graeme Farnell has been talking about has actually been happening during the last twenty-five years anyway, but not in any positive or managed sense. If you look at the numbers of curators in, say, medium to large sized museums there are generally speaking slightly more of them around than there were in the 1960s. But in the early '60s they represented 80–90 per cent of the professional staff of those institutions. Now they represent 40 per cent and the rest, the growth area of the past twenty-five years, is occupied by a majority of people now who are not curators but are conservators and educators and interpreters and designers and finance officers and all the rest. In other words, as the museum business has become much more complex it has had to add to the traditional perception of what a curator was, all sorts of new specializations, some of which have actually taken over from the curator roles that he or she should be doing.

This embattledness, which many curators today feel, is because they are not doing key jobs any more, and museums are not helping curators to redefine what they do. There may still be a further process of specialization ahead of us in which for example we start to get scholarship and interpretation broken apart in some sort of way. Consequently I think the word 'curator' is now so ill-defined, so I think this business of specialization is inevitably going to continue. I firmly believe that what we have to do is to manage the way in which this change happens in a manner that satisfies both the needs of museums and the needs of the individual staff members themselves.

VICTOR MIDDLETON: But I just wanted to comment very quickly on a point which you made which I saw as very important. That is the traditional curator role or traditional museum manager role, whichever you prefer, focusing on inward-looking towards the object, to identify its truth and to do it often with enormous passion. Now everybody from outside that ever advises museums (in fairness, perhaps because these are the museums that tend to pull in advisers and consultants), come across people in them who have enormous passion for objects, but which has become myopic and led them down inappropriate paths. I am not denying passion but I think it's not a recipe for success.

Neil's view, as I took it, was to focus on the outward-looking nature of the future. Outward-looking towards the public, because if they're not satisfied the danger is that the funds will simply disappear and wither for the reasons you said, and outward-looking to changing society: needs which are now actually coming very close to the way in which all businesses currently approach their mission within society. I think I prefer the expression 'dedicated commitment' to 'passion', because it probably means the same thing, but it's looking outward too, towards finding out which way to interpret collections to make most sense to a community which museums serve. But all of that puts an enormous amount of emphasis on a management role, on creating a general management curator. I think there's a danger, in a sense drawing the wrong conclusions from the words, and I can only endorse your last point: what is a curator? If he is indeed what you describe, the leader of the museum, by doing these outward-looking things and establishing priorities, brings us close to what we were talking about before.

TOMISLAV SOLA: The keyword in my own opinion for the future in our profession, is synthesis. This will bring us into some awkward situations because we don't usually expect it and we always talk about the decentralization. Instead, I now expect a strong move towards centralization which it will form. There will be some new common strategy, and a common approach. When I say common approach, I have three levels in my mind.

First, centralization, if we use the expression, will be on the level of the individual museum institution. This we have to face as our immediate task, because the museum is not coherent any more.

Second, the museum community, because it is at present diluting itself, and the third one would be on the level of integrated heritage care which would certainly include archives, libraries, all sorts of other public agencies, including communication agencies and such.

It has been said that there has been the experience of the SAMDOC contemporary museum collecting system in Sweden. This approach is very much on: it is very much functioning, and it has been an example of one of these centralizing effects, while at the same time effecting decentralization. May I say that SAMDOC stands in Swedish for contemporary documentation, that is a shortened version.

And I think what we are talking about is very much in line with what Georges Henri Rivière defined as an 'integrated museum', and which further developed into ecomuseums, but I would say there are still many other further variations of the integrated approach. To do all this we have to have a broad professional philosophy in the future – something which will really unite us on those three levels.

Discussion

MARK SUGGITT (Conference participant, Yorkshire & Humberside Museums Council): What I would like to do is bring up two points arising from Tomislav's paper and also from Neil's. I would like to endorse the need for theory, but I also think even more important is the management and implementation of that theory on museum staff. I speak as someone who has spent the majority of my working life in museums dealing with the mistakes left behind by other people: the collective failure which has produced huge backlogs of poorly documented, rotting material, and this occurred not because there was no theory about in previous periods. I was working in the social history field, and one thinks of Frank Pick's invaluable *The Form and Purpose of the Local Museum* published in 1938, or of John Higgs's paper on 'Folk Life Classification' in 1963, yet an awful lot of this damage occurred in the 1960s when these publications were around, and used in museum training. Somebody should have just dropped them in front of the curators of that time again and said: 'For God's sake, read it.' That is I think one very important point.

I would stress also what Neil said, that when we have these collections, if we have the money to look after them properly, there is the potential to produce what I think is the exciting prospect of multidisciplinary displays. Or we can develop new ways of looking at objects. Personally I would like to see more of the type of display which excites outrage and emotion, like, for example, Taste at the V&A, or Lost Magic Kingdoms – I think the more of those we have the better.

If we can do this and proceed with a lot more self-confidence, I think we will do a lot better, because it is a very real fact that when one or two museum curators are gathered together they will moan! One of the reasons why we are failing is that there are other people, often from other professions, who can come and say: 'We can do that' and museum curators can say 'Oh, but don't you realize ...' Given the very limited resources which the country does give us, we are doing a very good job, and if people would give us a lot more money we could do a lot better job.

I would like to tie in with something which I was asked to do yesterday by Lord Montagu, because at the end of that session he implied that possibly the independent models are the way forward. I asked whether that actually was right and I was asked to go away and find out from the Association of Independent Museums' exhibition stand how many independent museums in the UK don't receive any public subsidy. I went and asked and not unreasonably they couldn't tell me offhand. However, they did say that possibly two-thirds of their membership didn't receive any public subsidy, but also that these were nearly all very, very, small, and some of them might not get through the Museum Registration process and become officially defined as Registered Museums anyway. Going back to my final point, we are doing a very good job, but we need money and most museums can't look to the independent museum model to stand on our own two feet. Basically we are a rich country and the nation has got to make political choice as to how we spend our money: if the public money is around, as Neil says, we need a lot more of it.

CHARLES RYDER (Consulting exhibition designer): I agree with the point about public money: I mentioned it yesterday, and I think we also need to be a bit more stubborn in demanding it. When I was a young architectural student we had a professor whom we liked a great deal: he was very close to us in age and lifestyle and so on. Before his lectures he would fill the room with incense, he would play Japanese music and Poulenc and Carlos Santana and create an extraordinary atmosphere. This was the seventies, and we were all just finishing being hippies. It was extremely exciting. But the moment Gary's lecture started he was a professor, he was our teacher and he gave us as students what we needed by way of information. His technology was slides – relative to the nineteenth century slides are perhaps pretty sophisticated. But that was as far as technology went.

The point that I am making pertains to letting ourselves be museums. I don't know whether I need information when I go to museums. I like information science. I'm glad that Visa and Mastercard use informatics to keep my account straight, but for me that's enough. I took some students of mine, children, to the Metropolitan one day for a field trip and they were very quiet in the car on the way home and they said: 'Mr Ryder' (they were very nervous), 'in those statues why are all the people naked?' That's what they felt and that's what they cared about. They didn't want to know how the touch-screen worked. So I'm just wondering if we can let museums be museums, and perhaps try to live a bit more of a nineteenth-century life.

PATRICK GREENE (Conference participant, Museum of Science and Industry, Manchester): Picking up some points that Neil made about collecting and also the word that Mark Suggitt used about confidence – I'll have out with him our differences over independent museums over lunch! I would agree with Mark on the need for confidence. One of the areas of confidence we need to have, we being the international museum community, within which any two curators getting together will compare the desperate state of their stores, is that collecting is valid, and collecting is valuable. It is valuable because it is performed on behalf of society, and that means on behalf of people, and that means on behalf of users. But that takes us to the central point: do we encourage users? And the answer to that is, I fear, rarely. So why? – well really because of the

Discussion

conditions of our stores and the inadequacy of our information. So to improve that situation we need to make repeated public affirmation of the value of our collections, and stress that the potential value of our collections is much greater than their actual real value at the moment. We need repeated explanations, not amongst ourselves but to the outside world, of the need for collections: the need for accessibility to them and to stress their intrinsic value and values.

There might be some value, in talking of the long-term assessment of the value of collections and individual elements in collections, of introducing into the equation something like citation analysis already used extensively in evaluating published research. In other words, looking at the number of uses made by the number of different users of particular elements of our collection. This should not be the sole criteria of course, but could be used as one of the factors for consideration during decision-making on whether items are valuable or not for long-term preservation and conservation, and the use to which collections are put by all the categories of users.

Potential users are not at present well served and they are certainly not encouraged. It is very rare to see a museum including as part of its marketing strategy a promotion of its reserve collections and the infor-mation relating to them. So I would advocate not Neil's long warehouse with 25–50-year doors, which I think is more akin to the bunker, but advocate the concept of a well-used resource, which I think could be made possible by capitalizing upon the information revolution with which Dr Ghose and Dr Cossons both started their contributions.

EVELYN SILBER (Conference participant, Birmingham Museums & Art Gallery): I would like to take up where Patrick Greene left off. I tend to agree that the storage issue and the provision of information and access to the public is an absolutely key issue, but I come back to this point, in spite of my enthusiasm for a lot of what Neil Cossons was saying, to a couple of basic dilemmas. Unfortunately providing large accessible storage and the people to manage those stores on the spot, to take the public into them, to computerize the millions of records for all those objects and put right all the past weaknesses such as lax information, is not only incredibly time-consuming and requires quite a lot of resources, but it ain't seen as sexy. As far as our funding bodies are concerned, it's the things Neil Cossons defined as the non-collection-orientated activities: the changing exhibitions, the special events, the animation, the overall changing public face of the museum, that tends to impress funding bodies, because they see all this as providing an immediate attraction and changing attractions for the public.

Anyone who is involved as I am in promoting the museum and advertising its facilities knows to their sorrow that you can provide terribly good information about a new permanent display and try desperately to think of the hook that will catch media attention and present it and bring people in to see it and enjoy it, and you won't get the same kind of press enthusiasm, public enthusiasm or even in some instances political enthusiasm from your local authority or from national government that you may by doing an impressive temporary exhibition or special event. So I feel that it actually demands a lot from our national Associations and also from government to realize that we need consistent backing to carry many of these questions about public access to and really good conditions for storage, into practice.

One final note about the question of acquisition and disposal and length of time. I think it's perfectly true that as Dr Ghose described the logarithmic increase in rate of acquisition in some areas of museum collections does have to be given careful consideration, and possibly such a procedure which was suggested for 25-year, or 50-year, or 75-year assessments, with certain items being thrown away or discarded. But most people in real museum situations, particularly if they are involved with the fine and decorative arts, find that the situation is very different. For a start, today they are acquiring very little because they can't afford it – in fact saving the Titian has become totally irrelevant to their day-to-day concerns. They have also become incredibly vulnerable both to political pressure to sell things from the store because they aren't being shown, and also to the fact that changes of taste simply make past decisions taken with all the care, all the insight, and all the passion for the object you care to mention, look ridiculous to a new generation. So I do think that there are some strong differences in how we have to treat different areas of the collection.

PATRICK BOYLAN: I would like to throw one further question myself to Neil and that is: if what Evelyn Silber is saying about attitudes to behind the scenes expenditure is true, how is it that archivists got away with it? The average local Record Office in this country operates on between five and ten times the budget of the average local authority museum in the same area, serving about one-tenth of the number of users, and yet nobody questions this. Is it because the Record Office documents have been created by the greatest magicians of all, lawyers?

NEIL COSSONS: I don't know the answer to that, Patrick.

PATRICK BOYLAN: I think I know the answer, and that is that in museums we have shot ourselves in the foot, have we not, by telling everyone we exist to do everything but collect and look after collections.

Discussion

In marked contrast with this the archivists have been able to get away with it by saying: 'Our fundamental purpose is to look after our collections only' (in the case of my Record Office we have amongst other things $4\frac{1}{2}$ miles of documents that nobody will be allowed even to look at for 30–100 years because they are legally 'closed'), 'but because of this tremendous Public Records Act you've still got to pay £200,000 a year to look after them, even though no one is allowed to use them.'

NEIL COSSONS: Could I just refer to this business of the sexiness of the temporary exhibition, and the difficulty in contrast with this of selling to a funding body the idea of responsible documentation or storage.

If we leave aside the temporary exhibition and just talk about the permanent galleries in many of our museums, we have the opportunity in those spaces to do all sorts of things, to have object-rich galleries in which there is a wealth of information, with or without information technology systems, or to have object-thin galleries where drama or interpretation is the glue that sticks the objects together. But what we don't have when we look, for example, through the V&A (and I use that deliberately as an example), is a museum in which those galleries universally are attractive and scintillate. The objects are fabulous but they live in this dull and desperately worn-out environment.

The reason for that lies in the manner of funding, particularly for public sector bodies like the national museums or local authority museums: you have to bid for special funds when you want to do something new. Renewing a gallery should be part of the day to day operation of the business: it's not in fact something new, and you should be doing that all the time. The average life of a modern museum gallery is perhaps 10–15 years, and that implies that 10–15 per cent of a museum should permanently be being renewed on a rolling programme.

There are very few museums that operate like that because they haven't got the money to do it. But if you funded a museum on the basis that all those assets that were depreciating assets were depreciated on the basis of a conventional commercial balance sheet, you would actually be turning over, through the manner in which you fund, those assets and the show would always be new. The objects would be the same but the show would be new. You wouldn't need temporary exhibitions: you'd have police outside the door fighting the crowd. What we have in these big museums are museums that are worn out: completely clapped out in terms of their plant. The buildings are useless, the displays are tired and old, the place is dirty, and in among this are these fabulous objects. The funding base for keeping the show running ought to include as a part of the annual grant of that museum, the renewal of the museum asset itself, which is how any conventional, non-public sector type of organization would approach life.

Museums are in fact putting themselves out of business, because the perception that more and more people have of them is not what they have in the form of collections, but what they look like in terms of cobwebs, and that is going to spell their doom. So it doesn't seem to me that the issues lie between problems of collections versus temporary exhibitions, which can of course sparkle, and are the cheap, easy, quick-fix solution to get a few more people through the door. I believe what people really want to go the V&A or the Science Museum for is to see those fabulous collections, or the Science Museum, presented in beautiful, new, state-of-the-art galleries. They will go regularly to see the new galleries because if the same money that was going into those temporary exhibitions was used to put those new galleries in, there would be four new gallery openings a year in the V&A for ever, and that would keep the adrenalin going in the British public like nothing else on earth.

9 | *Profit and museums 1*

Funding, sponsorship and corporate support

Paul Perrot

I would like to start with a definition of museums as 'tomorrow organizations'. It seems to me that this aspect of our function is one that constantly has to be hammered home, for it is this I think that gives legitimacy to our existence and legitimacy to government at different levels to support us.

We are the custodians, collectively, of totally irreplaceable values: values which are both produced by humanity and materials that are the product of natural evolution.

In many, many cases, our resources are finite. Indeed our resources are the last of their kind, and thus I think that this places upon our institutions and ourselves as staff a responsibility which is quite different from that of the keeper of the Schatzkabinet of the sixteenth century or even of our predecessors in the nineteenth century, who still had the delightful illusion that the world was continuously expandable, that additional resources would always be found, in spite of Malthus, (by then Malthus had apparently been temporarily disproved), and therefore we could continue to exploit and explore *ad infinitum*.

We know now that this is no longer the fact, and that in so many cases the resources of which we are the keepers are those present resources and nothing else. That there will not be the great discoveries in the future. There will not be the unknown species that can be slaughtered in vast quantities and brought back and shared either in the trophy cabinets or, eventually, in the museum gallery.

And so this presents, it seems to me, totally different responsibilities than those that we had before, and it presents responsibilities and I think, as well, mechanisms to enlist the support of a far broader segment of the community than in the past.

I will say that it seems to me that there is almost a crisis of conscience that we are going through in the concern with the today while forgetting the responsibility to this tomorrow. Now this by no means suggests that today should be ignored. On the contrary, I think that we must find new ways to involve the population at every conceivable level. We must find every way to open our houses to larger audiences, to different audiences, to special interests, and to try to remove that kind of weight that has been upon some of our institutions, and particularly art museums, that they are the selected places for special kinds of people, for those who have been either anointed by fortune or by birth or been anointed by special knowledge.

These resources are the product of societies as a whole in the past and we have a responsibility to share this with society as a whole in the present, but our ultimate justification is to make sure that these things are there, and understood, and preserved and studied for the delectation and understanding of future generations.

I can get quite romantic in speaking about museums for they are, it seems to me, a kind of vote of confidence that there is a future for the species. Otherwise, why are we spending so much effort to study the principles of conservation and so forth? And if that is the case, it seems to me that we have a far greater claim to the support of the public purse as well as a partnership with the private.

It would be indelicate of me to refer to the situation as it is apparently emerging in this country, for I know little about it, except that it is with some horror I think that one finds that the kind of spirit of progress, the kind of spirit of exploration that was so strong in the museum movement here some decades ago and from which people like me learned so much when they started up in the profession in the late forties and the late fifties, that this somehow may now be threatened by a lack of understanding of the fundamental value – political value – of the resources we have.

Now, the subject this afternoon is funding and particularly the impact of corporate funding. I would like to look at funding with some different perspectives. Different sources of fundings that are available and which perhaps are not, certainly in my country and many others, have not been exploited possibly to the extent that they could be. One of the most easy, in a sense, is individual membership. For example, the museum can develop a core of persons throughout the community and its environment who for a very modest sum can be interested in belonging to a museum and contributing to it that small fee every year which allows for certain benefits and particularly a bulletin or information sheet or whatnot.

Now, fund-raising of that kind doesn't produce large amounts that can be put on the balance sheets because much of it is awash, but the result is a nucleus of supporters throughout the community and this can have enormous value, not only in appealing to the public sector, but also to the corporate sector. And, of course, there are the various classes of individual memberships which go from either $15 or $10 or $8 or whatever one might count to the higher levels of membership which can provide then an income which is larger than the cost of keeping the programme in operation and can contribute to the balance sheet.

Now, among these forms of support is corporate memberships. The ordinary corporate membership which may not be very large is, I think, extremely important. First of all one becomes a member of an organization (it generally takes an earthquake or something rather severe for the membership to be dropped) – and secondly it provides the museum with an entry within the corporate establishment. This entry has two advantages: not only is it continuous but also the funding is for general operation. It is not something that the corporate member can target specifically as being of immediate advantage to his firm or any individual of the firm – it is a kind of doing a public good and serving the community.

This is quite distinct from the support of specific projects such as exhibitions, and particularly blockbusters, in which the corporation by definition has a part in the selection. And this part in the selection is most often silent; they generally don't say anything, they profess to be totally uninterested in the subject. But we on our part are very interested in the subject that is going to appeal to this or that kind of company. And so the result of that is that there is, or can be, a loss of independence, a loss of perspective that can lead us to do the things that are popular, to do the things that are going to attract the largest visibility. These may not be the things that are most important either for our institutions or for the furtherance of knowledge.

In my little abstract of some of the things I was going to talk about I mentioned exhibitions on Van Gogh. I don't know how many exhibitions of Van Gogh I have seen: I love Van Gogh, I think he is wonderful, I think he is marvellous, but I think that we have capitalized on his missing ear a little bit too much. And the corporate world has caught hold of that ear and I think the more we give it to it, the more they will want to hold on.

I think that the mechanism by which we can avoid these pitfalls possibly brings us back to my first comments about the importance of the clear definition of what our purposes are and being unswerving in presenting them and defending them.

We obviously have great need for additional support. In my country, there is probably far greater plurality in funding sources than there is anywhere else. And this is due in part, I think, to our peculiar form of government, which has its roots in this particular island but which has been transmuted in such a way that we have absolute balance in the three branches of government. That kind of balance is also found in our institutions. It is found in that peculiar offshoot of this island which is the Smithsonian Institution. This is a federal instrument totally supported by the federal government but to whom the federal government has never suggested that it do this or other things. The reason it doesn't is because within the mechanism of government the Smithsonian has a totally independent status over which none of the branches of government has control, but the ultimate control, at least theoretically, remains in the citizens' Regents who are appointed by joint nomination of the House and the Senate.

Now this kind of balance that we have in the largest members of the museum family, we find it occurring in different ways in other types of museums, whether it is the Metropolitan Museum whose building is owned by the City of New York, whose maintenance is assured in part by the City of New York, while the museum is legally in the private sector, which provides the trustees, the supporters and the private fund-raising effort that maintains a substantial part of the curatorial and research staffs and makes it possible to carry out the research activities and the publications which that museum is so well known for.

It is this kind of balance that I think is important, and it is through this kind of balance that one avoids some of the pitfalls of over-domination from one side or the other.

In the United States we now depend very heavily on corporate support, but this is far less large than anybody thinks. It is substantial in terms of annual memberships and it is extremely visible in terms of support given to major exhibitions. But as has been recently published in the States, there is clear evidence even on the part of those corporations who have played such an enormous role in supporting exhibitions, that these corporations, while they maintain and are indeed totally removed from the selection process, make it quite clear that there are certain kinds of subjects or certain kinds of geography that they would not be interested in supporting. For example, a representative of Mobil has said that they would only be interested in supporting an African exhibition if it dealt with an area of Africa in some way or other in which Mobil was directly involved. IBM has said that they will only support an exhibition in a city in which there is a very major IBM presence, either in terms of manufacturing or more importantly, even, in terms of sales.

And so, to avoid this kind of overemphasis that can be had in terms of the blockbuster through the major support of an exhibition, it seems to me that we need to do much more to sell the idea that the museum is an instrument for the service of the total community and that as part of this community, both in the large and small cities, the company has a role to play to enhance the quality of life for all, at relatively little cost.

Now, the dependency on the blockbuster has been well documented by some of my major colleagues who have been privileged to be in cities large enough to attract the kind of support that I have mentioned.

The Metropolitan Museum, now, and in the words of its past Presidents, present President and present Director, is dependent, to a very large extent, on the gate money that is brought in by these major exhibitions, which are only possible because of the support given by the corporate sector. A museum like the Art Museum in San Francisco faces exactly the same kind of problem but perhaps to an even greater degree. If they don't have the blockbuster they just don't make their budgets.

A museum like the Field Museum in Chicago has begun to rely, ever since King Tut showed the way, more and more on corporate involvement, but there they have managed to achieve this on a yearly basis as part of the overall budget process. I think that this is something that we must definitely, in my country as well as elsewhere, emulate.

I have mentioned the absence of influence on programming with the exception of course of the self-censorship that the museum itself exercises upon its selection of subjects for exhibitions and exhibits. This can be insidious if the process is allowed to repeat itself time and time again, because then the flexibility of the intellectual independence becomes mortgaged for something else. And it is this intellectual independence, this freedom of being able to present different points of view, this freedom of being able to show the unpopular, to extricate those things which are of great importance to society, which may offend this or that segment of the industrial world. But that freedom must be maintained.

Indeed, it must be maintained in all sorts of museums and particularly those museums that are concerned with contemporary, technological and scientific development. Far too often I have walked into a science museum or science and technology centre and seen a glittering exhibit provided by this or that industry that would make one think that this was the only industry, the only company that produced the product or gave this service, and furthermore presents the subject in such a biased way that one is totally incapable even of understanding the technologies involved, let alone understanding its social ramifications.

Few museums that I know of have dealt with the problems of pollution or with the problems of overpopulation or so forth since it is clear that to do those subjects properly would require corporate support and in many cases corporate support would not be available. Although they might now, I don't think that Exxon would have ever considered at the time sponsoring or funding an exhibit on the hazards of the kind of exploitation that has been going on in Alaska. Not that the exploitation of Alaskan oil is not good in itself, but it has consequences and I think it is the role of museums in all their variety to try to demonstrate what are the consequences of past actions, how they affect present life and what impact they may have on the future.

There has been mention, regretfully, of the censorship, as it were, or the weight of government funding in certain parts of the world on the selectivity of what one shows. If there is the kind of diffusion of the funding base that I have alluded to, I think that this, to a great extent, can be avoided. Certainly there are some governmentally funded museums, such as the Smithsonian, that have been able to present very unpopular subjects. I salute them, since I was part of their family and they are doing it far more often now than they did in my day, and so there has been progress. But I think that that progress is based not only upon the changed perception of society and possibly the changed evolving perception of government, but particularly because of the sense of integrity, the sense of research permanence, the sense of dependability, that the institution itself has acquired.

I come from a city (Richmond, Virginia) which was the capital of the Confederacy. Fifteen or twenty years ago it would have been extremely difficult to have an exhibit in my community that would describe in detail the situations that occurred in the nineteenth century and that led to the war between the states. We now have a museum that is doing so. It is doing so and it is doing so with funds that are provided by the private sector, by industries that some years ago never would have thought of doing such a thing. I don't think they are doing it from a sense of penance, or doing it from a sense of moral obligation, as much as they are doing it from a sense that the institution that is presenting these exhibits has achieved a level of intellectual maturity and an intellectual neutrality. The Museum can look the facts in the eye and present them clearly without any advocacy, but rather as elements that are there to make an audience think and to make an audience understand better how it got to be where it is now, and through looking through that part of the telescope, be able to project how much better things could be in the future if those lessons of the past were learned.

And that's indeed the kind of things that I think our museums should do. I think that the necesary partnership can be achieved with industry, with the corporate sector and with the private sector as represented by individual members.

Now, I would like to dispel the notion that the kind of funding that has come to museums from some corporate sectors in the United States has been so large as to solve problems. It certainly has not been, but it is growing. As it has grown – and I am going to come back for a moment to blockbusters and to the very major exhibitions – we have had to pay a price. This is the price of the disruption of regular activity, the price of downgrading in the eyes of the public our own resources, whether those be the resources of the National Gallery, the Metropolitan or any of the major museums.

Our public now is beginning to expect the razzle-dazzle, the things that will attract the full-page advertisements in *Time* magazine (or double-page as Philip Morris generally provides), and I am grateful to them because we appear in those pages quite often and it doesn't do any harm to our image. But the fact is that these major exhibitions do present that other problem, and they are only justifiable in my view if a commensurate effort is made to demonstrate the values of the things that involve ourselves and that we are trying to interpret.

The special exhibition that comes in from outside should be the vehicle through which we stimulate a greater awareness and a greater understanding of the local resources. The local resources are either the institution that hosts the exhibition or those other resources and values which are disseminated throughout the community. And I think that if we do it this way, if we project this, we may have a fall-out effect, in that industry will become more sensitive to the collective need rather than to the individual need.

Discussion

CLAUDE LABOURET: In response to Paul Perrot's paper, I would begin by saying that museums need a leadership with strong beliefs in values and of mission, and they need strong leadership as well as expertise in their scientific or artistic approach. Once again I remind you that I belong to the business community, but I am going to betray the interests of the business community because I think that where the same degree of leadership exists on the side of the museum as well as on the side of the political people, and of the business people you have to speak to, then you will have a fair and well-balanced give-and-take game. You are currently bargaining money against something that business people attach a great value to. When you are speaking to business people don't forget that one way or the other they feel inferior to you socially and intellectually, and what they are buying with their sponsorship money is acceptability in the world of art and culture. They are bargaining for their acceptability and prestige, so I am aware that you are right, Paul Perrot, but I don't think the danger is really very big, if you stand up for what you exist for.

PAUL PERROT: That's why I emphasized at the beginning of my talk the purposes and the vision of what a museum is about. I think that if we are really convinced of this then we have an argument, we have a weapon. We don't need the shilly-shallying that goes on in some places, the willingness to allow our halls to be used for purposes that are totally foreign to all the purposes of the museum institution, the accepting of this or that industrial exhibit because it's free when it may provide very little information and fit very poorly within the whole context of the museum. I think that it is that kind of surrender which is absolutely fatal. It's fatal for the museum director to surrender his values to the Museum Board just as much as it is for the Board to surrender the museum's values to outside pressures.

That doesn't mean that sometimes one doesn't bend, but it seems to me that we expect the same kind of independence that the academic community has. We don't hear these kinds of commercial or similar pressures being applied to universities to the extent that we think they apply to museums. I don't think that university types would stand for it, and I think that we should be exactly the same. And coming back to the university parallel in our earlier conversation it seems to me that the representative from the House of Commons made a very interesting and important comment that museums should ally themselves, not physically but intellectually, with the higher learning establishments. It seems to me that we are the university of the tactile. If we consider ourselves to be outside that broad humanistic fabric then there is no reason why we shouldn't be treated by others as outsiders to that fabric. But we have a flag and I think we should continue to wave it.

PATRICK BOYLAN: I think we are back again to that notorious new entrance to the Los Angeles Science Museum through the Macdonald's hamburger joint. Of course it isn't just a museum entrance sponsored by Macdonald's: what I found offensive was the fact that there is a closed-circuit video link to the computerized chip fryer as well, showing you the wonders of modern food technology according to the Macdonald doctrine. From my viewpoint, if you'll pardon the expression, I found it impossible to stomach that.

BARRY LORD: I think Paul Perrot's comments on the interfaces between museums and the private sector are very well taken, as are the cautions that he offered. These are especially relevant in the UK where there tends to be a kind of rosy picture at the present moment about the way in which sponsorship and other outside funding is being presented as the long-term salvation of museums, not entirely borne out when one is actually working with it. And as Paul says, there is a price to pay for this in terms of outside pressure which does build up over the years, and one begins to see the differences.

One aspect of Paul's comments earlier on reminded me of a significant difference between North American museums and those here in the UK and I think elsewhere as well. This is the tradition in North America of the membership base for the museum, so that we see a museum as actually consisting of a large number of members counted in the thousands or tens of thousands who then elect members to the Board, perhaps not all the members of the Board but certainly there is normally a portion that are elected from the membership. Indeed in some cases all of the Board may come from that membership group, and it gives the membership a very direct role and involvement. Here in the UK the closest that one finds to that are Friends organizations that are sometimes consulted and sometimes involved in the museum in some way, but who don't consider themselves the actual constituency of the museum itself, unlike the typical situation in North America. When one comes to Paul Perrot's point about the importance of corporate membership I think we really don't have a parallel for that in the UK and elsewhere. This seems to be very much a North American phenomenon, that type of membership.

Now it may be that we'll see that approach developing in the UK in the twenty-first century. I'd be interested in hearing comments from British museum directors, whether they see that as something which might be developed or whether it is going to develop out of Friends organizations or not. But certainly in practice it leads to many differences. Even among your independent museums, typically run by a Trust, you have about a dozen members on the Trust but you don't have, typically anyway, a constituency of thousands of members who elect their representatives to sit on the Trust. Even if you have a Friends organization it doesn't exercise that kind of direct constituency, and then you rarely have the North American membership breakdowns of corporate members, family members and so on. So that's a significant difference, and I really don't know at the moment whether that is something that is going to spread to museums outside of North America or whether it is going to remain a North American peculiarity.

The other dimension which one might just touch on, which I don't think has been mentioned yet, is something that our consultancy is seeing very much because we are involved in the planning of new museums in the UK as well as the US and Canada, and that is the mixed-use phenomenon, that is to say where the private and public sector get together to their mutual advantage to develop a new museum or the extension of an existing one. Whether the museum development is funded by Macdonald's in a shopping plaza or sometimes a little more subtly through work with a developer, we have seen situations on the positive side. For example, a museum that was buried in a rather hopeless old building in a neighbourhood where the market potential was extremely limited, was able to sell that property, use the money as their share of the investment in a new property with residential and commercial dimensions to the building, and then became tenants, with a 99-year lease in a new building. These arrangements gave purpose-built facilities that were excellent, so that the museum was able to take much better care of its collections, with a far vaster market potential and sharing with the private sector in the promotion and development of the new site. We see this increasingly in North America and possibilities being explored in the UK. This is a phenomenon that we might just note for now but which is conceivably something that we will see a great deal more of in the twenty-first century.

PATRICK BOYLAN: Sadly, in the UK local government sector that can now only happen in Scotland and perhaps Northern Ireland. Up to March or April 1987 ministers were actually urging local government to go in precisely the direction of joint development and development gain, but on the 14th June that same year the local government minister at half-past-ten at night suddenly banned all such schemes from midnight! Apparently some authority in North London had done some pretty silly things in terms of an assets swop so everyone suffers and now there is no way we can do this any more. Indeed now we have a wonderful situation under the latest government regulations that if a private sponsor gives you a capital gift or a long lease of a new building free of charge the local authority is still deemed to have purchased the freehold value at the full market price as far as its capital spending limits and so on are concerned. Certainly the inconsistency of government policy in relation to precisely this area, to say nothing of similar confusion about tax deduction regimes, etc. has been and remains a problem.

PAUL PERROT: I just wanted to take further a curious phenomenon. As Britain is looking toward us for better ways of doing things, our Treasury seems to be looking towards the UK for ways of doing them differently. The result is that the great cornucopia that had been available to American museums through the tax laws has now become shunken to a tiny little something. Gifts to American museums have dropped 60 per cent as a result of these new tax laws, amd gifts of appreciated properties have gone. I think that again we need to make a very major effort to demonstrate to the public authorities how short-sighted these changes are, because the resources that are given to museums by the private sector are indeed what have made our museums what they are today. They have a tremendously strong economic presence in the cities where they are located, they attract tourism: a major exhibition in New York City may bring in $100 million of extra tourist visits, not to the museum but to the community. What you are saying is what could have been an example for so many is now beginning to lose that quality: this is a strange phenomenon.

PATRICK BOYLAN: I am sure Paul's statement would be regarded as wonderful news only about $2\frac{1}{2}$ miles east of here in Parliament and Government. The government's agenda for its objectives for its second ten years that has been set by ministers recently makes it quite clear that the achievements of Britain in the direction of the philosophy that has become known world-wide as Thatcherism, are to be exported to the rest of the world. The European Community countries ought to know that the British official policy for 1992 has been stated as to enable the rest of the eleven countries in the Community to gain the benefits of our recent achievements in that direction. When I was asked what the British government's position was and I was invited by French colleagues to go and speak on 'Museums and 1992' in Bordeaux just a few weeks ago, I was told that 1992, the open Community market, is an opportunity for the rest of the eleven countries of the Community to adopt the benefits of Thatcherism; and the other 1992 agenda, I was told, is the permanent elimination of Socialism from Europe, which I am sure is something that will go down very well with the socialist governments of Greece and France and one or two other places.

PAUL PERROT: In the USA, in contrast, we think that by 1991 we will have reversed our current trend towards Thatcherism!

LORENA SAN ROMAN: I want to refer to the situation we have in Costa Rica in relation to not only the culture of the museum but also in our national parks and conservation. What we do is that the government defines with us a national strategy. It began to work about three years ago and really we had been very excited about this. What we have been doing is to create private fund-raising foundations for the museums, and one for the national parks, and the government approved this. So we are obtaining money from abroad, and the government have put its money towards these outside dollars. For the first five years we receive the interest on this fund, and after five years we receive finally the actual dollars. In this way we are receiving money from the European Community, from other developed countries, and from private enterprise. They support two main lines: education and conservation, so the museums can go into both education and conservation while the national parks concentrate on conservation.

Also, to make things easier for American supporters, we created the Foundation of Costa Rica in Washington so that private supporters and all the foundations of the US that give the aid to foundations in Costa Rica can do so with tax deduction in the United States, whereas giving money directly in the beginning was not tax-deductible. I think that Costa Rica in the last three years and especially in the year after the Nobel Peace Prize, has obtained a lot of money from the developed countries in relation to ecology, education and conservation. Also, because of this, the private enterprises of Costa Rica are beginning to think seriously about the aid that they need to give to the education and conservation areas.

VICTOR MIDDLETON: I was just thinking that possibly among the audience here, one of the key issues is how do you start to achieve some element of sponsorship or a greater element of sponsorship than you've got already. How do you get some of the benefits which Paul Perrot described and perhaps above all, how do you minimize the fact that there are probably some constraints and fund-raising costs associated with it?

I thought I would make a couple of comments on this, because whilst there are exceptions, typically if you look at museums whether independent or in the public sector, all their needs usually intermingle: their revenue needs, their capital needs, the needs of the collection, and the opportunities associated with capital revenue and collection usually intermingle. What you end up with is a feeling that at the end of the day there is a prospective shortfall, or there is a lot the museums could do if they had some more money. Sponsorship is often approached as a way to get an injection into the existing budget in order to make it work for another year or two. Well, if you start from there, and again I am agreeing with others on the panel, I suspect you may be doomed to failure. You can't make an effective argument for sponsorship unless you divide the two streams of the museum business into their cost and revenue components. It is a good discipline anyway and by that I mean looking at the collection first and foremost, to determine what are the minimum levels of cost simply to maintain its integrity, the minimum level to provide safe access and the minimum level to display and interpret. And once you have identified those you can proceed to the opportunities for new developments, and some of the things I think Neil Cossons was talking about earlier on.

If you then look at that other stream, which is defining the new capital and the revenue streams to the extent that they are open to you, be it through admission charges if you have them or trading if you have it, I think you can then define and draw up a prospective list of sponsorship opportunities. If you have such a list, at least you have got a background on which you can construct an argument: it's the same business in the sense that if you went to a bank for a loan you'd expect to be asked for some information as to what you are going to do with it and so forth.

I actually think that over the next decade the social consciences of businesses will be there to be tapped if the argument is strong enough, and I think museums do have a couple of very powerful assets on their side. One of them is their identification with particular places. They make unique contributions to certain locations, and if that is a location shared by a particular business then you can tap a community conscience to develop income which can be used in ways which you can determine. So I believe strongly that if you have a plan which in any other field would be called a business plan, and have a clear view as to what you would do with this sponsorship, you won't avoid all the pitfalls that you mention, but you would be well on the way to a start, and I do believe that this conscience, morality if you like, is actually there to be exploited.

DONALD HORNE: Just a small point to take up and extend slightly the suggestion that Paul Perrot made that there might be more co-operation between universities and museums. I think that idea could be further extended.

Several years ago in Australia, a series of what you might describe as conservative red-neck backbenchers in the opposition party had something of a guerrilla attack against grants being given to university people, to artists and to scientists. This was quite successful and they felt quite pleased about it, but it did them a certain amount of damage. On this occasion what was most notable was that none of the scientists spoke up for the artists or the academics, and the academics didn't speak up for the scientists or the artists and so forth, although all had in that context a community of interest. I support very much indeed your suggestion that universities and museums should look to their common areas of interest, and I would simply say that you should add to this also scientists, general intellectuals and artists of all kinds. All of these groups of people are actually in the business of creativity, appealing to the imagination, conceptualizing, and of creating alternative realities through which we exist as human beings. Yet to hear them speak, often to mention the kindred groups by name is to be abusive: 'academic', can be used by museum people, scientists and artists as a derogatory term, and a university might boast 'We're not a museum.' I don't know about the experience in other countries, but certainly this can be one of the most destructive areas at a time when people are going through all these money problems, fiddling around thinking they know how to manage economies. These people have interests which are so clearly similar that they should not be so concerned with exploring their dissimilarities.

IAN SPERO: I want to make a few points.

First, some of you in museums may not be aware that when you talk of social conscience, and appeal to an organization's social conscience, because you want to tap into that budget for social funding, most of the bigger companies you are talking about in the UK who are known to sponsor big events have two budgets, especially the banks, in some cases the building societies. They have a budget which is for social concerns and conscience, and the money is distributed according to the panel who are in charge of distributing that money. The same might be true of a very large oil company – it's still a decision-making process, and the decision might depend on who you know, and of course if you are a big London museum you are more likely to know more people with the relevant power than if you are a regional museum, but I think we are still talking about a nationwide problem.

Then business organizations have the other budget, which is the marketing budget. That in turn is broken into above and below the line. Above the line is TV and the other kinds of visible things you see, posters etc., while below the line would be things like direct mail, public relations and image enhancement. In order to tap into that budget you'll have to speak to the company in a language they understand, which is about communication. I think that that's the common denominator here: if you wish to communicate with the public, you also wish to communicate with business. Business in turn wants to communicate with the public and they can do it via museums.

Since my company has been involved with museums here, we have received on a regular basis sponsorship proposals from museums. They've done their work and they've written down the sponsorship benefits and the prize you will get for your money. But this is not enough because if every museum and gallery out there were to send these proposals out to all the companies in the land you would still not get the funding that is required to maintain the country's museums from the sponsorship. It's more a question of understanding what the business requires in return. A problem that we have encountered with museums in the UK is a lack of interest in marketing: there are very few museums and galleries in the UK who really care about marketing. It's not intellectual, and marketing is a dirty word in some cases, which is quite naïve.

Comparing America with the UK and comparing like with like, and assuming we could make certain US-type programmes work in the UK, you still won't ever get the same kind of reaction here because the public's perception of museums is totally different from the public's perception of museums in North America; young people go to museums in North America. Young people enjoy going to museums in North America. It's easy to buy tickets: you actually have tickets. I was surprised to find that when I wanted to see an exhibition at an American museum I had to buy a ticket which specified the time that I had to actually go to that museum and when I got to the museum I was told which door to go in and I was directed around the museum in a manner which I didn't have to think about too hard. It was pleasant, I didn't keep on walking into dead-end streets and it was a very pleasant experience.

Now that might all sound very 'so what?'. The point I am coming to is I think the core problem in the United Kingdom, and one which really should be solved, if you want to acquire the sponsorship, because sponsorship isn't the beginning of the commercial contribution. The beginning is that companies have to be happy that they can actually communicate with their target market via museums and galleries. We are involved in quite a lot of cultural sponsorship – we do a lot with orchestras – and know that they are more comfortable working with orchestras, because business understands orchestras. Orchestras have a different image, and I think that museums in the UK should use Museums Year as a catalyst for a similar change of image. It's just a start – we are changing perceptions very slowly, but it's a big job to do.

I feel there should be an industry-wide public relations campaign following on from Museums Year. Instead of everybody being very concerned about their own individual institution, which is fair enough, there should be a gathering together and a force to actually make 'museum' a good word, and to make people want to go to museums, to make young people want to go to museums, one of the primary objectives of course of Museums Year. In short, I am saying there should be in the United Kingdom a fully-fledged effort to communicate with the general public and let them know what is behind the doors of museums and galleries. More galleries and museums should have marketing expertise, and it may be possible to get the private sector to help you there, sponsorship or secondment to support a marketing person within an institution. I think creativity and a combined strength in marketing effort is what is called for. I can only talk for the UK and this is just, as I say, an outsider's observation.

PAUL PERROT: One comment was made earlier about the membership in American museums voting for members of the Board. There are some museums where this happens but it is by no means prevalent in the circumstances that I know.

The Metropolitan Museum, the Toledo Art Museum, my own museum in Richmond, may have 16,000 or more museum members each, but they do not vote except through their presence in the museum, and the comments that they make about this or that part of the activities.

One aspect that I think is extremely strong in our country, and again is based upon historic precedent, is voluntarism. Our museums have enormous numbers of volunteers who assist in many, many ways in providing an interface to the public as well as assisting in curatorial and other departments. Now this is free labour, this is given labour, this is wonderful labour because it is given from the heart, not necessarily from a social visibility. But it does have another great advantage. It provides another way of infiltrating various aspects of the community. For example, among our volunteers in the Virginia Museum we have the wives of presidents of some of the major banks and several of our major companies (some in the Fortune 500). These ladies are behind the information desk regularly, providing services for a morning and an afternoon a month or being in the sales shop (which they run entirely themselves by the way, and that sales shop produces over $\$\frac{1}{4}$ million profit that is given to the museum every year). But this is voluntarism and I think that we should not say that this is a totally United States phenomenon.

I think that as the population world-wide grows older, as we get more interested in the so-called leisure time that I have been hearing about ever since I came into the museum world, the great challenge is going to be leisure time for the masses as well of course the managers. Of course perhaps the masses don't have any leisure time, because most members of the family have to work to make a living these days, even at the managerial level. But this aspect of voluntarism has enormous promise in many parts of the world and I would think that it would have particular promise in this country, and I don't believe it is particularly prevalent at the moment. And I would think that this would be something to look at in the twenty-first century.

As to the other aspects of money making, there is of course the museum shop, and as some of us saw last night in the Science Museum a beautifully conceived shop that was strategically located and one didn't feel trapped by it. They had a superb selection of books and it was totally comp-lementary to the Museum, providing the kind of intellectual continuity to whatever had been stimulated by a visit to the Science Museum. Certainly these are aspects of fund-raising that can be exploited as long as they are done with a clear view of the guiding star, and not to become waylaid into stocking the kind of products that have nothing to do with whatever goes on in the museum.

The museum is being used by industry or by corporate sponsors as a place for entertaining: in the United States a corporate member of a museum can be entitled to use a part or all of the facility once a year for an event. This can be very disruptive unless it is properly controlled, but it is also a source of income and it is a source also of disseminating the values of the museum to sometimes enormously wealthy people who have all sorts of degrees of experience, who have never even set foot in the place, but who will come in for the first time on account of the corporate hospitality event.

The counterpart of that – the downside as we say – is that we must make a similar effort to attract other segments of the population and make them feel that they too can have entertainment at the museum, that is to arrange an open house from time time to time where a fruit juice is given for free and where one can bring the family and spend an evening. Unless this is done then the museum falls back into the trap of exclusivity and becoming the province of certain social segments, and that is something that I think we all agree we need to counteract. Our primary interest should be to reach those that haven't been reached by the museum before, to give them a greater sense of perspective, a sense of life, a sense of place within the scheme of things, in the sense of what they were or might have been and what they can draw from that.

VICTOR MIDDLETON: To support Paul Perrot's view and in fact to slightly disagree with a point that Mr Spero made, because the evidence that I see which staggered me most (so I checked it half a dozen times before I used it), is that the group that doesn't seem to be going to museums to anything like the extent of the others are the over-50s. I originally assumed it would be the other way round. But in fact it's a third of the under-24s that visit museums once a year, a third of the 25–34s, it drops at the moment to about one in five of the over-55s and it drops to not much more than one in ten of the over-65s. Now that's an extraordinary finding. That's true in this country across a whole range of museums, so the problem is to bring in the active, affluent, totally indifferent over-50-year-olds (an age-range that includes some of us on this panel!) and get them to volunteer and play their part. This must be a major marketing consideration, to work out how you do that, but it is a big opportunity.

GEOFFREY LEWIS: In direct response to that, if you examine the UK attendance figures five years ago you will find that the drop-off then was at 45. It is now at 50. I think this is very encouraging.

PATRICK BOYLAN: It's the same people: they are not going now, and didn't go five years ago!

KATHY ZEDDE (Conference participant): I represent one of the provincial museums in Canada. I would like to draw attention to two aspects of corporate funding or corporate sponsorship that we have been experiencing in Canada. I would be interested afterwards, because there are a lot of different countries represented on the panel, to find out whether or not the same has been experienced and how they dealt with it. The first point is the fact that a lot of museums in Canada are very excited about the prospect of corporate sponsorship and are treating it as the flavour of the month etc., but upon further examination many have already come up against a brick wall and have had to discount the prospect of any kind of corporate sponsorship. This is largely because the nature of Canadian geography and the Canadian economy means that there are huge parts of Canada that are completely rural at the moment and will remain so. In these areas larger corporations simply don't exist or they don't feel it would be worth their while in terms of exposure to sponsor a new type of endeavour by museums. Museums in those more rural areas of Canada really are still floundering in their efforts to try to find plural funding.

The second cautionary note about corporate sponsorship concerns the ramifications of which corporations they choose or select to sponsor endeavours such as exhibits. The particular example I am thinking of happened in Canada in a museum which I was involved with there – the

Discussion

Glenbow Museum in Calgary. It sought corporate sponsorship to mount a major exhibit to coincide with the Winter Olympics. Because of the nature of the economy in that province, which is based almost exclusively on the oil industry, they selected a large oil company to be the corporate sponsor for that exhibit. Unfortunately that particular company operates in an area occupied by a native group that was involved in land-claim disputes with the government. The exhibit was then criticized by that group for selecting that particular sponsor, and a huge boycott grew up surrounding that exhibit and threatened its existence. So I think that the ramifications in terms of public perception as to who museums choose to sponsor their endeavours is something that museums have to keep in mind when they look at corporate sponsorship.

So I would be interested to hear whether or not any of these types of situations have occurred in any of the countries represented on the panel and if anyone has any advice for museums who find themselves in this sort of situation.

MYFANWY HORNE (Conference participant, Australia): I come from Australia and I visit a lot of museums, and there always comes a moment in an illuminating and interesting conference such as this one when somebody has to say: 'Yes, but...' I have got some anxieties and I suppose the way that I would like to examine them would be to start looking at objectivity, objects and curatorial responsibility. But to start off with I would like to make a very subjective statement. That is that I believe in the idea of museums.

Now, everybody in this room believes in the idea of museums, otherwise I presume they wouldn't be here. But I am old enough to have had the sort of history training which presented to me the idea of the Dark Ages and that saint who sat on a rock: he had a large book in front of him and he was protecting knowledge as the hoards swept in, kept only away from him by the water that surrounded his island. I think that there have been various bits of the Dark Ages moving around the discussion of the idea of the museum that has taken place today, not least the fact that there is the concern about sponsorship, and what sort of sponsorship you can have, and what sort of demands are made upon you as far as sponsorship goes.

One point that Paul Perrot made, and it was one that has been given serious consideration as we have been examining these issues, is how do you provide for the other side of the objects? The Science Museum where we were last night presents, to me, a wonderfully optimistic view of the machine: but as Paul Perrot pointed out there is another side. This is an important side in terms of looking at the year 2000 and beyond that, and in terms of what communities want. You have said this in terms that I would use myself: we are living in a world that uniquely understands the possibility of technological consequences. In fact it is almost medievally religious in the terms of understanding that Hell is polluted water, or Hell is plastics that won't go away, and I really think that museums do have a very strong responsibility to provide the alternative view.

If museums are anything, they're not organizations gathering in large numbers of people, operating within the tyranny of the audience turnover: they still remain organizations which are there to be temples of enlightenment. They are there so that people can go along and look at them either as viewers or research them as scholars in order to find out things which will perhaps make life in the future more as we would want it to be than it has been in the past. I think this is a very important function of museums.

To move on to objects now: Barry Lord has made this point, but if anyone is going to be involved with museums they have to have a real passion for objects. Other people have tried to redefine the word passion, but I think passion is a good word and we could perhaps stick with it. But what are objects? In themselves they are nothing. Objects in museums present craftsmanship, the ideas of human ingenuity, genius, patterns of our social and cultural history, but they are not if they are just presented as a chair or a carriage or as a steam-engine or something: then they communicate nothing. They are there in order to stimulate people to think of them being fashioned by human people, and I would like to extend the idea of objects. It seems to me that in talking about our cultural heritage, museums, with their concern for the object, leave out an enormous quantity of what our cultural heritage is, and this really does worry me. As somebody that has a passion for words rather than objects, though I can find a sort of passion for objects in me as well, it seems to me that there are vast resources that museums should be using: they are resources of our literature.

For example, I don't know how an ethnographic museum can put on a display of Japanese culture without letting people know that Japan has a very long literary history. In fact in the tenth century they were writing the sort of novels that Jane Austen was writing in England in the eighteenth century. I don't know how you could put on in a War Museum an exhibition of the First World War without having poems of Siegfried Sassoon and some of the other War poets. I think there is a real reason for seeing words and extracts from novels as being part of objects themselves, that should be up on walls along with other objects. They should be there in order to make people realize that there are other aspects of culture apart from the object. I have this passion for the word; other

Discussion

people have passion for music and for other aspects of what are considered our cultural arts, and I think they all have a real place in our museum culture.

The other aspect that I was going to talk about is curatorial responsibility and I think that I have said something about this in terms of trying to present both sides of the story, and I shall end with a short anecdote on this. Some time ago in Sydney there was an exhibition put on by a British pharmaceutical firm which was about medicine from witch-doctors to general practitioners, something like that. And there were various objects. In order to give it an Australian content there was a little bit about the First Fleet and how good the medicine had been on the First Fleet. There was a roneod sheet that told parties what the First Fleet was and I read through the sheet and thought: 'That's rather strange: First Fleet, 13,000 people. They would need high-rise tents to accommodate that number of people.' In fact there were only about 1,300 people in the First Fleet. So I raised this point with somebody, and out of curiosity I went back a week later and picked up the sheet, and there was still this 13,000. It was a misprint, something which we all do ourselves all the time – but nevertheless it was an extraordinarily gross error in terms of what was being handed out to schoolchildren. This seemed to me to be a basic curatorial responsibility: if you are going to put on a not very good exhibition you should at least check all the way through that all the information that is going to be given out is right.

KATE THAXTON (Conference participant, Museum of Richmond): I want to say first of all that I am not anti-sponsorship in any way. I come from a museum which was set up partly with sponsorship money and we have a gallery run by volunteers, most of whom I think are over 50.

However, having gone through that experience I do have grave concerns about how much sponsorship is expected to do in museums at the moment. There does seem to be a common feeling among many people on the management side of museums that they could probably do more than I think they should. The baseline of the museum is its collection, the curators' research of that collection, and the custodianship of those objects. What a sponsorship economy in museums is going to bring about, I think, is a much more selective view of what the museum can do. Basically, it would mean you have to get as many people through the door as possible. Really, what sponsorship can do is be the icing on the cake as far as possible, and allow us to do things that otherwise we would not be able to do, with the other regular money we have.

Profit and museums 2

10

Options and unique commercial opportunities for museums now and in the future

Frans Verbaas

Almost ten years ago now, coming from the business community, I was appointed to my present post with the Museum Year Pass Foundation (MYP for short). Founded by the Dutch Museum Association and the Ministry of Cultural Affairs, we, as an autonomous and non-subsidized organization, concentrate on stimulating visits to the Dutch museums. The issue, or sales as the case may be, of the MYP through about 500 museums and national tourist offices is one of the methods which we apply, besides regular promotional campaigns via the press, television programmes, radio programmes, television spots and numerous *ad hoc* activities like organizations of the National Museum Weekend, these again are some of the items we are using to stimulate the museum visits.

In funding these promotional activities we are financially supported by the sponsor of the Foundation, that is to say the Robeco Group Investment Company in Rotterdam. Yearly, we have about 250,000 cardholders using the Pass. The gross annual turnover rose in 1988 to about 6 million guilders which is nearly £2 million, I think. This amount – and that is one of the most important things and I think also one of the things which makes our Foundation special – we pay out to the museums associated with us after, of course, the deduction of the running expenses.

Ten years ago I was appointed by the executive committee of the MYP Foundation which then, and also now, could be described as progressive: progressive in a large number of areas, among others in the area of commercial activities. Yet, by these very same people I was regarded as a stranger in the company – we say as a strange duck in the water but I don't think that is proper English. I did not have a museological background but a financial-economic one, supplemented by diversified training and courses in the fields of marketing and public relations. As a matter of fact, I shall never forget that in the final round of interviews, in which I found myself with another candidate, the president of the Dutch Museum Association asked me whether I ever visited museums. My answer then was: 'Well, no sir, but if you will appoint me now then you can imagine that I will certainly do that from today on.' I am sure you can imagine that the majority of the staff members of the museums in those days probably had developed even worse impressions about me.

Coming from the business community, where broadly speaking the question in the end still is a matter of economic objectives such as profit, increase of market share and, to take another example, competitiveness, it quickly became clear to me that these were subjects about which little or nothing at all was known within the museum sector. Indeed, it was rather unseemly or 'not done' to think about these kinds of questions, let alone discuss them among each other openly. That is only logical because the majority of the Dutch museums, and I assume it is not only in Holland but also in this country and in other countries of the world, were financed by the various givers of subsidies such as the state, province and municipality. There was a healthy national economic climate, and culture, especially our museums, flourished as never before.

Nearly ten years on, the executive committees of the museums, at least in the Dutch situation, now spend a large part of their time on talks about possible privatization, financing the budget, raising revenues or the number of museum-goers as the case may be, and similar matters. In other words, the executive committees of museums talk and think almost daily about those matters which only ten years ago hardly were reflected on, or about which thoughts were rarely exchanged. In a way the next century is already here where options and unique commercial opportunities are concerned. And, you will understand, in this new framework I have not been a stranger in the company for a long time now.

In the Netherlands visits to museums have increased enormously over the last few years. In 1985 the museums were visited by about 15 million visitors, in 1986 the number increased to 18 million and in 1987 visits rose to a record number of 19 million. The figures for 1988 are not yet known, but expectations are that the 1987 number of visitors will be reached again. The number of MYPs issued by the organization is also an example of that. I have already mentioned the number to you annually, and this is now about 250,000. This is in contrast with other forms of cultural expressions like performing arts, drama and cinema attendance. For that increasing interest, numerous explanations can be found: people, either involuntarily or not, have at their disposal ever-increasing leisure time, the media are capable of raising a lot of public interest, and the education services' pursuit of helping young people cross the threshold of the museum at an early age is paying off.

But there is more. It is astonishing that such a large number of the public choose the museum out of the varied offerings of entertainment and information. It is remarkable that the exhibit keeps its footing in the flood of media. The real exhibit apparently has a magical effect, on account of which it is impossible to replace the museum collection by reproductions and copies 'indistinguishable from the originals'. The exhibit arouses emotions which vary from an ostentatious tantrum leading to the destruction of a work of art, to quiet aesthetic pleasure. How topical ostentatious tantrums are, many a person in The Netherlands, and possibly a number of you, were recently able to observe when a number of seventeenth-century masterpieces in the Dordrecht Museum were destroyed by a visitor.

The exhibit lends extra support to the imaginative powers where a representation of a culture from somewhere else or the past is concerned. The exhibit arouses romantic feelings which can lead to considerable financial sacrifices, such as is shown for instance when a shipload (which happened two years ago) of common china was sold at an auction for extremely high prices just because it came from a shipwreck of the East India Company. The exhibit is a carrier of information which keeps its footing amidst the gigantic supply of information which television, radio and various periodicals pour out over us daily.

In order not to go under, modern man must shield himself against an over-abundance of information. Apparently the exhibit succeeds in piercing that protective shield. Museums keep those objects. It is the task of the museums to keep objects in good condition and to preserve them. This preserving need not occur in an ivory tower, but can take place under the eyes of a varied public.

And that brings me to my subject: 'Options and unique commercial opportunities for museums now and in the future'. Don't accept from me that I can tell you in twenty or thirty minutes how to earn money, which way you have to work, but I think it is good when I try to explain that there are some conditions which have to be met within the museum, within the organization, which make it possible to operate successfully. Before being able to employ the museum successfully in aid of the purposes of commercial objectives, a number of basic conditions ought to have been met, of which I shall elucidate two.

Firstly (and most of them have already been talked about yesterday and today) is that the museums ought to be able to get down to their original tasks, that is to say the function to collect, the function to preserve (among which I include conservation and restoration), the function to document or, to put it differently, the scientific treatment of the museological collection, not only for the sake of those objects, but to make those objects function so that a museum can meet what in my opinion is its primary objective: to confront man with his own existence. A director of a museum in Northern France once said: 'A people that doesn't know its past will not know its future.' The fourth function of museum presentation also fits into the framework.

As far as I am concerned those, conditionally, are points of departure in order to be able to carry out other activities. This will also notably be of importance when we look to the situation as from 1992, that is the Europe of 1992. (I understand yesterday from Patrick Boylan that currently England isn't co-operating that much in relation to the Europe 1992, but on the other side of the North Sea we still think there will be a Europe of 1992 – an integrated European Community). What that exactly entails is not equally clear to everybody. It means that we will transfer our economic and our political sovereignty to supranational and inter-governmental bodies at a quicker pace. The inevitable and unavoidable consequence of this will be that, at the end of the integration, we will only be able to propagate our national identity by means of our cultural identity – the museum will be the guardian of our own cultural heritage and thereby of our own identity. And, once again, the scientific treatment in its broadest sense of the collection is of essential importance.

Secondly, and also other speakers talked about it yesterday and today, the internal organization or the management within the museum sector ought to be adapted to the present-day situation. This means that the concepts which I just mentioned to you, to wit market share, competitiveness, staff policy and other concepts from business administration must not be unknown to the executive committee of a museological institution. This will not be easy to achieve because obviously, let us be honest, old museums just never have been confronted with management problems.

Of the present generation of directors and staff members of the museums, often very highly educated but only in areas such as history, history of art, classical languages and anthropology, one cannot expect them to master these matters from one day to the next. The education they received definitely gives no cause for that, aside even from the fact that managing an organization also requires a certain mentality.

When we speak of options and unique commercial opportunities then we are in fact also speaking of the corporate culture of the museum sector, which ought to be adapted to the present-day situation. By your leave, I would like to elaborate on that. The concept of culture has many descriptions and meanings. Whenever the culture of an organization is spoken of then probably nobody will want to have a further specification of the concept but would wish one of the description we provide, or, as the case may be, of the contents of that culture. In this framework culture is often described as the 'common values' which an organization holds. The clearer the corporate culture, the clearer the identity of the company and the stronger the staff member feels, or is able to feel, connected to the objectives and activities of the organization. Corporate culture and personal objectives can then grow more towards each other. In situations in which no clear corporate culture exists, or when within the organization it is a question of several cultures, an identification problem will quickly arise for the staff members.

They cannot test their personal objectives and make them conform to the common values of the organization. The personal values and objectives will differ from one staff member to another so that differences of opinion are going to arise at the level of personal opinions and values. And that is more or less the present situation in a large number of museological institutions. There is a need for the organization to change, for the temple of culture to change to a market-orientated organization, while maintaining the original tasks of the museum.

The process by which one reorientates a company towards a market has been compared with teaching an elephant to dance. Both are difficult, cost a lot of time, demand a lot of attention and sometimes lead to a limited result. Because, once we get this elephant dancing, many will be moved, but few will praise the elegance of the dance steps. A number of conditions are also attached to any change of corporate culture, of which I would like to mention a few to you.

Firstly, the so-called 'top-down' approach. In this, change in culture starts with the executive committee which will have to spread, or, as the case may be, radiate it to the rest of the organization. The management ought to give the example itself.

If one wishes to make use of commerce, then one will also have to behave in this manner. For instance, and it is a very logical one, if one wishes to emphasize that the customer – that is the visitor to your museum – is always right, then the director shall have to vacate his parking space directly next to the entrance for visitors and will himself have to be satisfied with a space at the edge of the car park. The management must be the personification of the new corporate culture.

Secondly, acceptance by staff members. The changing of a culture within an organization can almost never be a one-man operation. The staff members will have to actively co-operate, have to endorse, have to work together and assist propagation.

Thirdly, changing is difficult. Every change will have to take into account the fact that first one must unlearn the old, or, more subtly put, the old must be integrated into the new, before one can acquire new principles. To unlearn is more difficult because many think that they will be accused or that they were previously doing things wrong. Moreover, it holds that the corporate culture is usually composed of many aspects and that the implementation of a change requires a multidisciplinary approach. One cannot leave it to the head of the finance department or the head of the personnel department. It requires a combined approach. For those who will attend the ICOM general meeting in The Hague in August/September of this year, a special assembly within the scope of the multidisciplinary approach will be organized, partly on the initiative of the Secretary of the MYP Foundation and former chairman of the CECA Committee of ICOM (Committee for Education and Cultural Action).

Fourthly, new values cause uncertainty. The acquisition of new values and new behaviour leads to loss of certainty. This phenomenon can occur particularly in the somewhat older co-workers. They shall turn away or, alternatively, resignedly submit to the changes. They say: 'Oh, present practice will last my time – I will retire within a year.'

In respect to these points I can give you a practical, and in my opinion, good example of a project that partially failed because a number of the points of departure drawn up just now were not complied to. Half-way through 1986, on the initiative of the Dutch National Tourist Office, 1988 was proclaimed as a so-called 'Year of Emphasis', and 'Holland, Land of Museums' at that. A number of organizations participated directly in this initiative, including the Dutch Museum Association and the MYP Foundation, albeit that the Dutch Museum Association and the MYP Foundation were already having second thoughts at the time. The intention was that the Dutch museums were to point out their existence to the public in 1988 by means of special exhibitions based on some seven themes, supplemented by museum flags, with courses for museum employees who afterwards could thereby operate in a more customer-friendly manner.

A marketing and public relations model, worked out by the National Tourist Office which also had already been applied to 'Holland, Land of Water' and 'Holland, Land of Music', was superimposed on the museums and on 1 January 1988 the 'Year of Emphasis' was festively opened in the presence of the Dutch Prime Minister. Well over 500 museums were to put in an appearance during 1988. I shall not elaborate too much on this promotional action but I can tell you that, aside from an incidental success, the results were broadly speaking disappointing because the Dutch National Tourist Office didn't have sufficient (or perhaps any) knowledge in the framework of culture and of museums in particular. No, almost no account was taken of the corporate culture of the museums, with the fact that the museums are not univocal and simple, but pluriform and complex. I shall touch on this again later.

To speak of options and unique commercial opportunities is to speak of corporate culture. But it is also to speak of marketing, and it will not have escaped your notice that there has been much grappling concerning the typification of marketing. Perhaps in the end the clearest definition is the once again revised version of the American Marketing Association: 'Marketing is the process of planning and executing the conception of ideas, goods and services to create exchanges that satisfy individual and organizational objectives.'

That much grappling has occurred about the definition is not only attributable to the fact that marketing is a relatively new concept. It is even more attributable to the growing awareness that the focus is no longer on the supplier but on the interaction of the supplier and the consumer instead. This was also mentioned today.

In the business sector, marketing is completely integrated. In softer sectors, including the museum sector, 'marketing-mindedness' is catching on, often under pressure from funds drying up and competition personally experienced. Central government and local government, whether hesitantly or not, pull their own weight. It is thus that one already speaks of 'city marketing', 'public private enterprise', and privatization piles on even more and suddenly confronts people who had until recently lived in a marketingless era with angles, starting-points and aims which to them are brand new and of a different nature. Grosso modo, the cultural sector adopted and still adopts a cautious and sometimes even aloof attitude.

A fundamental view of the relationship between culture and marketing has – to this day – not been developed. In the world of culture the fear still lives that upon embracing marketing, culture is reduced to a pack of washing powder. At the time it was probably also not really necessary for the culture in my country to reflect on marketing. The interest in and the demand for museums began to develop almost autonomously, successfully, visits increased and the financial situation did not yet give all too much cause for concern. The financial pressure which is experienced today has not yet presented itself in a powerful way.

Now, it is not the case that I am saying that nothing was done in the area of marketing and commerce within the museum sector. But I am saying that there was barely any fundamental action based on marketing-mindedness and based on a marketing-orientated mentality to speak of – even today.

The thought that one is practising marketing when one lets the canteen or organizes 'La Grande Parade' (which was a very huge exhibition to mark the departure of Mr De Wilde from the State Museum in Amsterdam a few years ago) is a misunderstanding. Marketing is founded on a number of cornerstones. The most important are: thinking and acting with the consumer in mind and adjusting supply to the wishes, and considering the needs and expectations of, the public in order that an optimal interaction is effected between supply and demand and between supplier and customer. What is also essential is that there is some consistency to speak of, a co-ordinated aggregate of activities and a command of the instruments of marketing, of the marketing mix, to the fullest possible extent.

The Americans attribute four elements to the marketing mix (four is more easy to remember than nine, I think!) and moreover, saw to it that all four started with a 'p' – so that it couldn't be easier. Product, price, place and promotion, together form the illustrious quartet. Repeated attempts to expand the number of p's were warded off by a shield of determination. An imminent aspect of marketing is that it is not an isolated, not an independent entity. Marketing is strongly interlaced with business management or, alternatively, organizational management. One who places the marketing ruler next to culture cannot be certain that what have up to now been cursory ventures have taken place between marketing and culture. Broadly speaking the world of culture still does not excel in thinking and acting with the public in mind, although I now make haste to say that within the Dutch museum sector, and undoubtedly also in your country and in the United States, evident progress has been made in this over the past few years. Relating to this, I was still very surprised yesterday evening to see in the Science Museum that they have a special Press Room – the first that I have seen in a museum in my life.

The key question then, as far as I am concerned, is whether culture and marketing, as widely interpreted, culture and its unique commercial opportunities can and must share the front door. In order to be able to give an answer to this, the boundaries have to be defined first, and only then – perhaps – lifted or, alternatively, to be shifted. Let us try to go through the matter systematically to some degree. I just said to you that the project 'Holland, Land of Museums' failed in part because it was not realized that culture, our museums, are not the same as 'Holland, Land of Water' and 'Holland, Land of Music'. For a start, we cannot and we may not generalize. Culture, the museums, are not univocal and simple, they are pluriform and complex.

Even the best fine-tooth comb will only help us a part of the way. In my opinion, the largest common denominators do not exist in culture. There are too many forms of culture and cultural institutions with backgrounds, intentions, significance and publics which are too varied. Fassbinder cannot be reconciled with Van Focquenbroch, a cinema club with a film museum, Amsterdam with London or York with Cardiff.

We cannot generalize, so it is difficult, if not impossible, to pronounce a general opinion. Perhaps it would be a good thing to commission a research institute to substantially investigate the area of tension between culture and marketing, supported by people involved from the academic community and from the field, from culture, marketing and communication and by research, including qualitative research and public opinion research.

So, you will hear no pro-marketing plea from me today, in general terms, and most definitely no missionary role. What keeps me from doing this is my understanding of the exceptional, vulnerable way in which culture figures and ought to figure in our lives and in society. This is not to say that I would begrudge the museums a large and increasing public. On the contrary, daily I do nothing but make it clear to people that visiting museums is a must. But the spiritual values incorporated into culture give cause for caution. Those values may under no circumstances be devalued. Not much imagination is needed to recognize that a commercialization of culture, of museums, possibly fired by unsuitable marketing activities, could promote the sort of erosion of values which is not desired.

Culture, on the other hand, ought to attempt to become as broadly based in society as possible, but not at its own expense. That is, museums ought to try to acquire as many visitors as possible, but not, again, at the expense of their standards and values. The autonomy of culture, authenticity and integrity may under no circumstances be reduced. The intrinsic values and the significance of culture, of museological institutions, are, however, widely divergent. That is why the answer to the question whether we should involve ourselves in marketing, or what the options and the unique

Options and unique commercial opportunities

commercial opportunities are, need to be individual ones for the time being. That will not be easy.

Firstly, the process of deliberation ought to occur honestly, without prejudices and fear in respect of marketing and commerce. Furthermore, the phenomenon of marketing has to be viewed in the correct proportion and in its entirety, including any possible consequence for the artistic supply, for the product and for the 'assortment'. It will have to be checked to see whether and to what extent the museums can bear a marketing operation. A practical problem in forming an opinion and in decision-taking is that within the museum sector there is still too little marketing affinity and know-how available, while in the marketing world and in commerce in general little feeling for and understanding of culture exists.

I am not saying that the museums ought to leave everything as it is. They cannot afford to do so, if only because they are being confronted to an increasing degree with the marketing activities of others, such as sponsors for instance.

Besides marketing, there is also the issue of public relations which did, and sometimes still does, provide piecemeal information at a high level of abstraction. Other means of communication, including advertising, were hardly given a chance. A warm tie, a strong bond with the public and supporters, is still not pursued enough. Announcements are made but there is no communication and motivation; partly due to lack of funds but also due to lack of impelling interest. (Mr Spero was also mentioning communication just half an hour ago.)

What must take place is communication and motivation. That is not the same as launching onto the world posters and folders which further intensify the information overkill to which people are exposed. Communication and motivation means delving into extant and potential publics. They involve the recognition of information needs and the capacity for absorption, the formulation of and execution of a close-knit communication policy, the recruitment of and the co-operation with suitable people with a broad experience in communication. Communication and motivation involves renouncing art-historical jargon where this remains incomprehensible.

Communication and motivation means coming closer out of conviction and means making an attempt at conciliation out of conviction. If the points of departure which have just been formulated above are complied with, the numerous options and unique commercial opportunities are available to museums.

Discussion

VICTOR MIDDLETON: I, as I think as you know, declare a belief in marketing in its widest sense as you described it, and indeed sometimes it is almost a passion with me if I might say that. I am not sure marketing has too many converts here. The only point that I would make and I don't know whether Frans Verbaas disagrees with this, but marketing in my view doesn't tell curators what to do about their collections, it doesn't tell them how to conserve things, it doesn't tell them what to display, and it doesn't tell them in what direction their scholarship has to go. I think curators with their passion know best about the integrity of their collections, and so they should, and they know best about the conceptualization of storylines and displays: I think that's the fundamental basis on which museums operate.

But what marketing does, and in this I support what Frans says, is provide information about what is actually possible and achievable in relation to the public as customers, whether they pay or not. That I think is its principal contribution. It indicates what revenue is achievable and it helps you to understand how far you achieve the public impact which you declare to be your objectives. So I think marketing knows best about what the visiting public want, what they appreciate, how much they learn and what they are willing to pay for. If you then bring in the curatorial integrity of the collection with the contribution of marketing, it may not be the best of both worlds but in a pragmatic world it is as close as you are actually going to get.

My final point is that if it is difficult to put over that message to curators, I suspect it is going to be even more difficult to put it over to trustees. As more and more museums go over to a trustee status I think the ideas of teaching that particular elephant to dance, Frans, has got some very interesting implications.

PATRICK BOYLAN: But I think you are both making the assumption that marketing is unidirectional, i.e. towards expansion, more expansion, and further expansion, whereas in fact it may be that marketing has to be used to change the product in quite different directions. Taking an extreme case, much of the fabric of the Palace Museum (Forbidden City) in Beijing has been virtually destroyed physically in the last eight years since it was open to the tourist public. The Chinese authorities are now using what are really marketing techniques to reduce by two-thirds the number of visitors per day going through the Palace, in order that it may survive physically to the beginning of the next century. So you would

Discussion

accept that marketing can be used to change direction, for example to change a museum that currently is attractive only to 7-year-olds, and make it attractive to grown-ups as well (or perhaps instead)?

VICTOR MIDDLETON: I would, absolutely. Marketing is the hand-maiden, if you like, of objectives. It helps you to form objectives then it helps you to achieve them. It doesn't tell you what to do: I have also been to the Forbidden City and I think you are right. In that case, what has been happening has been a failure of marketing – it's not a triumph of it. You can make marketing work in two directions. If you want to stop people smoking, which of course many people do, then you use marketing techniques. It's as simple as that. The objective is to stop smoking by employing the same techniques that persuade people to smoke. Similarly if you want people to drive better, short of shooting them if they don't, you've got to use persuasion techniques and that's marketing as well. So I agree with you.

BARRY LORD: That's a lovely image, marketing is the handmaiden, Victor. I think the anxiety in some people's minds is that the care and feeding of the marketing handmaiden sometimes takes over and it becomes something else – I won't elaborate the metaphor.

Two points I think about marketing to reinforce what Patrick [Boylan] was just saying: that it is very important to distinguish between a market analysis and a market strategy. Very often the assumption is made that when one does a market analysis that the implications for the museum are clear. In fact, the same market analysis can be used for absolutely contradictory market strategies. If the market analysis shows that the museum is currently serving a particular market well then the museum might draw the conclusion that it should get busy on the other markets and focus its attractions more on other segments of the market, or it may reach the conclusion that, yes, that is precisely our niche, concentrate on it and do it still more.

Of course this is equally true of private companies when they do market analysis, but the assumption is often made that once a museum market analysis is done, the museum has to take up the recommendations and I think often the people doing the market analysis tend to make that assumption too. So I think it is very important for museum professionals to be armed with the distinction between market analysis and market strategy so that they can say, 'Fine, thank you very much for the market analysis, now it is time for us to decide what our market strategy should be.'

Coming to my second point, in developing a market analysis there have certainly been situations where marketing does become something more than a handmaiden. There is an anxiety about the contradiction between the market-driven institution on the one hand and the research-driven institution on the other, and it is at least possible, rather more than hypothetically, to paint those alternatives.

We have had an example in Toronto this year where the Royal Ontario Museum spent about a million pounds on a major exhibition on the history of baseball. It happens that this year we are opening a vastly more expensive new baseball stadium and the Toronto baseball team is moving into it, so there is a great deal of interest in baseball and the exhibition was obviously planned for this season. It got universally panned by the newspaper critics who are now finally (after many years of neglect) paying enough attention to museums to review exhibitions, and the press said that this was an entirely market-driven decision linked to what was happening to the baseball season. A long list pointed out other subjects which the museum might have spent a million pounds in doing an exhibition on. (I think the origins of the list were probably in some of the curatorial departments of the Museum, because some of them were the pet projects of various curators whose exhibition plans are pushed a good many years in the future.)

That brings me again to the point of a research plan. I am really convinced that this is the correct approach for the museum when it comes to determine its market strategy, and moving to avoid becoming a market-driven and to remain a research-driven institution with sensitivity to the market which Frans Verbaas has been describing. In order to do this the museum must have a research plan which has been developed in consultation with its full curatorial staff as well as with the community it is serving, and of course based on what its collection consists in. This should show where its unique contribution can in the field of scholarship over say the next twenty years. Then, given the parameters of that kind of plan, one can say, 'OK, given that sort of plan, we have the marketing strength – what kind of mix can we make that will really serve our market segments or take us in the way we want to go?' It is that kind of responsible planning of the overall research base that seldom goes on when museums start to discuss marketing. It is usually a relatively optimistic matter of following this whim and that, and that then leads to great dissatisfaction among curators, the public, and among critics who say the museum does not have an agenda of its own, only that of its sponsors. I think that's really a critical thing for museums to keep in mind in the next century as we undoubtedly embark on a great deal more involvement with marketing.

Discussion

DONALD HORNE: I think we all know that marketing is something we can simply fall back on. I used to be for a while a director of an advertising agency and the Board would sometimes look at the stuff we were going to say to the client. My first question would always be: 'Is it going to do him any harm?' As to whether it will be good or not is always a matter of experiment.

I think that what one should remember above all else is that there is an element of show business in museums, if I might use that expression, and I don't mean show business in any derogatory sense. Obviously museums have enormous intellectual and cultural significance and that must not be denied. But in the final analysis, greater than marketing is an idea from the people running the museum that out of all those objects for which they have their passion, and all those stories they would like to tell, all those ways in which they would like people to look at the objects, they have got to think what they are going to do with them. They've got a store full of stuff; how are they going to put it together? What kind of ideas or concepts or appeals will this project to people in the 1990s, and really if that is happening, then marketing becomes a bit easier. It's a question of amplification and direction and mediation and translation and analysis and assistance, but there's that element of showmanship above all. I can think of some famous museums that have difficulties in Britain at the moment and in other countries where that has been the element that has been missing. As long as one recognizes that there is absolutely nothing derogatory in the idea of showmanship when one writes a book, one writes a play, one gives a lecture in a university, or whatever it might be. One is concerned presumably with arousing the curiosity and interest of people.

TOMISLAV SOLA: Visiting the trade exhibition associated with this Conference, it occurred to me to think about the inventiveness of those people who are trying to please us, and I have I think a nice idea. Let's say somebody comes across an idea to produce conference eye-stickers that will actually be attached to the eyes, so that one could actually sleep while you have your eyes open and staring all the time. Perhaps you could also add another sort of apparatus like this, although I have no solution for snoring! Now I don't say this just to joke. What I would like to say is I think we are producing a lot of stickers mainly because of our bad conscience about our environment, including the concerns of business. There is really sometimes quite a good response but on that primary level, for example in solving some urgent problem that we see or some possibility to get into their viewfinder.

But I wonder whether an alternative strategy would be better? If we are not trying to please businesses, solving their problems, but probably trying to have them in our viewfinder in our work, and try to value them as well, with their work, their actions, their approaches and so on. Then they will find themselves within the beam of our spotlights. Then they could react probably in a different way, not really expecting that our museum product would please them or flatter them, but probably we would be seen as being really concerned.

What I mean to say is that it is to do the same thing with business that we have been doing in our reactions to our public. At first we tried only to please them, to give them the product that we supposed they would accept and want. Then we put our public into our museums, talking about them very much. Georges Henri Rivière put it accurately in saying 'The museum is the mirror of community.' Now, when the public recognized themselves and their needs reflected in our museums they probably got more concerned with our case, with the case for museums.

I would say that this is the strategy that we should follow again, this time with that world of business that we actually expect some help from. Let them recognize themselves in our museums, in our collections, and especially in our exhibitions. And when the business community recognize themselves in museums: their fortunes, their contribution to this civilization and so on, then there probably will be enough concern for them to be motivated to get closer to us, and probably produce some additional effects together with us. I do hope I was clear enough in putting across this complex idea in my English!

MAX HEBDITCH (Conference participant, Vice President of the Museum Association): You will recall that back in the 1970s the Association was producing models for the museum services which envisaged a structure of public national museums, county museums, and district museums, a concept of service which was based on the traditions of the welfare state, education, health and so on. Are we quite certain as a profession that we do actually want to abandon that model in favour of what is essentially a public limited company? That seems to me the direction in which much of this Conference has actually urged us to go. This may be the direction we have to live with eventually, but are we actually certain it is the right one?

PATRICK BOYLAN: Back in 1973 we took a very definite decision in Leicestershire that we would call our new structure a county museum service and not a county museum. We meant it to be something different then, and I think that that is still a crucial difference. My most serious concern about the image of museums presented over these past two days,

Discussion

expressing my personal view now, it is that the interdisciplinary museum has hardly had a showing at all. Of course Tomislav Sola has stressed interdisciplinarity as a role, but we have tended to look at individual museums as reflecting René Rivard's pejorative view that most professionals and governing bodies tend to look at a museum as a building which has a collection in it and which is visited by people, but I believe that museums should be much wider than that.

And I think there are lot of areas of museums that have perhaps done rather badly during our discussions. For example, we've not really discussed natural history museums; we've certainly not discussed the crucial role that I see museum services having in relation to environmental issues, certainly at local and regional level and indeed at national and international level, beyond an incidental glimpse of that part of Lorena's operation in terms of the environment and environmental issues in the Costa Rica National Museum. So I think there are many things still outstanding, and if we had another four or five days we could certainly go on them. I think Max [Hebditch] has raised a very interesting question, in relation to the model or vision of what a museum should be. I have argued quite recently with the Arts Council's senior staff that they seem to have a social work model of what they do. They even use social work terms and they only know what the needs are of their own particular 'clients'; the people and organizations in the arts who actually manage to survive without problems are not in contact with them, so they don't know what's happening in those areas. But perhaps the same is true in the museum field. We have got a parallel in the UK. We claim to have a National Health Service, but we actually have a National Illness Service, and the healthy organizations and the healthy individuals are never seen by the national bodies, the Arts Council, hospitals and so on.

IAN SPERO: My interpretation of Max's question is 'market-driven or not?' Would you say that is what you are saying: whether museums are driven by the public or market-driven? My contribution to the Conference this afternoon was saying there should be market forces at work. There have to be market forces at work because museums have to appeal to the public, you have to draw the public in. There is a specific museum that came into my mind as you were talking. I won't name it because it is a national museum that I visited in the 1970s when I was a wee lad. I have a wee son myself now who is 4 years of age and I thought 'This will be fun, I'm in that part of the world in a hotel and I'll go back and see it. Won't that be great?' I went back with my wife and son in hand: we walked around and it hadn't changed one iota in ten years, yet it's a national museum for its own particular industry and a very popular one at that. Now I know damn well, having lived in America, that this wouldn't happen there. The restaurants were appalling, absolutely bloody awful, and it would not be allowed: in fact it would have been closed down, because the food was atrocious.

You in museums are appealing to the public, so if by reacting to market forces you get better restaurants and a better museum there's nothing wrong with that. It doesn't mean to say that you're not fulfilling your objective, which is educating the public and everything else that goes along with it – the knowledge factor. That's why I took my son in there. I wanted him to learn about these particular exhibits.

DONALD HORNE: Didn't you say the museum was popular?

IAN SPERO: It's extremely popular.

DONALD HORNE: Perhaps the public don't want it to change; perhaps they want it to stay the same. My experience of Britain is that foreign people still like visiting it.

IAN SPERO: My experience of Britain is that the British will take what they get. My company does the Egon Ronay Guides and that's a great example, food. Now Egon Ronay has personally gone out to change that but thirty years ago people accepted what they got: the British are like that. They're a bit better at reacting to poor standards now, but they mainly get what they're given, and they'll go back for more if there's no alternative. But in this particular case it is the national museum and therefore if you want to take a child to see history of (I won't say where) you would go to this place.

DONALD HORNE: I was objecting to the idea of market forces them-selves determining matters because the questions are too complex for that, and it is simply true that people sometimes do prefer the kinds of things that haven't changed. The point is, surely, that market forces are not going to determine anything. If you're running a museum you can't sit around and wait for market forces to do it for you. You have, as you suggested, to try something else out, and what you try out may be based on analysis of markets etc.

In this land of myths there are no markets. There are semi-monopolistic situations and highly intractable socio-economic circumstances in which fortunately governments continue to intervene, so that there can be choices such as having real museums as well as the Royal Britain exhi-bition which I went to see the other day. I am pleased to say there were a great deal less people there at that awful thing that's been put up near the Barbican at a cost of £6 million than at even the worst museum. It is obviously going to go down the drain though I am sure it was highly market-researched.

IAN SPERO: Just one point – market forces: I interpret that as the spending of money in someone's pocket, that's all. Whichever way you interpret it, it means how somebody spends their money or their time.

VICTOR MIDDLETON: Markets are people and I can't understand why 'market economy' in some ways is used as a pejorative term: serving people and serving communities is a good thing. People are in communities and they are also markets; it is the same blessed thing.

May I also comment on the welfare model which came up? Welfare systems tend to degenerate into giving people what's good for them and losing touch with what people actually want. It always comes back to the question – who decides what's good and whether people have choices, and I am only repeating what Neil Cossons said earlier on. If they choose not to go to museums for any reason then museums will lose the bulk of their *raison d'être*. So marketing is not forcing things that they don't want down people's throats and making them pay, it is helping to understand what people in communities actually want and how to respond to this. If you don't give what they want to them you get *glasnost* in Russia, which is precisely a people rejection against the models that have been forced upon them.

PATRICK BOYLAN: Can I just take that one up? Who is to be the spokesperson for future generations of users and scholars and visitors that are not going to be born for some hundreds of years, but to whom we as curators believe have a clear responsibility? We are extremely rude about the Ashmolean Museum which at the end of the eighteenth century burned almost all of its natural history collections, including the only stuffed specimen of the extinct dodo. Nowadays we think this was a pretty disgraceful thing to do, but nobody at that time cared about the dodo. There wasn't a local market force and people demonstrating as they do about the restructuring of the V&A or the introduction of admission charges of the Science Museum, there wasn't a market for that. And who is going to play God in relation to those future generations? I made the point early today about my Record Office with its $4\frac{1}{2}$ miles of documents that nobody is allowed to see by law for several decades: what is the market force in this case?

VICTOR MIDDLETON: Here's my best answer. I think because we don't live in a world in which there is a God which is going to make us a final arbiter and tell us what to preserve, I think those who are responsible for these things, and I am obviously including your good self, have got to fight with all the passion that you can muster and all the integrity that you can muster, for the sake of things in which you believe. That's the only way anything gets done in a democratic type of society, and having mustered your fight I still think you are then left with a responsibility for explaining all this to the public and involving the public. This is also part of the same process of understanding, and here I am agreeing with you. Sure, what I think marketing helps you to do is interpret your visions, basically to bring them alive and persuade people of your own beliefs. But I think you've got to listen to the market/public and I think that's the main point.

BARRY LORD: I want to just come back to Max's question which I thought was a good one, but I think is a little bit to the side of the direction in which we are going at the moment. I don't think the question was only about marketing. I think the issue of the extent to which the museum is responsive to the market is one thing, but I thought there was a somewhat broader question implied, which was the model of the museum structure. It is interesting to me because I was trying to refer earlier to the very different dynamic in North American museums due to the museum's membership, and I take Paul Perrot's point that in many cases they are not actually elected, but that wasn't really my main point. It was that whether they were involved with the establishment of the Board or not, 16,000 members in a city of your size is a powerful economic and political fact in that community, backed up as you say by a voluntarism which gives you volunteers who are, possibly not in number but sometimes in their particular connections, another powerful political and economic fact. I am struck, as I work as a museum planner and consultant here in the UK, by the absence of that membership force in, let's say Leicestershire or any given constituency, which would give you a very different world to move around in.

Now, to come back to the question, I think that the reason in North America why we have inherited that kind of thing is that the original model there is that the gallery or museum was very much a social cause, originally for a very small class and then gradually broadening out in terms of the social class that backed it, to serve all the people, and is still so today. I find working particularly in the United States but particularly in Canada that we're largely dealing with people who are absolutely convinced that their community must have an art gallery or a museum, or the best gallery or a better gallery than the other one or something of that kind, and to them it's a Holy Grail. To bring culture to their community is a cause. So that really was the model for the museum business in North America.

Discussion

Here you have an equally powerful and I think very important model, which Patrick Boylan referred to: that of the museum as a public service. The very use of the term Museum Service is a very powerful term, that we don't use in North America, and I am so impressed by that here. It is a totally different concept. It isn't the idea of a social cause, it's a social service as one expects sewerage and the NHS and so on. That's the status of it. These are two very different models and I don't know the extent to which the membership and voluntarism aspects of the American model can be transferred here: I am very dubious about that. But they are two very different models and, interestingly enough, in our own time they are being superseded somewhat by a third model which is the museum as a small business, which I think was the point of the question. Is the model of the museum as a small business a completely satisfactory model?

I think it is useful to identify that as a separate question because all three of those models: the public service, and the social cause and the small business, can all benefit from market analysis and market strategy. There's nothing wrong with that. There is no reason why your social service museum, even your national museum, could not be made more responsive to market forces and still remain a social service, so I think it is useful to distinguish between those. I don't think people should abandon entirely the strength of the UK museum as an accepted public service, because that has its own strength too and it is valuable to see that clearly. I think on balance that the transformation of both these models into the small business model, to a greater or lesser extent, is probably not a bad thing if it is done with proper planning and management, but it is useful to see how we are transforming one model to the other.

PATRICK BOYLAN: I think you are seriously underestimating the extent of volunteering and memberships even in some UK public sector museums. I have less than 200 paid employees in my service in Leicestershire but I have 450 accredited museum volunteers and over 1,000 people paying membership subscriptions to museum societies, and our various Friends in the different towns. Perhaps institutions that are so well supported in that way don't need to bring in consultants, so you don't come into contact with them! Perhaps consultants are in the sickness business not in the health business?

IAN SPERO: I just want to say that the role models you are comparing are different. In America, having lived there, they don't have the heritage and they don't have the culture we take for granted in England. I always took this for granted until I lived in America. When I came back I went to far more museums than I did when I was younger. I think it is a different attitude, so you can't really compare like with like in that respect.

PATRICK BOYLAN: I think Paul Perrot must be allowed to respond on the United States culture and even more so Lorena San Roman whose country was invaded by Europeans slightly before the United States of America, in 1495 I think.

PAUL PERROT: I'm not going to defend 1495 or 1492 or whatever, but rather challenge the notion that the museum is not a social service. It seems to me that it is essentially a service to society and a most important social service because it is not only the society of today, it is the society of tomorrow.

As to the marketing question, I think it is also very essential and you should know what the reaction of our visitors is. We should know why they come and why they don't come, but before that I would like to have us look critically ourselves at our exhibits. In the United States and in Europe and this country, there has been an awful lot of visitor research. There has been an awful lot of putting the pressure gauge on the flat tyre, but the flat tyre should have been recognized clearly by the staff who were responsible for puncturing it and for doing such a poor job. Instead of that we have studied these things and I think that any amount of self-criticism, self-analysis, is absolutely no excuse for museums to sell the kind of slops that some of them do in their restaurants! It was like that in the National Museum in the United States at one time – I think we have improved it since then. One does need to have market research, but one does not need to have anything except to realize that one oneself is part of the public. Come down from your ivory tower and count yourself among the multitudes and then find out why the multitudes don't respond to us when we say we are one of them.

DON FILLEUL (Conference participant): I come from Jersey, Channel Islands, the offshore finance centre, where we have great trouble raising funds for our new museum.

I just wanted to say I was turned on to speak because of the remarks that were made about voluntarism. The fact is that in Jersey we only fairly recently began to have a professional museums service, since about eight years ago when we formed something called the Jersey Heritage Trust of which I am happy to be a trustee. Now the Jersey Heritage Trust was established in order to develop what was known as the Jersey Museum run by the Société Jersaise, which is an entirely voluntary movement, mainly of interested academics who were enthusiastic in everything from archaeology right up to ornithology, organized in a number of sections. They are a very important organization and they had developed over the years a fairly old-fashioned, but super, museum. Someone had of course given them the museum building, and all the various things that have

Discussion

happened to them over the years have come largely through membership subscriptions and bequests. And it was because of various remarks that were made about methods of raising money, because I am completely imbued with an honorary service, with the fact that you go and ask people for money for nothing, and only very recently have we thought about sponsorship from a commercial point of view, that I was interested to find no mention whatsoever from any museum organization of having anything left to it in the way of money or property or artefacts. I suppose you will say that in fact this does happen a great deal about the country.

But for instance in Jersey over the course of the last few years the Heritage Trust has been given a magnificent art gallery which is a converted chapel. If you have heard of the artist Sir Francis Cooke who lived in Jersey, his widow gave us his gallery and we in the Trust have now a magnificent and very large art gallery. We recently had a bequest of very large numbers of the finest private collection, I believe in the world, of snuff bottles. Now, because these snuff bottles had nothing to do with Jersey, with permission we flogged them at great profit in Sotheby's and we got $£\frac{3}{4}$ million, and that $£\frac{3}{4}$ million is going to be spent on the building of a superb agricultural museum formed from one of our old Jersey granite farm complexes. This sort of thing is happening.

I wanted simply to say that we believe it is our duty as a Trust and a museum service (we are led, incidentally, by a famous museum director; I think Mike Day was an Ironbridge man before he came to Jersey) to convert that dusty, fusty old museum we used to have into a place where everyone – our own people and visitors to the island – will want to come. We must have contributions from our government. We have to have money and we need $£\frac{1}{2}$ million a year, and we've asked them for £3 million for the new museum. But we believe it is our duty to stand on our own as much as we possibly can.

So we encourage bequests but we are also encouraging commercial sponsorship. We are trying very hard to make the museum a popular place and I think that if I have learnt anything this week I have been privileged to feel the pulse of how museums seem to operate here and I think that the international contributions have been marvellous. But I do hope that we all want to make museums lively places. And I think if there is anything to say for museums in 2000 and onwards it is that we want more and more participation by more and more people to make museums not dusty, fusty and musty, but the liveliest centres of social intercourse in our countryside.

PATRICK BOYLAN: We have run out of time but, with that last contribution, finished on a most appropriate note. On behalf of the Museums Association I want to thank most sincerely all who have made this major event of our centenary programme, Museums Year 1989, such a success: everyone who has attended sessions during these two stimulating days, our sponsors Rank Xerox, our organizing staff, all the panellists and above all our eight keynote speakers for their splendid and provoking contributions.

Speakers and panel members

(Details as at May 1989 from Conference programme unless otherwise stated)

David Best (Panel member)
A partner of Touche Ross Management Consultants, one of the United Kingdom's leading firms of consultants. Responsible for Information Management practice and has been involved in consultancy since 1977. Has done work with a number of museums including the Science Museum and the National Museum of Wales as well as various government departments and commercial companies.

Patrick J. Boylan (Chairman and editor)
Patrick Boylan is the Centenary President of The Museums Association and is also currently Chairman of ICOM UK, the ICOM International Committee for the Training of Personnel and the ICOM Subcommittee on Professional Ethics. After training and working as a teacher he has worked for the past twenty-five years in museums in Hull, Exeter and Leicester/Leicestershire, where he has been Director of Museums & Arts since 1972. His research interests are primarily in the fields of Quaternary Geology and Vertebrate Palaeontology and the history of nineteenth-century geological controversies, although he allows himself a small amount of time for research on the complicated relationships between French geology and French wine.

[Since 1989 an Executive Council member of the International Council of Museums, and from 1990 Professor and Head of Department of Arts Policy and Management, City University, London.]

Neil Cossons (Keynote speaker)
Director of the Science Museum, London – the National Museum of Science & Industry. For twelve years, until he was appointed Director of the National Maritime Museum in 1983, he was the first Director of the Ironbridge Gorge Museum Trust, Shropshire. The museum won the Museum of the Year Award in 1977 and was the first Museum of Europe

in 1978. Previous to this he was Deputy Director of the City of Liverpool Museums.

Neil Cossons is a Past President of the Association for Industrial Archaeology and was President of the Museums Association in 1981/2. He was the first Chairman of the Association of Independent Museums and is currently its President. He is a Fellow of the Society of Antiquaries and of the Museums Association, a member of the Ancient Monuments Advisory Committee and of the Historic Buildings and Monuments Commission, and of the General Advisory Committee of the BBC. He was appointed OBE in 1982.

Graeme Farnell (Panel member)
After a degree at Edinburgh and a postgraduate Film Diploma, worked in both independent and local authority museums before becoming Director of the Scottish Museums Council. Has been Director General of the Museums Association since 1986.

[Since 1989 editor and publisher of Museum Developments Ltd]

Mark Fisher, MP (Panel member)
Labour MP for Stoke on Trent Central. A documentary film producer and scriptwriter, and then Principal of an Education Centre in Stoke-on-Trent. A Staffordshire County Councillor before entering Parliament in 1983. Since 1987 he has been the Labour Party's 'Shadow Minister' for the Arts.

Saroj Ghose (Keynote speaker)
Director General of India's National Council of Science Museums, which has spent thirty years in developing a chain of interactive science centres and massive outreach activities throughout India. Educated at Jadavpur and Harvard Universities and trained in the Smithsonian Institution. Dr Ghose now concentrates on developing a new laboratory for research and training in science communication at international level.

Chairman of the Indian National Committee of ICOM, Vice President of the International Committee for Museums of Science and Technology and Member of the Executive Board of ICOM Asia-Pacific Agency, Dr Ghose has been the recipient of the Padmasree award from the President of India and the Indira Gandhi Award from the Indian National Science Academy for popularization of science.

[Since 1989, Executive Council member of International Council of Museums and Secretary General of the ICOM Asia-Pacific Agency.]

Speakers and panel members

Sir Philip Goodhart, MP (Panel member)
Conservative MP for Beckenham since 1957. Formerly a journalist with
The Daily Telegraph and *The Sunday Times*. Junior Minister at the
Northern Ireland Office and Ministry of Defence, 1979–81. (Involved
Ulster and Armed Forces Museums.) Chairman of Sulgrave Manor Board
which is responsible for the ancestral home of George Washington, and
Chairman of the Warship Preservation Trust. Author of *The Nation's
Treasures – A Programme for National Museums and Galleries* (1988).

Donald Horne (Keynote speaker)
An Australian author and lecturer who is Chair of the Australia Council.
Educated at the University of Sydney and University College, Canberra,
has worked on a number of newspapers and magazines in Australia and
has had an extensive teaching career at the University of New South
Wales as Senior Lecturer and Professor, Chair of the Arts Faculty from
1982 to 1986. He has written a number of articles and books, including
The Great Museum (1984).

Kenneth Hudson (Panel member)
Director and a Trustee of the European Museum of the Year Award
since 1977 and in that capacity travels extensively throughout Europe.
Currently preparing a Report for the Museums and Galleries Commission
on the possible and probable effects of 1992 on activities within the
museum field [published 1990].

Author of the UNESCO-sponsored *Museums for the 1980s*, of *Museums
of Influence* and *The Cambridge Guide to the Museums of Britain and
Ireland*, and of *The Cambridge Guide to Historic Places*, which appears
this summer (1989). His *Cambridge Guide to the Museums of Europe* is
scheduled for publication in 1991.

Claude Labouret (Panel member)
Graduate of Paris Law School, Ecole Libre des Sciences Politiques and
Harvard Business School. Has had a business career in publishing.
Member of the boards of several educational and cultural organizations.
Presently consultant and associate of Institut La Boëtie for research on
museums.

Geoffrey Lewis (Panel member)
President of the International Council of Museums 1983–9. Director of
Museum Studies at the University of Leicester 1977–89. Previously Direc-
tor of Museums in Sheffield and on Merseyside.

Barry Lord (Panel member)
Based in Canada, has served in various educational, curatorial and director's roles in Canadian museums and government programmes before initiating, with Gail Dexter Lord, the museum consultancy firm LORD Cultural Resources Planning and Management Inc., which has completed over 100 planning studies in Canada, the United States and the United Kingdom, where the firm provides the museum consultancy service for Museums Enterprises Ltd.

Victor Middleton (Panel member)
Victor T. C. Middleton graduated from the London School of Economics in 1959 and has over twenty-five years of marketing, research and academic experience at senior level. His career includes several years with international commercial companies and the British Tourist Authority, twelve years as a full-time senior lecturer at the University of Surrey (1972–84), and the last five years as a tourism consultant with a range of contractual agreements. His primary commitment is to Ventures Consultancy Ltd (Beaulieu) of which he is a Director. Author of *Marketing in Travel and Tourism*, published in 1988, and of numerous articles and other publications related to many aspects of tourism.

Lord Montagu of Beaulieu (Chairman)
Owner of Beaulieu Manor Estate and founder of the National Motor Museum. Founder President of the Historic Houses Association. Since 1983 has been Chairman of the Historic Buildings and Monuments Commission (English Heritage) which secures the preservation of ancient monuments and historic buildings in England. He has also served as President of a wide range of other organizations including The Historic Houses Association and The Museums Association.

Eric Moody (Keynote speaker)
Is currently heavily involved in the training of arts managers, including museum professionals, as Senior Lecturer in the Department of Art Policy and Management at City University, London. He has a background of teaching and in the arts as the former administrator of the City University Gallery and as a practising artist. His doctoral thesis was on the art market and the state – the relationship between private commerce and public support of the arts.

Paul Perrot (Panel member)
Paul Perrot has been director of the Virginia Museum of Fine Arts since 1984. Prior to that he was the Assistant Secretary for Museum Programs at the Smithsonian Institution in Washington, DC, a position he had held since 1972. Before joining the Smithsonian staff, he was a director of the Corning Museum of Glass in Corning, New York, for twelve years.

Speakers and panel members

A native of Paris, now a naturalized American, he studied at the Ecole du Louvre in Paris and at the Institute of Fine Arts of New York University from 1946 to 1952. He was named a Chevalier de l'Ordre des Arts et Lettres in France in 1982 and also received the Katherine Coffey Award in 1986, the highest honour of the Mid-Atlantic Association of Museums.

Perrot is a member of the Executive Committee of the International Council of Museums (ICOM) Committee of the American Association of Museums and has served as vice-president and is a past member of the ICOM Council. He is past-president of the International Centre for Conservation in Rome and is a member of the International Institute for Conservation of Historic and Artistic Works.

Lorena San Roman (Keynote speaker)
Bachelor in biology, Master's Degree in Natural Resources. Has taught at the Costa Rica National University since 1978 in different areas of the Natural Sciences, especially botany, agrostology and toxic plants for cattle.

Since 1981 General Director of the National Museum of Costa Rica, and, since 1985, Executive Director of the Foundation of the National Museum of Costa Rica – Anastasio Alfaro.

Since January 1988, Executive Director of the Costa Rican Committee of the Quincentenary of the Discovery of America and President of the Costa Rican Committee of the International Council of Museums (ICOM – Costa Rica) and co-opted to the Board of the International Training Committe of ICOM-ICTOP since November 1986.

[Now Director, Centro Ecológico La Pacífica, Guanacaste, Costa Rica.]

Tomislav Sola (Keynote speaker)
Studied History of Art and Journalism in Zagreb followed by research at the UNESCO-ICOM Documentation Centre and a postgraduate course in contemporary museology at Sorbonne University in Paris. 1974–81: Curator of Primative Art, Zagreb; 1981: Director, Museums Documentation Centre, Zabreb; Editor-in-Chief of Information Museologies ICOM. 1986: Member of Executive Council of ICOM; 1987: Lecturer in the Postgraduate Study of Museology, University of Zagreb.

Ian Spero (Panel member)
Formed Spero Communications in 1981. Today the company is retained as creative marketing consultants by a diverse range of UK and multinational organizations.

The Museums Association commissioned Spero Communications in the spring of 1988 to establish a marketing and sponsorship strategy for Museums Year 1989. The company were successful in aligning *The Times* with Museums Year and went on to devise the Museums Passport Scheme. A member of the Spero Communications group of companies – Info Publishing Limited – produced and published *The Times Museums Year Guide*.

[Awarded the PR Week 1990 Award for the Museums Year Campaign, for the best use of sponsorship.]

Frans Verbaas (Keynote speaker)
After studying financial administration, general economics, cultural pedogogy and several seminars and courses in relation to marketing, public relations and public affairs, F. Verbaas was appointed (1975) as Marketing and Charter Coordinator by an international airline, followed by an appointment (1978) as Sales and Marketing Manager at an international transport company.

In April 1981 he became Managing Director of the Museum Year Pass Foundation of The Netherlands. The MYP Foundation is an initiative of the Dutch Museum Association and the Ministry of Cultural Affairs and is involved in the promotion of the Dutch museums as a whole. It produces the MYP (each year approximately 250,000 pass holders), television spots, radio and television programmes, and printed media campaigns, and it organizes several other activities such as the Dutch National Museum Weekend.

He is Secretary of the Public Relations Committee of the Dutch Museum Association as well as a member of the Museum Public Relations Committee of ICOM.

Index

Index

Index

181   41MO   FM   6074
02/93   44393

DATE DUE

MCK RTD   APR 2 6 2006